# My Memories

Irene Martha Rosell Lamphear

*Irene Rosell Lamphear*

Copyright © 2011 Irene Lamphear

All rights reserved. No part of this book may be used or reproduced in any manner, stored in a retrieval system or transmitted by any means whatsoever without the express permission of the author.

ISBN Number: 978-1-60458-772-2

# Acknowledgements:

This was written with love for life, during any and all of my years.

I hope that family, friends, and neighbors will realize that they *did* influence my life in various ways recorded herein and even ways not written here.

A special thank you to Barbara (Rosell) and Nathan Wilkinson for the time spent at their Florida home. It was very comfortable to begin the writing of these memories in 1993 as I sat in the "Florida Room" or out-of-doors for many hours doing so!!

To: The Baughan Family in Washington State as I typed much of the first draft on their computer…and when help was needed, they were there to correct the problem and get me typing again. They constantly reminded me to "Save! Save! Save!"

To: Heidi Hart who edited my many, many first pages and urged me to continue.

To: Aaron VanHorn for scanning many photos that I hoped would be in the final copies of my memories (and they are!!)

To: Ron VanHorn, who painted the picture that was used in the cover art.

To: Bethany Hart; my heart is full of thanks and warmth for all her time and effort put into this book of memories. Anything that was needed computer "wise," she had to be "the one" doing it…NOT ME.

Thanks to each of you loved ones.
Irene Martha Rosell Lamphear

# Table of Contents

| | |
|---|---|
| My Arrival and Family | 1 |
| My Christmases~ Childhood through 1981-1982 | 3 |
| My Home, Yard, and Early Years | 5 |
| My Grade School Years~ Various Memories | 19 |
| Farm Life~ Chores-Milking | 26 |
| Gardening and Peddling | 33 |
| Working in Fields | 44 |
| Relatives-Friends-Fun Activities | 49 |
| Church Activities | 59 |
| Earning Money~ Baby Sitting and Berry Picking | 67 |
| Early Sparta-Our Home Town | 69 |
| High School | 74 |
| Selling 35 Acres-Building a New House | 79 |
| World War II-Thoughts and Memories | 82 |
| Mother Worked | 86 |
| Dating-Entertainment | 88 |
| Weddings-Rosell Girls | 91 |
| Employment~ Helms-Grand Rapids Brass-W.A.D.C.~ (Before My Marriage) | 96 |
| Camp Fire Girls | 104 |
| Babies- What a Joy | 109 |
| Family Activities with Friends and Family | 116 |
| Various Things to Recall | 118 |
| Tornado | 123 |
| Strawberries | 125 |
| Work~ Soil Conservation and Algoma Township School and Other Part-Time Jobs~ After My Marriage | 125 |
| Kids' Early School Days | 128 |
| Marti in Plays | 130 |
| Mis-Haps~ Stitches= Hospitals | 131 |
| Family Memories of Special Events | 134 |
| Grandma Rosell~ Train Ride | 144 |
| Get Togethers~ Extended Families | 145 |
| Bus Driving Years | 150 |
| Treasurer- Algoma Township | 161 |
| The House Fire | 162 |
| Grandma Rosell's Birthday Parties for Kids | 170 |

| | |
|---|---|
| Summer Campout | 170 |
| Baked Beans | 171 |
| Hay Rides- Extended Family | 171 |
| Kids~ Jobs- Etc. Through the Years | 172 |
| After College~ Kids' Marriages- Work- Families | 175 |
| Just General~ Those We Loved-Experiences Etc. | 181 |
| Rollin's Health | 193 |
| Rollin's Other Experiences | 199 |
| Irene's Health | 203 |
| Trips | 205 |
| Anniversaries | 275 |
| My Parent's Wedding Anniversaries~ September 24, 1919 | 278 |
| Retirement Parties | 279 |
| Odds... | 281 |
| 1997 | 283 |
| 1998 | 292 |
| 1999 | 296 |
| 2000 | 299 |
| 2001 | 301 |
| 2002 | 304 |
| 2003 | 305 |
| 2004 | 308 |
| 2005 | 310 |
| 2006 | 312 |
| 2007 | 314 |
| 2008 | 317 |
| 2009 | 318 |
| 2010 | 319 |
| ... and Ends | 322 |

# MY ARRIVAL AND FAMILY

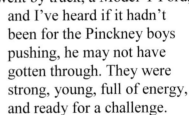

Myself as a baby

The night of a snow storm, or maybe it was even a blizzard, I was born. I remember my mother (Caroline E. Dieckman Rosell 1895-1990) telling me that my father (Reinhold <u>Malcolm</u> Rosell 1895-1978) went for the midwife, Mrs. Edith Blanchard. She lived about one and one half miles from their house. I was born in the house that is now 9852 Pine Island Drive, north of Fonger Road. Mrs. Blanchard lived on the SE corner of what is now known as Rector Road and Grange Avenue. My father went by truck, a Model-T Ford, and I've heard if it hadn't been for the Pinckney boys pushing, he may not have gotten through. They were strong, young, full of energy, and ready for a challenge.

My birth date is January 2, 1930. I was the third little daughter born to Malcolm and Caroline in the farmhouse they'd purchased in 1920. Awaiting my arrival were sisters Barbara Jennie (10-8-1920) and Imogene Helen (9-27-1924).

My memory doesn't have much to offer about my first years. I'm sure I received a lot of love from my parents and sisters.

My extended family was my Grandma Barbara Strunk Dieckman and Grandpa John Henry Dieckman. They lived in the suburbs of Chicago; Oak Park and Cicero, Illinois. Then I had a step-Grandma Josephine Englund Rosell Turnval, who for many years lived in Usk, Washington (My father's parents; father, Reinhold Rosell, died when Daddy was in his early teens, and his mother, Olga Stjerndahl Rosell, died when he was about ten years old). Grandma Josephine moved back to Grand Rapids, Michigan in 1941 and was a dear grandmother to me.

Aunt Irene Dieckman

Carrie Rosell and Josephine Turnval

Helen and Scott Holmes

Dieckman side of the family

My aunts and uncles on my mom's side were her sister, Irene Magdelena Dieckman, her brother, John William and wife, Erna (Heiden) Dieckman of Illinois. On dad's side they were sister, Helen Marie Rosell Holmes and husband, Dr. Scott Travis Holmes (Orthodontist) of Muskegon, Michigan.

Carrie Rosell and John Dieckman

There also were distant relatives who were special to me, "Uncle" Claes (Claus) Hackinson (Hawkinson),

Barbara Dieckman, Carrie Rosell and Barbara Rosell

1840-1940, and his daughter "Aunt" Jennie Hawkinson, 1877-1963. There was a special friend of the family: "Aunt" Martha Skareen, though no blood relation; she knew the Rosell and Stjerndahl's in Chicago. She met my mom while working at Story and Clark Piano Co. She then introduced my mother and dad to each other. She was one of the sponsors at my baptism. She always lived in the Chicago area, a maiden lady. There also were the uncle and the cousins of Dad, the Bloom family.

## MY CHRISTMASES
## CHILDHOOD THROUGH 1981-1982

Aunt Jennie's home was fascinating! She had many pictures on the walls, and oh, so many houseplants! I'd go from room to room and count them at least once each time we were there. Even later, as I worked the egg route, I'd count them. Aunt Jennie's yard usually had flowers blooming in it. Her home was 111 Hastings Street NE in Grand Rapids, Michigan. This home is still there. The expressway I-196 north wall is in front of it. (1997)

Christmas Eves were at "Uncles and Aunt Jennies." Oh, the feast, though I didn't like the Lutefisk; I did like the milk gravy on the potatoes. Lutefisk is a Scandinavian delicacy. Lutefisk (pronounced LOOT'-uh-fisk) is dried cod that has been soaked for days in water and lye. Lutefisk translates literally as "lye-fish" in both the Swedish and Norwegian languages. All the 'courses' of the traditional Swedish Christmas dinner were served, thus it was a long time for kids to wait for gifts. Finally when gift time came; I always received a gift from Aunt Jennie and Uncle, from Grandma Josephine (via Aunt Helen), and that special one from Aunt Helen and Uncle Scott. We went to Aunt Jennie's until probably the early 1940's. I can still close my eyes and admire the sideboard, with the skating scene, the narrow pantry room, the beautiful bedroom suite, and being able to go into the parlor (this room was usually closed).

One Christmas Eve at Aunt Jennie's I remember; it was such fun. Cousin Dick Holmes was little, but old enough to express the excitement of Christmas and gifts.

My mom and dad gave him a tricycle. What a squeal and how his brown eyes danced!

Uncle Scott told me that as a small child I didn't like men. He remembers a time when Aunt Jennie's cat, Buster, came toward me and I actually leaped onto his lap. Another occasion Uncle Scott mentions is, when as a little tyke I came to him and exclaimed, "Let me LING you LUMTHING!" (Translation: "Let me sing you something!")

Uncle Turnval had died in 1941, therefore, Grandma Josephine moved back from Usk, Washington. She lived about a year at Aunt Helen's, in Muskegon, then she moved into her own home at 430 Coit Avenue, Grand Rapids. We had our Christmas Eves at Grandma Josephine's from about the late 1940's or early 1950's until 1958. During part of this time Cousins Harry and Ellen Dufort, Bob and Lorraine came too (this home was torn down by the State when the I-196 Expressway was constructed, about 1961).

Travis Baughan, myself, and Rollin

Next generation at Christmas eve party

We began spending Christmas Eves at Barb and Nathan's then. We continued going there until about 1982. It seemed to have gotten too big, not only in number, but the younger families had to schedule times with the in-laws for all family gatherings too.

Barb always had it decorated nicely, though different from Aunt Jennie's and Grandma Josephine's. There were many candles and a live garland over the fireplace. A large pretty tree inside and the outside spruce tree always beckoned with its large number of lights aglow. The dining room table, plus three or four card tables in the living room were used for dining. We all participated in bringing food. I remember making little Swedish meatballs. I received the recipe from Maynard's aunt, Emma Klein. It had been used for the Lutheran Companion Smorgasbord at Mamrelund Lutheran Church. I usually brought a Christmas type salad too. Imogene brought Swedish brown beans and rice pudding. The pudding had an almond in it, which was a tradition; if you were the person who got the nut, you were the next to marry or to have a child. Aunt Helen brought a platter of 'smorgs,' sulta, potato sausage, and lingonberries etc. Mom brought her ever-delicious rye bread. As the younger generation became a family, they brought punch makings, hors d'oeuvres, coffeecakes etc. We all brought rich, festive Christmas cookies.

'Twas so much fun because there were so many little ones there!

## MY HOME, YARD, AND EARLY YEARS

The farmhouse was 'old' even when my parents purchased it. It was a two-story frame house, with seven rooms. It had a back room that was used for years as the laundry room. The kitchen had a big wood cook stove in it. There was a cupboard beneath the chimney height, where mittens, scarves, dust cloths, and shoe polishing stuff all had their own shelves! There was a dining room too. These three rooms formed a lean-to, off the east side of the first story. The dirt was dug from under this area to make a regular sized cellar in 1934. Under the rest of the rooms was a 'Michigan Cellar' (a Michigan Cellar was just a hole where the dirt was dug out of the area under the house. There were no walls of mortar and the floor was dirt). The living room and my folks' bedroom were also on the ground floor. Upstairs there was a bedroom on the south and a small bedroom on the north. The north room had an opening (trap door) to an attic above.

When I was little, we had a big coal stove (round or square) in the living room. It heated the living room and when the door to the downstairs bedroom was open it also was heated. The chimney from the stove went through the ceiling into the south upstairs bedroom. In winter, it took some of the chill from the air. We girls would take our turns dressing, or undressing, close to the stovepipe! Coal for the stove was purchased at the elevators, or an area, which was called the coal yard. The coal was shipped into these areas by boxcars of the railroad. When I was young there were two or three places to buy coal in Sparta. (We still used coal as we lived in the 'new house' 1274 Fonger. I would load coal at the elevator... only place then to purchase coal... after the morning bus route and bring it home to unload in a coal bin in the utility room!)

We three sisters slept in the south room some of the years. Later Barbara and Imogene had the south room and I had the north room. I had a bed that used a 'straw-tick' for a mattress. This was straw from wheat or oats that had been thrashed on the farm. The straw was changed four or five times a year. The huge mattress case

There is a pile of dirt behind "Aunt" Martha Skareen, Grandma Barbara Dieckman, Aunt Irene Dieckman, and me in front (1934) from digging the cellar.

was just like a *huge* pillowcase. What fun it was to pounce into bed the first time after new straw was put into it!

This house had a cellar; cellars were cool (known now as the basement). We girls would take the milk, butter, and leftovers to the cellar after each meal. Mother made homemade Root Beer. She used Root Beer extract and other ingredients, which had to age. We could hardly wait! It was put into Mason jars, which were sealed with jar rubbers and a zinc lid. It was such a treat, on a hot summer's day to drink this beverage for refreshment. It was used sparingly so it would last longer.

There was no running water or indoor bathroom in this house. For years water was carried from an outside pump by the pails full. After the cellar was dug under the lean-to; Daddy sunk a point into the ground for a well, under the kitchen. I think the well was only 23-27 feet deep. It was the softest water! A pitcher pump was then installed in the kitchen, on the counter near the sink.

The 'out house' was what we used all the years we lived there (that's the old two-holer). During the winter and at night, the use of a pail worked well. It was more convenient and comfortable than running out doors. Emptying this pail was one of our assigned chores. Many outhouses had a crescent moon cut out of the door and some had a star or two as well. Ours did not.

In the early years, there was no toilet paper (rolls) to use. I'll bet almost all rural outhouses had a Sears Roebuck Catalog in them. A person using the facility would rip out a page and with both hands crinkle it up to "soften" the page for use as we now use toilet paper.

I remember hearing on winter evenings, "Time to light the Aladdin Lamp!"

Oh, how it lit up the living room as dusk set in. Other regular kerosene lamps were used in the kitchen and dining rooms, as well as taking them to the bedrooms upon retiring.

There was always a time for the chore of washing the lamp globes. Sometimes they were blackened on a side or more with much soot, this happened when the wick didn't work well.

The kitchen floor was redecorated when the original pattern had worn off. The bare linoleum floor was a dark brownish-red. Mom would scrub it thoroughly and wait for it to be very dry. Then a coat of plain color was painted on it and let to dry well. A sponge was then dabbed into contrasting color paint and a design was made on the plain color paint. The color I remember was a green background and a cream light yellow was the "dabbed" color. Although this was an example of frugal living it was a clean and pleasant change.

Mom had two different painted, gasoline powered, washing machines, during the years. This was a modern convenience; many others still scrubbed laundry by hand. Imogene says that Mom ran her hand through one of these machines' wringers. At that time I was a baby and Barb was my sitter, diaper changer, etc.

In 1936-1937 Consumers Power Company brought electric to our area (it was at this time that the roads were given names and the houses numbers; I believe by Consumers Power Company). I remember coming home from school and switching on every light and switching it off again. What a modern convenience! This changed our living in other areas too. As money was saved for various electrical appliances they were purchased, over a period of many years. Probably one of the first was the electric pump, followed by the refrigerator, stove, washing machine, iron, etc.

The Great Depression was still apparent during my first years. I remember nothing of the worries or hardships. I do know that I was rationed one-half hot dog when they were served and even though we had chickens on the farm, I was given only a wing or drumstick. My mom always ate the back and neck (not much meat on these) but this left more for the family, or another meal. Yes, they lived frugally, most families of that era did; they were forced to!

The farm's back fence line bordered on my dad's Uncle Henry and Aunt Dena (Rosell) Bloom's acreage. Mother worked a lot in the fields so my sisters 'baby-sat' me whenever necessary. Mother did much of the mowing of hay, and raking of it in season. She also 'mowed' (distributed) away the hay in the hay mow (the place in the barn where hay is piled or stored). The hay was pitched onto a wagon by hand. Then a two tined big hayfork was pushed down into the hay load and locked. The hay came up on the hayfork and traveled on a track and was dropped in the mow and had to be distributed. A rope was attached to a whipple tree to which the horses were harnessed and they provided the horsepower to raise the hay to the mow, on a track. Horses provided the power for all farm work. In the fall, Mom would cut and husk corn. It was cut by hand, swinging a corn knife, which looked kind of like a large oversized question mark. Corn was then set up into shocks. A wooden frame helped form the shock so it'd stand and air would circulate within and about it. A foot down from the corn tassel the

Dad and we three girls

Judy Dieckman and myself

stalks were tied with twine. Yes, back in the 1920's and 1930's (as now) a lot of farm work was done by Mom.

On this farm we had two woodlots; one in the northeast corner, about one and one-half acres, and the other in the southeast corner, of about two and one-half acres. As a youngster I had a chore of going out to these woodlots and finding pieces of pine stumps for kindling (Mom called this *binka*) to light a good fire in the kitchen cook stove. The large water reservoir and the copper wash boiler (on the top of the stove) were always filled on Sunday night, ready for Monday's wash day. The fire was always hot on washday.

Those two woodlots carry other cherished memories. Among them; the many walks I took, the days in spring picking wild flowers, the finding of wintergreen and eating the leaves and berries, also eating the fruit of low bush blueberries. Oh, how I loved the out-of doors and nature! I knew where each species was growing and when they bloomed. What beauty, what freedom, what a creator is our God! I recollect too, how my sisters, as they were older; opted to take a Sunday afternoon nap instead of 'traipsing' out to pick flowers. A few years later I understood, a nap felt great!

I heard many times that at the time I was a baby and toddler that Daddy had a hired man named Luke Bannister, who was black. Imogene remembers he had a daughter who visited him at our home. She thinks her last name was Hardiman. She was a pianist and when visiting, she played my folks' piano and Luke played the violin. I checked the name Bannister in the phone book and talked to some of his descendants in 1996. I had cut out an obituary from 9-29-04 Grand Rapids Press (the deceased was Theodore "Bud" Hardiman) which stated he was a child of Theodore and Beatrice (Bannister) Hardiman.

I called a surviving daughter of "Bud" and she put me on a three-way conversation with her mom Noma.

Noma informed me that her husband Theodore "Bud" Hardiman was a grandson of Luke's. Yes, Luke played the fiddle, and various family members did play the piano. She also gave me the phone number of her husband's brother Lloyd, who lives in Mecosta, MI. I called him and he enlightened me.

The two brothers lived with "Grandpa" Luke on what's now 10 Mile Road, probably about one mile east of what's Vinton Ave. He also lived on Alpine Ave. south of 10 Mile Road. They moved back to Grand Rapids in 1940.

They went to Englishville School, south of 10 Mile Road (Teachers were: Hoag, DeVine, and Fox). The boys also attended Sparta High School, where his brother Theodore (who's obituary I found) played basketball.

These boys were "batching" it with Grandpa (Grandma had died) after their parent's divorce. At Englishville he remembers a Kellogg boy who's parents had a sawmill on 10 Mile Road. He bumped into this Kellogg again while both worked in road construction. They were both happy to see each other. Betty Courtade called and asked what I was doing. I said "working on my memories" and explained the above. She exclaimed "I was in first grade at Englishville when two black boys went there! Their name was Hardiman, and they were older! In fact, I have a picture of the students in front of the school!" Yes, there were the two boys!

I couldn't find the photo album of my mom's that had a picture of Luke in it. Therefore, I asked Lloyd (in Mecosta) if he had any pictures of Luke. Four days later my mail had a picture of Luke with our team of horses. The one horse had my sisters, Barbra and Imogene, and Elaine Klefbohm and the other had Randy Klefbohm and another cousin from Chicago.

Mrs. Jennie Doyle lived right across the street from us. She was always 'old' to me. She'd sit a lot of hours in a rocking chair and look outdoors. In the summer she'd sit outdoors, on her porch. I remember visiting her and Mom sending food over to her via me. Mrs. Doyle sometimes said to me, "I make myself oatmeal for breakfast, but the meals you bring over are so good."

This house, and the 35 acres, was owned by my folks until 1946, when they sold it to Anton and Betty Mieras. They looked at it Sunday, June second; bought it June third with the contract signed June 8, 1946. They were a young couple from the Grand Rapids area. He was employed by Gullmeyer-Livingston, a machine shop (my father knew some of the Gullmeyers from when he boarded at Aunt Jennie's as a young man in Grand Rapids). Mieras' lived there until they sold it in 1963 to Joe and Marge DeMute. DeMutes sold it in 1981 to Jerry and Lonnie Geers who are living there now (1993). Mieras' put in a bathroom where the back room was, and the Geers changed the house by putting a stairway to the basement on the south end of dining room. They fixed a playroom for the kids in the basement. Lonnie Geers had Mom and me up to see the house, and Lonnie enjoyed hearing its history from Mom, this was in about 1984. Mom really enjoyed that visit too.

I remember having three large hard maple trees in the front yard. We children played many hours in their shade, or in the leaves. Two of the trees were growing quite close together. The roots-above ground and the trunks formed a little oval shape. My playmates and I would carry water out to it and fill it. We then played we were fishing and we also dropped small pebbles into it, to see the little ripples. Rope swings were attached to high limbs. Two were with notched boards for seats, and the other swing was a single rope tied around a tire, that was discarded from a vehicle. We would 'pump-up' ever so high and reach other branch leaves with our toes! In the tire swing we'd turn round and round and get dizzy. This tire swing was one we laid on our tummies to swing in. Swinging was a pleasant-fun time.

Many hours were spent under the trees playing; play house, dress up, dolls, tea parties and the like. The trees are gone now; all submitting to winds of strength. They stood many years straight and strong!

Carl Fonger, myself, and Judy Dieckman

In the fall, one can never forget the piles of raked leaves, and there were several huge ones! We kids, all, had fun running through these piles and watching the leaves fly, or jumping up and down in the soft humps of color. Then best of all, was probably, being Jack or Jill in the box as others would cover you completely with leaves and we'd emerge from them laughing gleefully and brushing leaves from our hair and our clothing. Sometime during my early years, from six until who knows when, I would lie on my back beneath the trees and look through the leaves. They sang various melodies of their own as they moved, thus letting different scenes dance above me and within and above them. To this day I still enjoy this simple wonder. Cloud watching was always fun! Just lie down and watch the white, fluffy puffs move through a clear blue sky! It was always neat the way the formations resembled a train, an animal or other objects. It also was amazing how quickly or slowly clouds move and how fast the formations change.

Relatives and friends came from the Chicago area and they always parked their cars under the big trees.

I was quite young when I had an earache. Mother put some warm oil into it. I do not remember having any more of them. Maybe this is why I have sympathy for children who have earaches. If my memory is correct, I was still in the seven-year crib in my parent's bedroom (I snicker at this entry but this is vivid in my mind). I was probably nine or ten years old when I had the mumps. I remember sitting at the dining room table and coloring with my new crayons. The coloring book was, "Gone With the Wind;" I colored many long flowing gowns.

In 1937 Aunt Irene Dieckman took Barbara, Imogene, and me around the Upper Peninsula and into

Wisconsin, to the Berner's (my Grandma Dieckman's sister's family: Milly and Dick Berner). We stayed at St. Ignace, Michigan or at least we shopped there. Barb bought Dad a souvenir and thought it was Indian made but it was made in Japan! I took with me the Dy-Dee doll I'd received for Christmas. I'd give the doll a bottle of water and she would wet and I'd change diapers. This doll was a constant companion of mine.

We visited the scenic Wisconsin Dells. We took a boat trip and saw the rock formations as a guide pointed them out to us. It was beautiful and fascinating to me as a seven-year-old. As a tourist attraction, I'm sure that it is much, much, more commercialized now.

Rosell girls and Berner cousins (Wisconson)

Milly and Dick Berner had four children (first cousins of my mom). There was Lillian, Arthur, Edna, and Eleanora. Edna was very faithful in corresponding with my mom until she died August 21, 1989. She played the piano at my mom and dad's wedding. I still correspond with Lillian Berner Schnoor who lives in Medford, Wisconsin. Arthur married Ruth, and they visited us when my folks were alive, as did two of their daughters. One daughter, Elaine, (Jim) Springer and daughters Wendy and Jodi brought Edna and her husband Carl Loeffler for a few days visit. This was when our son Bruce had a speedboat and we younger ones went to Wabasis Lake. In 1992 when Betty Mieras and we visited Wisconsin's House on the Rock, we stopped at Elaine's (not home) so we went to Ruth's and spent a few pleasant hours visiting, in Waterloo, Wisconsin.

Oh, another silly memory! My siblings knew I was afraid of (earth) angleworms. Soooooo in order to antagonize me, or to just have a bit of privacy they'd hang these worms on the outside doorknob and guess what? You're right! I'd scream a lot but they were on the inside and they knew I'd be staying outside! They also told me at various intervals that I was adopted. Oh, I never really looked into that probably due to paragraph one and two, of these ramblings! Another thing that we did was to tease Imogene by chasing her with a rusty 'dead' milk strainer pad, yelling it was a mouse!

My Grandma Dieckman died in 1936 in Chicago. I remember nothing of this except she died of cancer and suffered in the last days. Mother saved her last letters and they are in our home safe at this time. The first death I remember was "Uncle" Hawkinson's. He had been bed ridden for about nine years following a stroke. Little "Aunt" Jennie cared for him and in the latter years has a Mrs. Hansen helping. When I visited Uncle during this time, I always would go into the bedroom and stroke his hand and talk to him. The parlor of the home is where he lay in state. I remember going into the room and stroking his hand for many minutes as he lay in the casket. Upon turning around there was an adult or two in the doorway. They had observed me with my dear "Uncle"; he was ninety-nine years old (The custom was to have the body lie in state at the home. There was a wreath on the outside door, indicating this was the home of the deceased).

A main source of entertainment, after an electric radio was purchased, was the programs, "Jack Armstrong the All-American Boy," The Lone Ranger," and the American League Tigers baseball game. Prior to the radio, and also when we had one, the old wind up Victrola (phonograph) was used a lot. We had many records to listen to.

I began driving a car at age nine. At first I didn't shift from gear to gear. Then came a day, Clifford Lundin, who was helping us hay, was riding with me from the forty acres on Fonger Road, back to the house on the thirty five acres on Pine Island Drive, he said to me, "Shift this thing, clutch and move the gear shift!" Well, I drove from then on, in all the gears; the gears formed that trusty old letter 'H'. More regarding road traffic, etc. later!

Back then, one was licensed to drive at the age of fourteen years. I took my driving test March 3, 1944 with 'Bunch' VanDenHout, Sparta's police officer (later when I first subbed school bus driving, he was whom I subbed for).

I remember the first times I drove over/under the cement bridge on Pine Island Drive. This distinctive bridge was built in about 1924-26. This bridge appears to be narrow because of the tall sides and the canopy of arches. Therefore I drove with due caution. It is a landmark that many non-residents recognize. When we describe where we live, their comments inevitably are. "Oh, you live north of the cement bridge. How can you stand driving through that bridge all the time?" The width of the bridge can intimidate if one meets another car. However, through the years, I have become very comfortable driving through it... if I only had a penny for every time I've been over it.

For many years Pine Island Drive went straight north of the bridge to what is now 11 Mile Road, it then made a 90° right turn. It went east for about ½ mile to beyond where the present Pine Island is then it made another 90° turn to the left before meeting up with the present Pine Island 1/10$^{th}$ of a mile before my present home at 9400 Pine Island. At some point in time (1948-49) Pine Island was reconstructed. My sister's boyfriend (Nathan) drove over the embankment at the end of one of the 90° turns (11 Mile & Nestor). Could this have been the reason for the reconstruction? The 90° turns were eliminated and replaced with a series of long sweeping curves.

In the summer's heat I would many times be the one to carry a quart Mason jar or two of water to those working in the fields.

I remember going to the field to get Daddy for lunch and how, sometimes, he'd hoist me up upon the workhorse's back, with the harness still on and I could ride to the barnyard. One noon I was on one trotting along, as it came to the driveway it whipped in at a faster pace and I slipped under the horse. I clung to the belly strap for dear life! Mom saw me from the kitchen window, as the horse continued to the barnyard. She hurried to me, I was no worse for it, but I was glad my mommy was there!

I am allergic to hornet and wasp stings. I remember fainting two times when stung. One time was in our driveway near the back door. The other time was at Kresge's Dime Store, on Monroe Avenue in Grand Rapids, after the egg route delivery. There I was taken to the employees' lounge (of course, since that year, downtown Grand Rapids has completely changed).

I did have at least one year of 4-H. I don't know who my leader was. We hand hemmed two dishtowels and learned how to darn socks. I've really darned many a sock during the years and enjoyed doing it.

I hated to go to the dentist as a kid. I'm sure the chairs' arms were loosened by me pulling hard on them! I had many cavities, though I drank a lot of milk and had a healthy diet. When I was in my twenties the dentist said that soft enamel allows cavities to form more easily. My enamel didn't harden in my teen years when it should have. The drilling of decay used to be done with a slow drill that seemed to get hot the longer it was used…UGH!!! Now we have high speed drills that are water cooled. Another negative about the going to the dentist was that one's saliva would gather and I would almost choke before I could spit it out into a spittoon-like basin. Nowadays a suction straw is constantly removing water and saliva. Because of these advances, I no longer hate going to the dentist.

## MY GRADE SCHOOL YEARS
## VARIOUS MEMORIES

The rural schools were governed by a School Board: Director, Moderator (Treasurer), and Secretary. Daddy was the director for many years. During those years I remember driving over to Mr. J. R. Berger's to have vouchers or checks signed, also to Mrs. Millie Mosher's for school business too (they both lived on Fonger Road, west of Nestor Street. Berger's was the little white house on the south side on top of the hill; Mosher's was across the street on the North and to the East a bit).

These schools were further governed by Kent County Board of Education whose office was in Grand Rapids. The rural schools' records were stored in the County Building. This office coordinated teachers to be interviewed by the local boards as well as ordered and distributed materials and books used in the courses of study at the local schools (they did much more too, I'm sure). Mr. Lynn Clark was Kent County School Commissioner during my memory and his secretary was Grace Knoll. Many times, when in Grand Rapids, Dad would take questions in to be answered, to receive or give reports, to return or receive books or materials with me tagging along.

My teachers were: K- Miss Zada Meyers
                  1- Mrs. Louise Kiel
                  2- Mrs. Louise Kiel
                  3- Mrs. Jean Daley
                  4- Mrs. Jean Daley
                  5- Miss Kathleen Prater (then married)
                  6- Mrs. Kathleen Tyssee
                  7- Mrs. Velma Cook
                  Mrs. Velma Kaufman
                  8- Mrs. H. Anderson

    My education began at age four and two-thirds years in the one room school about one-quarter mile south of our home. The school was Chalmers, Algoma District #4. It was named for the donor of the land, upon which it was built, in 1886.

Myself and Joyce Barnes at 8th grade graduation

    The girls always wore dresses. In the winter, probably all of the children wore long-legged underwear. We also had snowsuits and boots as part of our daily wardrobe! The outside clothes were hung during school hours in a *boys'* or *girls'* cloak room. Our lunch pails were put on long shelves above the hanging clothes. We carried our lunches in various containers. Some of us had round metal pails that molasses or peanut butter was purchased in. Some used the bags that loaves of bread had come in. Many mothers made homemade bread all the time; ours did. We sometimes traded our bread sandwiches for the *yummy* store bought bread! The hairstyles were varied, from braids to straight, and then some were curled. The curled effect came from the curling iron, some different from today's electric ones. The curling iron was put down into the globe of a kerosene-burning lamp, (the handles holding on to the rim of the globe and the iron into or near the flame). When the iron was hot, the hair was inserted into the iron, as is done today, and wrapped around it.

    Outside the cloak room was a stand with a pail of water on it. It had a long handled dipper hanging from its rim. Students at recess, noon or with permission at other times, would dip into the pail for ones drink (the health department of today of today would really SCREAM, heh?).

    I walked to school each day. Almost every day, in spring and fall, the gravel road was scraped by the road grader. It was then County Road 633 and is now Pine Island Drive. This was done before our trudge to school and it was especially neat to walk over. My shoes always left their imprints. What fun! In the winter the snow was scraped or plowed, and we had snow banks to walk on and also play in! There were several kids walking to and from school on County Road 633. They, of course, were in various grades. Little to bigger in size!

    The one room school housed students K-8 and had one teacher. The school's enrollment was a larger number by far than the recommended number of twenty-five pupils per teacher in the 1980's and 1990's.

    My kindergarten teacher, Miss Meyers was the same teacher my sister, Barbara, had for first through eighth grade.

The desks were wooden, had an ink well hole in the top right corner (though I can't remember the *quill* pens **ha, ha!**). I did use the fountain pen, which had a tube that you filled with ink. One put belongings into the desk through an opening of the desk near your tummy. There were long *recitation benches* in the front of the room facing the teacher's desk. Students came to these benches for class assignments to be given. Here too, is where lessons learned were recited. Oral reading was done from these benches as well as all recitations and completed schoolwork. Math and writing examples were on one of many blackboards; two on each side wall and one in the front. Maps were on rolls, which pulled down to reveal the area of study in Geography or History. The portraits of George Washington and Abraham Lincoln were hung in prominent view. The flag stood in the front of the room and the "Pledge of Allegiance" or "The Star Spangled Banner" was a daily expression of our respect to it and our country.

The lights until 1936-37 were gas lights hanging from the ceiling. There were three on each side about four to six feet into the room from the side walls. These were lit only on the darkest days or for evening gatherings. Robert Fonger, who owned the store across the street, was the handyman who'd come over to fix a lamp or light the lamps when necessary.

The years in this school proved to be a learning experience and a pleasant one too! As you can note I had a new teacher about every two years. During the seventh grade Mrs. Cook left due to health reasons and Mrs. Kaufman replaced her. In eighth grade Mrs. Anderson taught me so much in both Math and English.

In the spring there was a *County Schools' Field Day*. Schools in a local area all competed in sports. One field day was at Foxville School (corner of Algoma

Foxville School

Avenue and Indian Lakes Road). Many events of running took place right on the gravel road. Several one room schools were in attendance, probably Morningstar, Foxville, Hull, Chalmers, Gougeburg, and possibly others. I remember the excitement of going to this competition. One year I won the *broad jump* medal, a pin. I'm wondering if I still have it. Yes, I do!

    Oh, it was such great news the day Cousin Richard Holmes was born (5/4/1937). I was in second grade and was dismissed from school at two-thirty. At seven minutes to four o'clock, back down to Chalmers School I went, to tell Imogene and of course, the other students, that I had a new cousin.

Reva Fonger

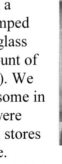

The school was across the road from Robert and Lottie Fonger's general store and home (northwest corner of Pine Island Drive and Fonger Road, it burned in 1960). They sold Texaco gas, from a pump near the road. This gas was pumped with a hand pump mechanism into a glass cylinder up to ten gallons (or the amount of gallons you desired, up to ten gallons). We could buy necessary groceries there, some in the old fashion bulk containers. We were always waited upon, as one was in all stores at that time. There was no self-service.

    The school kids could purchase tablets, pencils and candy there. We kids would always look at ten to fifteen or more tablets just to choose the cover page on top. Should it be a nature scene, a movie star, a cowboy, a picture depicting something historical, a Western scene of Indians and Cowboys, ohhhh, such a big decision! One even took a friend or two with, to help you choose. Another highlight was that as we kids played on the school ground, now and then, Bob Fonger would throw several hands full of one-cent candy pieces into our play area and what a scramble that would be! All getting a chance for free candy.

Imogene and Reva Fonger remember the Gypsy Caravan coming to this area. Reva remembers being instructed not to leave the gypsies in the store area alone, not even to check on something, for fear of shoplifting.

On the playground, yard games were Sitting Pretty, Duck-Duck-Goose; Tom-Tom Pull a Way; Eney-Iney-Over, and of course softball. At recess and noon hour, as one ran out the door, you could hear the calls for: "I get first," "I'm pitcher," "1st bat," "2nd bat," etc. Jail was the favorite all time game. Jail was, when boys caught girls and put them in jail and vice versa. The Jail was the southeast corner of the school, where the shed extended out from the school building itself. Woe, to be out on the playground when some boys found a 'walking stick'. "Run girls run, they're after you!" We had light soil in the area and many sandburs grew there. You guessed it; kids would chase each other with those sandburs too! Ouch, they could hurt!

In winter, during our noon hour, we'd all eat fast and many times go to the west a bit on Fonger to Mud Lake and slide down an incline from the road to the lake. Sometimes we shoveled snow off the lake and skated, either with skates or just on our boots. Another noon hour sport we enjoyed was sledding or tobogganing down at Hall's hill (almost next door to where we now live at 9400 Pine Island). This hill we used a lot. We built a snow jump. Especially with the toboggan we'd go mid-air and what fun it was. Me? I was screaming *a l l t h e w a y!* The teacher, for both of these noon activities, would ring a warning bell. That loud clear one that we knew so well. "Last one down the hill; gotta get going!" Bigger kids would pull smaller kids on the sleds back to the school. Hurry! Hurry! Hurry! All the way back to the school.

Kids going to school during my years; their last names were: Mapes, Harmon, Fonger, Kotowski, Badder, Smith, Schoonmaker, Nester, Morrison, Tokarzewski, Quackenbush, Truax, Kent, Montgomerys' grandchildren Peter Bean and Bonnie Anderson, Straus, Barnes, Majeweski, Hall, Stout, Sprik and probably others. This covered almost all the homes in the Chalmers School District of Algoma Township. Homes then were about an eighth to a quarter of a mile apart and all had about forty to eighty acres for raising gardens, cows, chickens, pigs, goats and sheep (some or all of these) on the farm.

When I was in about the fifth or sixth grade; they installed on our playground: four swings, a slide, and four teeter-totters. These were basically galvanized pipe frames. This was a great addition to our recess and noon hour fun. In winters' cold many of us got our tongues stuck on the pipes. Did you ever do that?

During World War II, ration books for sugar for the area residents were distributed from our one room school. Local persons were in charge and on those days only one-half day of school was held! People in charge were volunteers.

There always was a school Christmas program. We children were excited to be dressed in our best clothes. There were poems, readings, singing, and a play; all students from K-8 participated.

The Christmas tree for years was a live Cedar tree from the cedar swamp on the 'milking place' farm. The kids and teacher decorated it. The school, I'm sure, always had the construction paper chains decorating the wall areas. After electricity came these chains were draped between the hanging lights too.

We drew names for a gift exchange, which had a price limit. Because it was the first gift opened each year, it was a special highlight.

The rural school bell was rung when there was a fire in the neighborhood. On the "other place" (40 acres on Pine Island Drive and Fonger) there was a garage type shed behind the house which we rented out. One day shortly after school ended, this shed caught fire. The renter's children or their friends had been playing with matches. Chalmers School's bell was rung. Some neighbors thought that maybe some kids were still at school, fooling around. News somehow traveled and soon neighbors were coming with ten-gallon milk cans filled with water. The Township had one small fire truck at Camp Lake (area) which the water was dumped into when the initial water was used. The fire was put out and the building was not destroyed.

## FARM LIFE
## CHORES – MILKING

Cows were pastured in the summer, but in the winter chores entailed various jobs. I remember putting hay down from the mow through probably an eight-foot square opening in the corner of the barn. The height on a certain board indicated that enough hay was down. The silage (corn shredded in the fall while yet green) was the same way; up to the rungs of a silo door. Dairy feed (ground grain) was bought by the large burlap type feed sack at Grand Rapids Growers; they were located on Ionia Avenue (no longer there, the expressway took over). In the winter, the cows each morning had a manger full of hay, after being milked. Silage was fed to them at about four-thirty in the afternoon. A bushel basket was used as a measure for the silage. Most of the cows had a heaped bushel, some less. It was an art to dump this basket full over the top of the stanchion, and over the cows' head. Sometimes the cows were out for water in the barnyard when silage was put into the manger. A dipper of grain was dumped on top of the silage, like a yummy sundae. The mangers were always swept of hay shaft or whatever things the cows had left so that silage was pure silage! After the P.M. milking the cows again got a portion of hay.

At some point in time, drinking cups were installed for the cows. They nuzzled their nose into the cup and this forced a release valve, which put water into the cups. This of course had to be sometime after electricity was installed and it meant not needing to hand pump that pump 100-200-300 strokes to fill the big watering tank!

Oh, then of course the excretion, good 'ole' manure! It did have to be removed. Yes, many times I cleaned the gutter; I'm not sure at what age. A large scoop shovel is what we used; many times the liquid was shoveled into a pail and taken out to the manure pile, as this was less sloppy.

This is something on the 'kid-side' of me, while in High School. If I wanted to go to a basketball game at seven or seven-thirty, I'd get home from school and quickly change my clothes. Boy, then I'd go out, clean the gutter, put down silage, feed the silage, put down hay and would even milk 'my' cows while others milked 'theirs'. Get the picture? How could Mom and Dad refuse to let me use the car to go to the basketball game?

Another 'kid-side'. I slept in the north upstairs bedroom and my friend Joyce Barnes lived next door to the north. She had an upstairs bedroom on the south of their house. We'd have a given time and have a 'light signal,' from her bedroom to mine and vice-versa, to tell each other if we could drive to a game or a movie! These were the years! (1943-1947)

Traffic, on the roads back in 1934-1943, was considerably less (under-statement!) than now. I had a medium size dog named Wooly. He had the little brown

Myself with Wooly

spots above his eyes, otherwise was mainly black with a bit of brown and white. He was quite a pal! Part of my chores, at about age eleven, was to feed the young stock on the second farm (the forty acres, Pine Island Drive and Fonger Road, from here on will be referred to as the "other place") This farm was just one-quarter mile down the road. In the afternoon I'd hook a snap and chain to Wooly's collar and to the sled's rope. Then in the winter, with the gravel road packed with snow, he'd pull me on the sled to the barn.

Feeding these young calves and the two mules was an experience in itself. In the early morning it was a scary challenge for me. I was full of imagination, and worries! "What if a Hobo was sleeping in the hay?" "Or what if?" Shadows of nothing even stirred the imagination. So, when it was dark, I'd drive the Model-A Ford toward the big drive-in

Judy Dieckman, Sandra from Chicago, and myself

doors, I'd stop, and leave the headlights shining. It was a most welcome sound to hear the manger doors swing outward and then slam noisily as they shut back down. The mules pushed these doors with their noses. Those mules, bless that old Browny and Jennie, each would greet me with their noisy "HEEEEE HAW HAW HAW" and how could any hobo or anyone else hide in the hay with that burst of noise, without covering their heads with hay! What a memory (these mules Dad must have bought about 1940, from Bert and Mike Hawkinson who lived on Fruit Ridge Avenue near Mamrelund Lutheran Church).

I began milking cows at nine years old. Mom said, "Her sisters both started at twelve years but she begged and begged and we let her start at nine." I 'pailed' cows from then until after I graduated from High School and even while working in an office (some of the years the milking machine was used).

Milking the cows sparks some real memories. Usually I milked five cows. I had a rhythm that Dad said, "You must put those 'bossies' at ease because they just let their milk down." Memories include playing verbal games like: I'm thinking of, learning the State Capitols, multiplication tables and even Latin vocabulary in High School. I still remember many of the state capitols. We sang many, many hours; songs memorized by repetition. Some of these songs I still sing. My dad was whistling most of the time. We also whistled songs together.

Our herd was usually about twelve to fifteen milking cows and one or two dry, meaning they were awaiting calves. They were Jerseys. We had twin cows, Teeny and Tiny. We'd raised them from birth. Teeny was a great milk producer; Tiny was a poor producer. At one freshening-time Teeny gave birth to twin bull calves and Tiny a day or two later also had twin bulls. Oh, we were all so excited!

Whenever we had bull calves born we'd have one for veal. The others went at about three to seven days, as deacon calves, to the Rockford Livestock Auction. This was located about one-half mile south of 12 Mile Road on Northland Drive. Mr. Lyle Squires owned and operated this auction barn. Even in 1993, Lyle remembers the Rosell girls bringing over those Jersey deacon calves; I do too! The back seat cushion of the Model-A came out, the front passenger seat rolled forward and the calf or calves were loaded in. It was six miles to the sales barn and they wobbled around as the car rolled over the bumpy gravel roads. An employee or Lyle would grab the calf by the short rope, pull it gently, and pick it up and out of the car and to the ground. A receipt with a number was given to us and then we'd anxiously await the correct number of days for the check to come in the mail. Heifer calves of the better producers were usually kept. This would never have included any of Tiny's; remember... she was a poor producer!

All our cows were named. I remember one unusual name 'September Morn,' others were more common: Molly, Daisy, Lucy, Belle, Lolly, etc. We had a breeding bull, named 'Johnny Deiss' after the man Dad purchased him from.

My parents had purchased another 40 acres, which we called "the milking place." It was north on Pine Island Drive about one-half mile from our 35 acres (9852 Pine Island Drive). Each spring the dry and milking cows were herded up Pine Island Drive to this farm. One person always went ahead to the "milking place" and readied himself to head the cattle into the gate. This was done usually in late May. The cows, I'm sure, always enjoyed their new fresh menu of grass. They were left to pasture here all summer.

There was a creek that ran north to south through this acreage. It was at the rear of the long forty acres. Two other things of interest on this farm were a Cedar Swamp and a hill that, because of its abrupt height, was nicknamed Bunker Hill (it was from this Cedar Swamp that we for years cut our Christmas tree and also one for Chalmers School).

Milking time was always at the same time of day. Usually the cows were 'up' toward the shed area. The times they weren't there, apparently they'd had good grazing and had lost track of the time or for whatever reason. In the afternoon sometimes they might be back, back over the creek. This meant walking down for them, getting them to think milking time and get them to the shed.

Some days the cows stood in the creek to cool off or whatever. Whenever this happened or they crossed the creek their udders really were sandy dirty. Cows would always have their teats and udders washed before milking.

The shed was just that, a rickety little windbreak lean to. Four cows would be let into the shed at one time. We put grain into a square wooden box and as they ate, we put a chain around each neck. We then washed them, milked them and out they'd go again. The next group did the same. I was a fast milker. We each milked the same cows at each milking.

In the early morning, whether in the barn or shed, we were milking. My memory tells me I'd milk the cows as fast as I could, with my head in a kerchief, leaned against the cow. My eyes were shut, just hurrying to get done so I could go nap-back before getting ready for school. I had this nap-back thing down to a science.

Milk was milked into a twelve to fourteen quart heavy stainless steel pail that had a small oval opening. This meant the balance of the pail on top was covered, thus eliminating any extra dirt entering the pail. When one finished milking a cow, the milk was poured into a strainer

that fit into the neck of a ten-gallon can. This strainer was equipped with a strainer pad. The pad was made of layers of cotton cloth and shaped to the necessary size. Milk filtered through the pad catching any particles of dirt. We got a milking machine in later years; a Surge.

After milking, the milk had to be cooled down to about 45°. This was done in the milk house that had a cement tank, filled with cold water from the well. The ten-gallon cans were put into the water and with a long handle milk stirrer (used to circulate the milk) the milk was cooled. An old hand pump was used to fill the tank for years. We would count the pumps to 100, again and again, to fill this tank.

We sold milk to Grand Rapids Creamery and it was Grade-A milk. Our milkman was Burt Ross; he came to pick up our cooled milk at 7:00 A.M. You could tell time by Burt. It was only during the snowstorm of 1936-1937 that he didn't make the pickup for three days. Yes, milk was dumped into the snow, as we only had one extra ten-gallon can. The milk hauler always exchanged cans daily. Cans were emptied and sterilized each day at the creamery.

The Grand Rapids Creamery was located on Front Street just north of Pearl Street in Grand Rapids, and it was an interesting place to tour. I did it several times with my dad after finishing the retail egg route in Grand Rapids. We'd sometimes get sour milk at the creamery for the couple of hogs we raised for pork meat. We always, however, got an ice cream cone. Oh, they had a lot of great flavors for back then. The cones were cone shaped and every now and then, way in the bottom of one, I would find a little square piece of paper that said "free cone!" What a thrill to get one, all during the next week I thought about what flavor I'd choose. Through the years we received several.

It was probably 1948-1949 that Barb, Nate and the folks went to Wisconsin to see the Berners' (Mom's cousins). We were living on the "other place," and had about four to six cows to milk by hand as this barn had no hookup for the milking machine. The milk was now sold to a small local dairy, Stouts (my folks had sold the 35 acres in 1946). Imo and I did the chores fine, however one cow was due to freshen and early in the morning was struggling. We called Dr. Heyt (vet) from Sparta. He said to have boiling water ready when he came. He attached a rope to the calf and together he and I pulled, he positioned the calf and we delivered a stillborn calf. This was on a morning before going to the office of Helms Industrial Development Company in Grand Rapids, Michigan.

## GARDENING AND PEDDLING

We had chickens on the 35 acres on Pine Island Drive but after 1946 we had many, many more on the "other place." The building right in back of the house at 1274 Fonger Road (later called the shop), the east shed of the barn, the upstairs, and half of the downstairs of the barn, all housed chickens. This barn was torn down and burned by the new owner of the gray house in January or February 1995 (I cherish the watercolor painting that Ron painted and gave to us of this barn, shop, and brooder house).

Dad (and later Rollin and I) bought baby pullet chickens in February and May. This made egg production more even during the year as all of the hens were not moulting at the same time.

The corn and oats for chicken feed we raised. Chicken mash was made at the elevator in Sparta for years; then at (Bill's the Mills), Comstock Park Feed (this mill was completely torn down in late 1994 and early 1995. Great Lakes Granite Works and Patten Monument Company have been built there). Corn was shoveled from the corncrib into the pickup truck bed; the oats were bagged. At the mill the corn was shelled and weighed. The ratio of corn, oats, and supplements were then ground together into mash. In the coops, the mash was put into long wooden mash boxes and the hens would eat from this throughout the day.

One of the chores for chickens was the chopping of the ears of corn with a hatchet on a chunk of wood. Then oats were spread on the floor. The hens always had several pails of water in a corner too. There was a wooden frame to hold the pails upright. The cleaning of the coops was a chore. The manure is very high in nitrogen. Oh, the spring cleaning, after all winter made one's eyes tear due to this strong ammonia smell.

The eggs were gathered from the wooden nests twice a day. One time just prior to noon and the other at 4:30 to 5:30 P.M. The nest size was about twelve to fourteen inches square and high. The front had about a two to three inch board on the bottom extending upward; this kept the straw in the nests. Most of the eggs were laid in the morning. It was nice to have most of the eggs clean at gathering, however sometimes one egg was broken and the yoke got all over the rest, making it necessary to clean them. Eggs also needed cleaning if chicken dobby (this is what we called the chicken poop) was in the nests and the eggs laid in it. Sometimes there was a hen or two that *pecked* the eggs with their beak, breaking the egg and eating some of it. The balance of this egg was in the nest for other eggs to become dirty too. It was hard to pin point which hen did the pecking!

During the early years of processing the eggs for deliveries, we 'washed' the eggs by hand with a cloth in the sink or pan. They were then lined up in rows on old towels to drip dry. The grading was done on a little 'one' egg scale, weighing the eggs into the sizes of: small, medium, large, extra large, and jumbo. All our eggs were sold as small, medium, and large; anything over large just went into large. At the time the pullets started laying we also had pee-wees. Those eggs were so little and cute!

The way we graded changed in later years. Eggs were put in an area; rolled over a scale and disbursed onto a declined rubber mat to the small, medium, large, and extra large areas, oh, so much easier and faster!

In the 1950's, we got an electric egg washer. The eggs were gathered into a rubber-coated wire basket. The basket was then set into a somewhat larger galvanized pail with water in it. This was then set onto a base where an electric motor gently jiggled the base and the eggs rubbed against one another and they were cleaned.

The candling of eggs (like x-raying through the shell) in the early years was done with a small cardboard box with an oval hole (smaller than the size of the egg) with a light bulb in the box. The eggs were turned above the hole; the light from the box showed through the egg and showed spots of thickening or blood spots. White eggs were much easier to candle than brown ones. Most of our hens were the strain for producers (Linorcas and others). They laid the white eggs. Later the candling was done in conjunction with the above-mentioned grading system.

Eggs were put into thirty dozen cardboard cases, three dozen to a layer, during the years of our Grand Rapids deliveries. When I was quite young, my folks sent six dozen and twelve dozen wooden crates to Grandpa and Grandma Dieckman in Cicero, Illinois. When they returned the empty crates, they would have packed comics into them from *The Chicago Tribune* newspaper. Probably there were other goodies too, but we girls scrambled for the 'funnies.'

Baby chicks arrived at the Railway Express Office or the Post Office in Sparta. In later years we went to the hatcheries near Zeeland and Hudsonville to pick up the order. Those babies were so downy, soft and cute. They *cheep-cheep-cheeped* so loudly in the boxes as they were brought home. They also did this under the brooder. The brooders kept these babies warm. The brooders were fueled by kerosene with a galvanized canopy above the burner and the chicks huddled and ran around under it. We had three different size brooders and canopies. I know Dad and I would go check the heat and distribution of the chicks on both cold and windy days and nights. We always put cardboard kitty-cornered against the corner walls, so the chicks couldn't snuggle into them. Chicks were prone to crowding into corners closely and thus could and would suffocate.

It was fun to watch the chicks grow. They lost their down quite soon. Their first feathers came on the wing tips. Their little combs formed in a few weeks. We would sometimes have one to five roosters in with 100-200 of the pullets. Their combs were always bigger (taller) than pullets. Pullets began laying eggs at about four months. These hens laid eggs for about a year. Then we'd cull out the non-layers at intervals. Dad did the culling; we did the catching, most times at night when the hens were roosting. The culled ones, were butchered, feathered, drawn and sold. Dad chopped off the heads with a hatchet on a block, scalded the feathers and then pulled out the feathers. I picked 'pin-feathers' and singed the hair. Mom always 'drew' the innards; she could do it so fast-fast-fast. They'd have thirty-five to fifty chickens done by 2:00-2:30 P.M. Then many times, I'd deliver them to Aunt Helen and her friends in Muskegon for their freezers. People froze that many in their freezers (the latter part of above was during my early married years). The day before egg route day, we'd have seven to twenty-one chickens packaged, ready to deliver for orders received the week before. Dad and Mom seldom sold old hens to dealers buying live poultry. When Rollin and I had the chickens and egg route, we did sell them live. The chickens were caught and loaded into large wire cages and put on a truck to take for butchering.

It was in the spring of 1956, Dad had pneumonia, and I was responsible for the care and safety of the baby chicks. I remember it especially because I'd just checked the brooder and the chicks. I went and told Dad all was well (Mom was steaming him under a paper tent). I walked to my little gray house and said to Rollin, "It sounds like a roaring train southwest of here." The wind was carrying the sound of the tornado, probably hitting at Pine Island Drive,

Wakefield Avenue and Seven Mile Road in the Comstock Park, Michigan area.

    We always had a garden larger than was needed for the family. The excess was sold on the egg route etc. It was in the 1930's that Dad began a retail egg route. The raspberry and strawberry patches also offered additional sales. In those years homemakers did a lot of canning and Dad sold string beans, corn, potatoes, pickles, cabbage, cauliflower, and squash by the bushel and berries by the sixteen quart case; I was helping on the route when they still did a lot of canning.

    I was with Daddy delivering produce and raspberries and he told me to stay in the car as he peddled. Well, two ladies in the 900 block of Lafayette Avenue NE came out and asked me how much a quart of raspberries was. I told them, and they said they would buy two quarts, so off I went to deliver them. Bad move; Dad said, "If you can do one, just continue down the block from house to house, ask if they'd like to buy any raspberries or string beans." Thus started my delivering of produce and eggs. One of the things I remember about early peddling was if an item was 52 cents and a customer offered me $1.02; I'd have to give the two cents back and say, "Just let me make the change: 53, 54, 55, 65, 75, and $1.00, thank you." Yes, I finally caught on to the $1.02 reasoning. I do, however know it stumped many store clerks, especially before the age of computerized cash registers. According to my diary, at fifteen years, I delivered eighty to ninety-five dozen of eggs by myself on Saturdays, in Grand Rapids. Remember, drivers' licenses were issued at fourteen years of age.

    The red and black raspberry patch that I remember most was across the street from the two homes on Pine Island Drive to the south of the old Chalmers School (what's now the Algoma Township Fire Barn #1). The black raspberries with fewer rows were on the north and the red ones to the south. I picked along with hired pickers in the morning, every other day or every third day during the season. The rough part was that the pickers would go home at about 11:30 or noon, and the family always did the finishing up. Could this be why I never cared to pick raspberries as much, as an adult?

We had strawberries too. These I enjoyed every aspect of, and still do!

We planted hundreds of cauliflower and cabbage plants, many hills of Hubbard squash and also potatoes; the usual beans, carrots, beets and some melons, several flats (50 plants to a flat) of tomatoes. One 4th of July we transplanted cauliflower from the seed-row into the individual hills. Imogene and I hurried to finish this planting so we could go to Ramona Park. This was an amusement park on the West side of Reeds Lake, in East Grand Rapids (the park was torn down years ago). Nathan and Barb were going and we could go too!

At this time we also raised Italian Squash, long before it was known so well as Zucchini. Dad had been given some seed from Grandpa Dieckman who received them from his Italian friends in Cicero, Illinois. One thinks back; we had no recipes for the use of them as we do today. Many of them were large and we gave them to many ladies, some were sold. Now we know they are much better in the smaller size. The recipe I still enjoy most is the one my mom thought up when we had so many big ones; zucchini, tomatoes, bacon, onions and salt and pepper sautéed and simmered with a little extra water. Maureen makes this now and calls it zucchini soup; she adds more liquid than I do.

Our family and the people of the egg route could not use all of the produce raised. We sold many bushels of cabbage, cauliflower, potatoes, and squash to the neighborhood grocery stores, years ago before the self-service super markets and wholesale marts. I know we sold to one on Scribner Avenue (or was it on Turner?), one on Knapp Avenue (east of Plainfield), one on Spencer Street, one on Clancy Avenue, (one or two of these were owned by Stehouwers) and one on Alpine Avenue just north of Ann Street that a Glen Jewell was manager or owner of. These were in the area of the retail egg route or on the way home.

I know I was scared as Dad drove down a cobble stone, steep hill (Hastings Street) which was above Division Avenue. I know I closed my eyes, and thought, "What if the brakes go out?" This hill was dead end; a huge cement wall was the end. This was when I was younger, and before I drove down it myself! Just before the wall was a driveway into a group of about six houses, one was octagon, how intriguing. This house, as others, was lost to the freeway. We had about four customers in this area.

    We made many friends on this route. Some customers we had for the entire years of our business. I continued to help Dad after my marriage. When I was expecting my babies the customers were all so caring. As the kids grew they sometimes went with Grandpa and Mom; what a thrill to show them off. The egg and produce route continued even after my Dad retired. The chickens, Rollin and I continued to raise etc. Our Marti helped on the egg route through ninth grade, when we gave up chickens completely. Bruce and Maureen helped with various chores including the cleaning of the coops, feeding the chickens, gathering the eggs, cleaning them, grading them etc.

Names of the customer friends that stand out in my memory are: Friedricks on Livingston Avenue (they had built pianos in Grand Rapids); Messerschmidts, a childless older couple on Trobridge Avenue (he was a railroad employee and had so many collections: railroad stuff, stamps, coins, and they had a big table top music box that played from a large cylinder showing it's movement so beautifully, this was so unique); Frank and Helen Carle on Clancy Avenue, who were just like a great aunt and uncle to the kids. Helen and Frank were generous with gifts to my little ones. Marti was best known to them. Helen attended a play, "The Boyfriend," with us. Marti was assistant director and stage manager for this play while she attended Western Michigan University in Kalamazoo, Michigan.

Another was Mrs. O'Leary, on Clancy Avenue; I delivered the eggs to her and at one point she complained of bad eggs for two to three consecutive weeks. The next delivery, Dad went in and asked her where she kept the eggs. She opened the refrigerator and there were six to eight bags with a few eggs in each, way in the back of the refrigerator. These may have been, who knows how old! So Dad took all the bags out and replaced fresh eggs for the total number of eggs in those bags. He then said, "Please use up each bag completely and do not shove part filled bags to the rear, you'll not have bad eggs." For years, we put one dozen eggs in a # 3 paper bag and two dozen eggs in a # 5 paper bag for delivery. These bags were purchased from Shapiro Paper Company. We used very few cartons for many years. Then toward the last years we did use cartons more.

The Arvid Kianders, on Fairview Avenue had a lovely family of six children. Mr. worked for the railroad. One of their daughters was a Martha. Years later, one daughter, we learned, lived in Ketchikan, Alaska. Mr. had died and in the obituary was listed Ketchikan, Alaska. I called Mrs. Kiander for the daughter's address before going to Alaska in 1981, but I forgot to call her when the boat docked there a short time. This family also had an article in the paper in 1993 about a family reunion, which would be including family from Europe. Funny how one spots names, and can enjoy an item as such. After I read this in *The Grand Rapids Press*, I called the lady and we had a nice visit, it was the Martha aforementioned. Then, in 1995, in the anniversary section of *The Grand Rapids Press* one of the Kiander boys and his wife's anniversary was listed. I sent a congratulation card. It was about three weeks later, on a Sunday afternoon; they stopped and visited us.

    The Trofasts on Eleanor Street; I worked under Mr. Trofast at Grand Rapids Brass and Wolverine Appliance Distributing Company. They became customers when I worked for him. Their next door neighbors were John and Elaine Flikkema and children. Later Rollin and I bought cars from this John and still later in the 1980's and 1990's from their son John II and grandson John III (VanAndel and Flikkema Plymouth/Dodge, on Plainfield Avenue).

    Many years we delivered items to the Russell's on Boltwood Boulevard, east of Monroe Avenue. This home was a mansion. It stood on a wooded piece of land. It had a large porch on the west side with the beautiful large white column pillars. The drive went completely around the house. They had a lovely yard and flowering trees,

The south face of the Russell house.

 including my favorite the Redbud or Judas tree. I remember using the kitchen entrance for delivering. Right next to the door (back of the door, when the door opened) was an old General Electric Refrigerator with the unit sitting on top. They had this as long as we delivered eggs to them (1964). Most people by then had new and more modern ones; they apparently felt it was serving their needs.

Mrs. Russell's maiden name was Comstock, one of the wealthier families in the early years of Grand Rapids. She received the house through her mother's side of the family. These Russell's, at the time we delivered eggs, had

The south-west side of the Russell house.

a machine shop business as well as the business of supplying water to the residents of the North Park Area.

A big thrill came at this stop once in probably 1962-1963. Marti and her cousin, Ruth Ann Wilkinson (Deters) were delivering the eggs. Mrs. Russell (maybe after the girls mentioned the big house), offered to show us through the mansion.

Wow! The beautiful long dining room table and the huge buffet (sideboard) were massive. In the buffet was sterling silver (36 and 24 place settings; also many silver serving pieces). This buffet also held the linens; tablecloths that extended to what seemed like eighteen feet or more. Mrs. Russell so graciously showed us all these things. She told us that her grandmother would entertain many people with a formal dinner on a given evening. The following day she'd instruct the cook and maid to fix up the leftovers and she'd invite another group of people as guests for that evening.

The other rooms were beautifully furnished with furniture of the quality and beauty that Grand Rapids was famous for.

Then came the thrill of going to the third floor. The ballroom with its eleven foot ceiling was huge. It extended the length and the width of the entire floor. There were window seats at the windows with old velvet covered photo albums at each. The albums were full of the old tin type pictures, family members and friends from babies to the elderly. What charm!

Such a lovely setting, such a beautiful historic home (really lived in) and such a sweet little lady. This was something that Marti and Ruth may keep as a memory.

This home had been sold probably in the 1970's or 1980's. I did wonder if it were now apartments. In about 1989 or 1990, my sister Barb and I were riding around (Nate and Rollin were to the Old Engine Show at Buckley) and I drove into the yard. A lady was coming down the back steps (the same ones I'd used many times). I introduced myself and she did too. I told her of my wondering; she said, "No, we have redecorated but we are a family living here." I thought, how nice!

One more thing I shall not forget while on the egg route. I was on Plainfield Avenue, a few houses north of Knapp Avenue, at the time (1962) the first man, John Glenn, went into space. He flew the Mercury mission called Friendship 7. It orbited the Earth three times. The customer asked if I'd like to stay and watch it be launched, of course on T.V. What technology. What an advancement in aerospace!

One area of our route was up on a hill to the west of West River Road in Comstock Park. These homes were lovely; some bordered where Greenridge Country Club had been for years. We nicknamed it 'snob hill'; as always these were among many of our sweetest customers.

Marti and I were on the egg route when I got word that Aunt Jennie had died. She had died during the night before but I did not hear the phone ring (both the Mieras family and Duforts did; we had a four party line then). It was January of 1965, it was cold and we'd had a sleet storm; the roads were very icy. Bruce called us at a customer's home and we called him back for the message.

## WORKING IN FIELDS

As stated in chores, we had a team of mules. I spent a lot of time in the fields with them. Imogene and I dragged, cultipacked, disced, and cultivated with them; can't say I ever plowed with them.

Seed corn was shelled on winter evenings. The straight-rowed, large ears of corn, which were harvested the fall before, were the ones we used. The 'silk end' was shelled off and the kernels were fed to the chickens. The balance of the ear was shelled for seed. This was done by hand.

When a field was ready to have corn planted it was 'marked'. A mule or horse pulled a long two-by-two piece of wood with pieces of metal slanted downward to the ground, leaving a line. This marker was pulled north and south and then east and west. Where these lines crossed is where the hill of corn was planted. The corn was planted with a hand planter. Some of the planters had two compartments one for the seed corn and one for the fertilizer; both dropped down for each hill. The cornfield thus marked, could be cultivated in either direction and sometimes we even did it diagonally.

We all helped plant corn by hand, taking turns by the hour or so. Corn plants broke through the soil and soon weeds needed to be destroyed. One thing I remember well; a day that Dad checked on how we were doing cultivating the corn. He instructed us that it'd be better if we pushed down on the right handle of the cultivator, thus the loosened dirt would pile onto the weeds between the two to four inch tall corn plants. The next day he again checked. This time he praised us for a good job (years later as I drove the school bus, I remembered how great it was to have praise given to us back then, and I tried therefore to give praise to the kids on the bus routes).

Aunt Irene Dieckman

Corn was used for silage as well as husked grain. The husking of corn is described some in the area of "My Earliest Years." Silo filling was usually a co-operative effort with neighboring farmers. Full stalks of corn still in the live green state were cut in the field and thrown onto wagons; it was then transported to the silo filler (machine). It was hand thrown onto an intake belt and then went through a teeth-like mechanism that shredded it. This shredded corn was then blown up a pipe by the machine, to the top of the silo and it fell down into the silo for winter's use.

We raised oats, wheat, and hay besides the corn. Oats and wheat in the early years were cut by a binder, which tied them into bundles. These bundles were then shocked by leaning the tops together and the butt ends of the bundle flared out at the bottom. Thus the grain finished drying. When it was dry, it was threshed by threshing machine. In later years, we had the grain combined by a farmer owning a combine (this was known as custom work).

I have a vivid memory of Daddy one-day, during a drought year. He stood in the seven or eight acre oat field with his arms uplifted; his voice shakingly said, "God please, please send us rain, or these oats will never head out, I trust you Lord." He turned; tears were streaming down his cheeks! It made an impression on me; one I'll not forget.

HAYING= The windrowed hay, put there by a dump rake, was pitched into piles. It was loaded onto the wagon by thrusting a three-tine hayfork into the pile and heaving it onto the load. The person on the wagon placed it. This was quite an art and how it was loaded (tied in) told the end result; whether the load stayed on or whether it slipped. Quack grass was a slippery combination to load (the old dump rake Rollin just dismantled this summer 1993).

The first hay wagon I recall was on steel wheels. Dad bought the rubber tired one in 1942; that was modern!

The hay loader was the next phase of 'haying'. The hay loader had tines fixed to cross bars, which picked up the hay from the windrow. The rope-geared conveyer would then move the hay to the top of it and drop it onto the hay wagon. We used the old dump rake for years while using the hay loader. The windrow was never an even amount of hay when the dump rake was used; 'ugh' when a large bunch came up the loader. The side delivery rake was such an improvement for windrowing. We'd borrowed one a few times or had it custom raked and later Dad bought one.

To load the hay, the tractor had the wagon hooked to it, followed by the hay loader. All three straddled the windrow and the hay was picked up and loaded. There were usually two people on the wagon. It was 'kinda' fun and definitely a challenge; as one needed 'sea legs' to balance since the fields were not level or a stone stuck out of the ground (stones are all over in the northwest corner field of Pine Island Drive and Fonger Road).

Once in the aforementioned field, I was driving Roy Lundin's John Deere tractor with the hay wagon and loader hooked on. In the corner area was an electric pole and guy wires on it. It seems I was intent on watching the machinery in back of me and I was under the wire (in other words, between the pole and the wire going to the ground). Dad and Roy had a laugh over it as they guided me straightforward as far as possible before letting me turn. Alone, I'd never have made it; as I know I felt panicky.

Dad hired boys of the neighborhood to help with haying, when pitched onto the load, when loaded by the hay loader, as well as later with bales. These boys' names were Arnold Quackenbush, Elmer and Oscar Badder, 'Tut-Tut-Tony' (Roy) Harmon, Bud Fonger in the earlier years. Possibly the Mieras boys and Montgomery boys or those of that age helped in the latter years.

Hay bales were just that. Hay was raked with the side delivery rake (it made neat even amounts of hay in the windrow). The baler compacted it into bales. The older Allis Chalmers baler put out round bales and the John Deere baler put out square bales. They said the round ones shed rainfall better, if rains came before it was picked up.

As mentioned above, the fields were stony. There were some huge rocks; Dad called them 'donecks'. Many were seen just surfacing the top but who knows how huge they were beneath the ground.

At the time Pine Island Drive was re-constructed (to become blacktop) Dad told of a huge rock being buried in a hole dug from the roadway. Rollin states that Dad said it took two cranes and a bulldozer to place it into the hole (Rollin adds the machinery was not as large and powerful as today's-1993).

The other fields had smaller size stones. These were from small cabbage head size, on up to the too large to lift size. These were picked up yearly I'm sure. The hayrack was taken off of the wagon and planks laid over the frame with eight-inch sideboards put on it. These stones were heavy. We'd take a swathe about fifteen to twenty feet on each side of the wagon and picked up the stones. The family did a lot of this picking, and neighbor boys were hired to help with it too. The larger, too heavy stones were rolled onto a stone bolt. This was made with two by fours. It was about five feet long and about fifteen to eighteen inches wide making a cradle into which we rolled the stone. It had handles, and a person on each end of the bolt carried and hoisted the stone into the wagon.

Sometimes if all of us were on one side of the wagon, we'd play the game hit the deck. The stones we picked up and threw; some landed well; some bounced off; some missed and flew beyond the deck of the wagon.

Many of these stones were used in stone work at Olin Lakes and a lot of stone went near the bridges on Division Avenue south of Fonger Road. Dad was always willing to share all these stones!

Many neighbors remember Rosell's team of mules with the girls holding the reins. We could ride Jennie, the light brown one, when Dad first bought them. Browny, the dark brown one, we could not. I broke him and it was not difficult. Kids would come to our home in the evening or on Sunday and we could ride these mules, bare back of course. Our city cousins and friends thought it was great, and needless to say we did too.

My parents bought a used 1941 Fordson tractor later. I continued to do discing, dragging, cultipacking, haying and I also plowed. I always got a real dark tan, as dark as an Indian. I really enjoyed the various work, because I was always happy out-of-doors!

The word Indian reminds me, when working the fields, especially plowing, with the horses or mules my dad, and sometimes we girls, found several arrow heads. It always was a thrill and special treat to show these. Bruce still has some of these arrowheads.

### RELATIVES- FRIENDS-FUNACTIVITIES

Friends of earliest childhood included Reva and Carl Fonger, children of Bob and Lottie (owners of the store across from Chalmers School). Carl was one month older than I, and Reva probably two to three years older. There was Bonnie Lou Anderson and Peter Bean, grandchildren of Forrest and Belle Montgomery; Marian Mapes, daughter of Joe and Emma; Lena Badder who lived with siblings and her mother; Ilene Tokarzewski, daughter of Gust and Josie; Arnold Quackenbush son of Glen and Ethel. These were kids I played with prior to attending school and in my earliest school years.

In my third grade year Joyce Barnes, (younger brother Doyle and parents Chris and Grace) moved into the Montgomery house on the hill, just north of 9852 Pine Island and Evelyn Straus, (two younger sisters, Leona and Mildred, parents Leo and Katherine) moved into Tokarzewski's, the stone house. Keith Hall, (older sister Barbara, older brother Frank, and parents Frank and Galena) moved into the house on the northeast corner of 11 Mile Road and Pine Island Drive, the former grandpa Quackenbush farm. Bud Fonger (Howard Tate) moved into a newly built house with his parents Lyle and Reha Fonger. This house is on the northeast corner of Fonger Road and Pine Island Drive.

What excitement it was to have these new kids in school, especially Joyce and Evelyn right next door about one-eighth of a mile to the north. I sort of chuckle, each of them and I had nicknames in grade school. Evelyn was called 'straw bag' (from Straus), Joyce was called 'Barn Cat' from Barnes, and I was 'Feed Bag,' because I was Swedish-Swede.

At about 8-12 years old I can remember some of the teenage neighbor boys filling a bag (like a 5# or 10# of flour), and placing it on our gravel road. As some cars passed it, they'd stop and figure that they'd retrieve it. The boys quickly reeled the string or rope they'd tied onto the bag and the driver would not find the bag. The boys were hidden in the brush back of the ditch area. No harm done, but I'm sure there was some laughing or chuckling.

In seventh or eighth grade many of us kids got two wheeled bikes. Wow! My 'crush' was on Bud Fonger at this time! We, along with others took many bike rides down to the bridge on Grange Avenue and west on Fonger Road to Division Avenue. These were gravel roads.

A summer fun activity, at about age eight was going swimming at Olin Lakes. Cousin Ellen Dufort or my sister Barb would drive us there on the hotter days (my mom never drove cars). The resort had dressing stalls and baskets to check in clothes. It had a floating dock to swim out to. I'm sure I couldn't swim then, but the others, Cousin Ellen, Barb, Imo, Lorraine and sometimes Bob, did. I played in the shallow area. This lake had a cold temperature! It was a real treat to go there.

In the Olin Lakes area was a road to a few cottages. Down this road there was a lot of stone work; a wall, an arch, other creative stone work and a garden of flowers. It was beautiful. These stones were hauled from the forty acres of ours at Pine Island Drive and Fonger Road. There had been many various size stone piles in the fields and also a 'thrown-piled' stone fence about one-eighth mile, along Pine Island Drive, south of Fonger Road. As stated before, Daddy was always willing to share the stones, after all, the next year and each year hence there would be stones to take their place!

Kids of the neighborhood played softball on our various home fields. Anyone free just called one another and we got together. These games included kids from Algoma Grange too. Those most frequently together were: Jim and Sue Ringelberg, Carl Fonger, Bud Fonger, Evelyn, Leona, and Mildred Straus, Gordon McIntyre, Evelyn and Dale Darling, the Brantner boys, Mary and Helen Couturier, and others. Depending on the number of kids there, determined if we played teams or workup (this was probably the years 1944-1952).

In the winter we skated on Mud Lake, on ponds in the area, or on the Rouge River flats near 11 Mile Road. Many times Martin Ringelberg went skating with us. We played tag, and tree tag, skating around the trees. We skated on ponds in Dufort's woods too. All the Duforts skated well. Boy, how I envied those who could skate backwards. I did good to just skate and did my ankles ever ache! Skates of 1993 have so much more support. Sometimes we built fires and roasted marshmallows!

SUMMER= Friends, like Evelyn Straus, were outdoor kids and enjoyed being active. Leo, her father, was a fisherman in his spare time and it rubbed off on Evie. She and I spent many hours up on High Lake (located between Rector Road, Pine Island Drive and 13 Mile Road) fishing. Others who also fished with us were Doyle and Joyce Barnes, Imogene and my dad. At the time we fished here, there were no homes around the lake. There was a tree-lined shore and then an opening of about fifty to sixty feet where we launched the boat, on the east side of the lake. It was a rowboat with oars and a homemade anchor of cement. As one fished, one landmark we knew was an old wooden dock on the south shore, others may have been the number of trees in a group. The dock was undoubtedly built by owners of acreage who swam from that point. We went fishing mornings, afternoons or evenings. The fish we caught were Bluegill, Sunfish and Perch.

We used this lake for swimming too. More kids swam than fished. We swam on the east side where we shoved the boat in. It was peaceful; we'd listen to birds, watch turtles, look into the blue sky and view the varied white clouds to see what images we could make out of them! What memories!

This also was the lake that men cut ice blocks from, for the summers ice supply. I know Bob Fonger's store had an ice shed to the rear and side of the store and dwelling. The ice blocks were packed in sawdust and therefore were insulated, melting very little. This ice was used in iceboxes and areas to keep food and perishable products cool.

Evelyn, Joyce, and I were very close during our elementary and high school years. During the years, besides going fishing, and playing ball, we went on bike rides, played at each other's homes, went hiking, and picked flowers in the various woods. The woods were clearer of briars and underbrush than now, as cows grazed in them. We went to movies, and to school games.

Barnes' had a (pump) player piano with many rolls. Evelyn, Joyce, and I (and even more Joyce and I) used to play that for hours and hours. Our feet pumped those pedals so fast as we sang the songs over and over. A few I remember well were "Star of the East," "Oh Holy Night," and "Yes, We Have No Bananas" and countless others forgotten by name.

Both Mrs. Straus and Mrs. Barnes sewed a lot. They made all their daughters' dresses. Joyce's mom helped me sew my eighth grade graduation dress. It was a light pink eyelet, pretty material; Joyce's dress was the same. We would look alike! I only learned as recently as August 1992 (at Joyce's husband Roy Waldron's funeral) that it aggravated her so; that her mom gave me so much time and instructions and that she expected her to do more on her own.

VACATIONS WITH RELATIVES= Many years in the summer when I was quite young, I spent some time with Grandpa Dieckman and Aunt Irene in Cicero, Illinois. Also, with Aunt Erna, Uncle Johnnie, and Judy in Oak Park and Wheaton, Illinois. This was always a treat, the little country girl in the cities! They always planned special things, and it was always great fun. Even the sidewalks were intriguing to me!

Judy had a friend Ruth whose mother and dad were deaf mutes. Ruth and they spoke in sign language. It was a whole new experience for me to observe. It was a very special time to be with Judy and play all day long with no chores to do!

In 1943 Joyce Barnes and I went to Grandpa's June 4-12th. We left Grand Rapids by train at 11:30 A.M. and arrived at Chicago's Grand Central Station at 4:50 P.M. On Saturday night we attended the WLS Barn Dance (WLS was a Chicago Radio Station with strong power; it was heard easily at our home and gave farm reports etc. Another strong radio station out of Chicago that we listened to was WMAQ). At the Barn Dance many of people we heard on the radio, we saw perform in person. The ones I remember most now were Lula Belle and Scotty, singers, and Red Folley. On Sunday we went to Sunday School at the Italian Mission (it met in an old store) and to church at Gethsemane Lutheran Church, where I was baptized as a baby. Sunday afternoon we went to Brookfield Zoo with Clara Behrens. Clara also took us downtown for dinner at the 'Top of the Town' restaurant. We visited other relatives, the Klefbohms (on Daddy's side). We rode the 'L' (elevated train) downtown and that was fun. We could look down on street traffic and at the second floor of houses. We went to Riverview, the amusement park, with Grandpa and Cousin Mary Boomgarn. We really had a fun-

The "L"

filled day. The roller coasters, the fun houses, the water chutes, and all the rides that are similar to the parks of amusement today. We went to Aunt Erna and Judy's too. We took in a matinee movie and just had fun, fun, fun! We came home, with Aunt Irene and Grandpa, by car.

I also vacationed a few days to a week at Aunt Helen's in Muskegon, during the summer. Here I once embarrassed my two sisters. We'd just eaten a big meal and Uncle Scott and Aunt Helen were taking us to the Lake Michigan beach. We were passing an ice cream place and I said, "Oh, I'm *sooooo* hungry." My sisters could have died! It was always fun to go there; the boys were little, and fun to play with, and to go to the beach to swim, jump the waves and make castles in the sand, what fun!

Dick Holmes spent some time at the farm many times. Some of these times were when he was quite small. Uncle Scott and Aunt Helen went away on one or two of these occasions. I remember little Dickie being lonesome for his mommy and daddy and how he tried to keep back the tears. Randy also spent time with us, on the farm. It was fun to have them with us. One word that Randy said incorrectly was *berr-ee-i* for berry. He'd want to go to the raspberry patch to pick them. I'm sure the boys enjoyed just being with, and feeding the farm animals etc, as I can't remember doing any special things with them. Of course, the picnics and usual activities we did.

One weekend after high school, while working in the office, Garnet Wiltenburg and I visited in Chicago and went both ways by train.

My grandpa Dieckman came each summer and spent about four months with us. It was hot in the upper flat where he and Aunt Irene lived, in Cicero, Illinois. He would sit in the shade of our maple trees on the hotter days. He helped with many odd jobs, but I remember him helping with various preparations for canning. I can picture him peeling peaches and pears under the trees. He was a big man, had a rather gruff voice, was clean-shaven, with quite bushy eyebrows, and most of the time he had a corncob pipe in his mouth. Mom told me that when I was small I would not make up to him. Maybe it was due to not seeing him often, maybe because of his gruff voice or, was it I did not make up to men?

He was a carpenter by trade. He had blueprints of the barn, which was built in the late 1930's on the "other place." He pre-cut the beams, rafters, studding, etc. I think jobs were still very scarce and help was plentiful. It seems like Harold Hine, Mike Traxler, and Joe Mapes were some who helped erect it. Dad paid them some money but also with eggs, some meat, potatoes, and other produce; this meant food on their tables.

Irene, Barbara and Imogene Rosell, and Lorraine Dufort

After the Duforts moved back to the farm of Great Uncle Henry's, (Great Aunt Dena had died many years earlier) we were together even more often than before.

Sunday dinners often were eaten at each other's homes. At afternoon chore time, in both cases, some went home to do them and then back for supper lunch. At Duforts after supper, Cousin Harry would get out the bones, (from a little cupboard door on the side of the open stairway) and fascinate us, as he played various tunes on them. They were placed between the fingers and then the fingers moved with a speed that the bones knocked together, playing a tune, with just the right tempo. To me, then and now, it was quite an art. We'd sing and enjoy songs of faith, of country, of the south and just plain silly ditty songs and choruses around the piano too.

Those Sunday afternoons we kids would play games, etc. In the winter, we many times skated on the ponds in the woods or went to Newaygo Sports Park to toboggan. What fun!

In 1942, we went tobogganing on a hill on the east side of Algoma Avenue about three-quarters mile north of 10 Mile Road. It was here that I pulled a ligament. As I recall, the toboggan was loaded, legs were not yet placed and we began going down. My legs were caught up by someone in front of me, but as we approached a stone pile and brush at a good rate of speed; my legs were dropped. The one leg gathered snow and twisted backwards, under the toboggan. I was pulled up the hill on the toboggan and we all headed home. I was laid up for many days healing this leg.

We also (on packed snow) went bobsledding down Algoma Avenue itself. Bob Dufort made the bobsled. We'd slide all Sunday afternoon in the cold weather and enjoyed, enjoyed, enjoyed!

In the 1930's and 1940's the neighbors visited and played cards at each other's homes. Kids always were brought along. We played together out of doors and indoors too. Sometimes we played cards, board games, hide the button, hide and seek, catch, and softball. Transportation and economics were reasons for the close togetherness of neighbors. Indeed these were close friendships. The neighbors I remember most through various years were Fongers, Tokarzewski, Halls, Duforts, Harmons, Montgomerys, Barnes, and Ringelbergs and probably there were more.

The Erik and Hilda Lundin family lived on 13 Mile Road east of Algoma Avenue, up the hill on the north side. The children of the family, who I know best, are Dorothy (Sven Nelson), Gertrude (Henry Sprik), Cliff (Mable) and Roy (Ruth). Erik built this lovely large home. I remember the big kitchen, with the island work area and I think it had a utensil circle above it. The other rooms were large too. Roy and Ruth lived with Erik and Hilda. Roy worked in Grand Rapids for many years. Roy and Ruth's children were younger than I was. Evelyn was the older, Delora the younger. We were together quite often. We played hide and seek, play house, dolls, and board games. At my home we played under the maple trees with our dolls. I had a doll bathinette. We'd give our dolls baths in the water, dress and re-dress them. I also had a double decked doll bed (now called bunk beds). We had such fun, being 'moms' as we played house. Later Roy and Ruth had two boys, Arden and David. (I knit a pair of booties for Arden. This was my first knitting project, and I remember them being *sooooo* big for a baby. Ruth remarked so graciously, "He'll grow into them!")

Algoma Grange, #751, a farm organization, was a place that farmers discussed political issues, as well as the betterment of farming in general. It was organized on February 22, 1899 with 57 charter members. Algoma Grange membership covered our township farms, and possibly some outside of the township. It was a source, too, of neighborhood social events. The Grange met every second and fourth Saturday night. The meeting was held, and then there was lunch, visiting and card games. The lunch usually consisted of a variety of sandwiches, cakes and jell-os. A 'supper committee' furnished it. Members were put on the committee on a quarterly basis. There were people who didn't farm who were members too, in later years.

We kids always ran up and down the wide area stairs. I would never venture a guess of how many times parents told us to slow down or stop, but did we? I'll bet not! Upstairs there was a big meeting room off the two ante rooms and wow, how we'd run and then slide on our shoes in that big room. The floor was waxed as a dance floor.

Mock wedding

Many times after the supper someone would play the piano or fiddle (or both) and one of the Grangers would call some of the familiar Square Dance Calls and the youngsters and older people danced. They also played polkas, waltzes and shoddish and people were on the floor dancing. I remember Joe and Tony Elsner, how they could dance!

Rollin as a bridesmaid and Marti as flower girl.

Some years, in the winter, they held dances or Pedro (card) parties on the opposite Saturday nights of the meetings. The public came to these. I don't know if there was a charge for the dances unless there was special music, but there was a charge for the card parties. This was to raise money.

Families belonging changed (minus or plus) through the years. Among ones I remember: are John and Millie Mosher, Irv and Hazel Pennington, Jake and Minnie Pennington, Jack and Marie Pennington, Clarence and Erma Pinckney, Maurice and Jessie Post, Lynn and Dorothy Post, Van and Rena VandenBrock, Joe and Tony Elsner, the Hockelborn family, the Bowlers, Hugh and Bea Long, Bob and Lottie Fonger, Mart and Dorothy Ringelberg, Bert and Fern Martin, Brut and Betty Mieras, Don and Arlene VanderHoff, Arnold and Grace Hetland, and Ed and Eva Grant. There of course were more.

Note: it was through Kent County Pomona Grange that I met Rollin--more on that in dating.

Our Marti, Bruce, and Maureen were in various programs at the Grange. They had parts in skits and sang; one song was "C-H-R-I-S-T-M-A-S" and another was, "Two Little Piggies in the Pigpen." Kids and families planned the programs for many of the meetings.

## CHURCH ACTIVITIES

My Christian Education began, of course, at home. Both of my parents had a lot of faith. Prayers and bible stories I'm sure were a part of my early life.

I was baptized at Gethsemane Lutheran Church in Cicero, Illinois by a Rev. Wike. This was where my mom's parents lived. Aunt Irene Dieckman and "Aunt" Martha Skareen were my sponsors.

My Sunday School years began at Algoma Baptist Church on Grange Avenue. I must admit, as I have before, that I remember very little before I was five or six years old. My sister Barbara has stated that she and Imogene were so proud of their 'little sister,' as they took me to Sunday School. I'm sure she's also stated that I brought them some embarrassment.

Joyce Barnes and myself at confirmation

In 1936 Mom and dad (who were both Lutheran) began attending and joined the congregation of Mamrelund Lutheran, just off Fruit Ridge Avenue on Lutheran Church Road, Kent City, Michigan. I think I can remember hearing that Grandma and Grandpa Dieckman loaned the folks some money to buy a car so that the family could ride together to church. It was a nine-mile drive from our home.

The church building sat on a knoll and its white frame and steeple were very picturesque. It was after we started to go there that the men of the church dug out the basement. The labor and teams were all volunteers. The mules mentioned in the 'Farming' pages here, I believe were used. They were then owned by the Hawkinson brothers. This was a big project making much more space available for church activities.

I had devout Sunday School teachers some of whom I'll list: Emma Youngquist, Mae Nyblad Shaw, Neva Casey, Mable Kriger, Ann Nyblad DeBoer, Irvin Stouten and others. I seldom missed Sunday School and church. My Sunday School perfect attendance pin had the number eleven in it.

Barbara and Imogene were confirmed in a large class. My class was average; I was confirmed May 28, 1944.

Summer vacation Bible school was held for two weeks. It was always such fun and a learning experience. Due to the distance, my parents could never transport me daily to attend. Frank and Lillie Holmquist offered to let me stay with them so I could attend. Mom mentioned several times that she thought I liked most foods, but learned from Lillie I didn't. Could it be I thought I could 'get away' with not eating foods I didn't care for?

The hours were from nine to eleven-thirty each morning. The lessons each year had a theme and the teachers, eager to tell us all of God's love, did their job well. We had a recess/play time, outdoors if weather permitted.

During these years the church had a Junior Missionary Society that youngsters (probably up to 14 years) attended monthly. We met at different homes on a Saturday afternoon. The only leader I remember was Marian Johnson (Mrs. Kenneth). Each month she and probably a helper, told of missionaries on the foreign fields, read us Bible stories and gave challenges to take with us. Bible verse time was always a competitive time. Boys and girls came in large numbers to this. This gave the congregation's kids a time together for fellowship, other than only at Sunday School. The lunch time treat was always an anticipated joy!

Another learning experience was the summer Bible camps. The Michigan camp, which I attended, was on the east side of the state, near Brighton, Michigan (1944-45-46). The youth from Mamrelund probably went at different weeks. Friends I went with were Eloise Callen (Jewell) and Joyce Barnes (Waldron).

We had good speakers (many times missionaries home on furlough) and Bible studies. We had hikes, swimming, camp fires, lesson time, and sing-a-longs. This is where I met a friend from Flint. Her name was Joan Rudland who married Gunnar Anderson. We remained close, though we did not see one another often, we did correspond. Joan died in about 1985, of cancer.

I was at this camp in August 1946, when one of my girl friends and I hitchhiked home! I wanted to see my newborn nephew, Daniel John Wilkinson. I was an Aunt!

One year Marian Holmgren and I went to Conference Bible Camp at Cisco Beach on Lake Geneva in Wisconsin (July 14-22, 1945). We went by ferry from Muskegon at 1:00 A.M., arrived in Milwaukee at 8:00 A.M. We took a taxi to the bus depot and left by bus at 12:20 P.M. and arrived at Cisco Beach at 3:00 P.M.

We attended three to four services a day/night. We played volley and softball, walked the beach, went on speedboat rides (probably dull compared to the speed's of the boats in the 1990's) had campfires and sing-a-longs.

At Mamrelund Lutheran we had a Junior Choir led by Esther Saur, organist and choir director for years. Some months mothers helped. As years went by I sang in the adult choir. Choir members (who sang for years) were: Harry Dufort, Frank Holmquist, Charles and Elsie Roberts, Neva Casey, Althea Klein, Fred and Emma Klein; then we of the next generation Imogene, Lorraine Dufort, Lucille Holmquist, Carolyn and Lorraine Bjork, Joy Lonnee, Charles Clement, Norma Johnson, Ione and Arnold Johnson and many others in both age groups.

    Esther gave a Christmas party at her home each year. The refreshments were always the traditional rich cookies and pastries. A new one was the Rice Krispies date ball, rolled and then dipped in chopped nuts. It was the first we had ever had them and they have been popular ever since.

    Luther League was the Youth Group after confirmation age; it was active with meetings and fun activities too. There were many kids in it. Some were: Carolyn, Lorraine and Don Bjork, Lola and Oscar Anderson, Imogene, Lorraine Dufort, Bill Nyblad, Joy Lonnee, Lowell Johnson, Keith and Lois Stream, Ida and Maynard Klein, Franklin and Mary Ann Wegal, Charles, Ellen, Carol, and Maurice Roberts, Marian Holmgren, and others.

    Highlights of annual fun times were: decorating the full church, with live garlands (the boughs were twisted around and woven into strands of binder twine and tied) and a big, tall, beautiful tree. We always went Christmas caroling to the elderly and shut in. The meetings had Bible studies, speakers, prayer, etc. The Easter Sunrise Service was so inspirational. For years it was held on the east side of Long Lake at the County Park. A portable organ (that had been used at carnivals) was borrowed from Arzie Pinckney of Sparta. With a beautiful sunrise (if not-mist-rain or snow) and Leaguers dressed for 6:00 A.M. weather; we recalled Christ's resurrection and the promise of eternal life to all who accept Him as their Savior. There was a message, songs of praise, and prayer. Following this was breakfast of bacon, eggs, juice, hot chocolate, and rolls served at the park by a committee of mothers.

I was given the opportunity, on February 9, 1947 to be a delegate to the International Luther League Convention held in Los Angeles, California.

The Michigan Luther Leaguers went to Chicago's Grand Central Station and met with other states' Luther Leaguers. A chartered train was boarded there for the trip. In other cities, on the way, more cars were added to the train.

It was a great experience. There were devotions, Bible studies, singspirations, (at train depots and on the train) meeting of new friends and some planned games. Some of those riding the twenty-eight car train were Esther Olson (Sherman) of New York State, Marian Sauter (Williams) of Galesburg, Illinois, Norman Olson of Chicago, Illinois, and Melvin Anderson of the Upper Peninsula of Michigan.

Myself at the Colorado River

On our way out we visited Utah's state capitol and Mormon Square (2-11-47).

The Rev. Wesley A. Samuelson

Rev. Westly Samuelson of Bethlehem Lutheran, Grand Rapids was our chaperone. Rev. Wilton Bergstrom was the Synod's Youth Director and it was he and his staff that planned our itinerary. Some of the outside extra highlights were: a trip via boat to Santa Catalina Island; I was sea sick on the way over. We went to Tijuana, Mexico one day. On our trip back home we stopped at the Grand Canyon's South Rim. I walked down the trail with Melvin Anderson (from Michigan's Upper Peninsula) to the Colorado River. We started out with eight in our group going down, but six of them dropped out. There were other groups too, a few of them made it to the river. There were drinking fountains on the trail but several weren't working. It didn't matter much on the way down, but going back up was different. Going down the Hairpin Trail, we started at an elevation of 6700 feet above sea level and at the river it was 3000 feet. The trail is eight miles down. I took off a jacket and a sweater and went in my blouse. At the river it was 92°. That was fine because with one's feet in the Colorado River one cooled off quickly. It took two hours and forty minutes to reach the river. Coming back, I felt it was drudgery; climbing altitude wasn't what it was cracked up to be. I saw it snowing upward, the air temperature made this. I got very tired. Melvin went ahead; it was about 3:30 P.M. I had to stop; I rested with my head in my arms, kneeling against the stone guardrail. I must have fallen asleep, as a counselor who was checking for kids on the trail awakened me. He gave me two sections of a large Hershey candy bar and told me to keep hiking when ready. He was continuing down the trail. We saw twelve deer on this trip. We had a banquet that night, I drank water, and more water, and more water! (Remember, we had no food and very little water on the trail.) The ones who had made it to the river were asked to stand: I was so tired!

    The next day showed the effects of that, never to be forgotten, sixteen-mile hike! I was so stiff and creaky. I had to be helped up the steps of the train.

The convention theme was CHRIST IS ABLE messages were:
>To keep us steadfast in the faith
>To build strong homes
>Power to live by
>Christ for America

There were singspirations in the lobby of the Figueroa Hotel. Up to 500 of the registered 2,200 Leaguers filled the lobby, and adjoining hallways and stairs; singing to many of the guests. There was a talent quest and many entered it. Certain groups performed skits. All were good. Special music, such as the choir from the Pacific Lutheran College, rendered musical numbers.

I stayed in the Clark Hotel on the third floor. There were five other girls in the room. From the hotel window we looked across a busy street and then down into an alley; it was from here that I saw a 'Bag Lady'. We girls witnessed the lady taking food from the garbage cans and putting it into her bags. None of us had ever seen anything like this, and it impressed each of us.

I taught nursery class with Lorraine Dufort for years at Mamrelund Lutheran. The class was held in the kitchen of the old white frame church on Fruit Ridge Avenue and Lutheran Church Road. The children were two and three years old.

Mrs. Eli Roberts (Sadie) had the class before me. She was a grandma of great faith and a devout Christian. I felt I was to fill someone's shoes that I could not. I told her this. Her reply was, "If you only teach these little ones to bow their heads, fold their hands, and pray, you are teaching."

We had long wooden tables that double decked and came apart. We took them apart and the children sat around them on their chairs. These tables when decked served as work areas and serving tables for banquets, wedding receptions, and gatherings of the brotherhood and ladies aid groups.

The lesson period consisted of a Bible story (with a leaflet of same story going home with the child), a paper punch out or color sheet, praying and singing. There were usually twenty-two to twenty-five in the class each Sunday. Kids in classes: Terri and Ann Averille, Pat and Nancy McCune, Keith Burgess, Karen Hanson, Bill and Barb Longcore, Charlene Clement, Mary Ione Johnson, Royal Allen Klein, Leroy Klein and many, many more.

The opening service of Sunday School was in the large basement room. Classes then dispersed to the sides of the big room (the frame, three section dividers at first separated the classes, later the accordion room dividers) and to the kitchen. I led the opening service for many Sundays and I remember how those kids sang, especially the motion songs. I hope they remember some of the choruses now.

Rollin and I were married in the white frame, Mamrelund Lutheran Church. The new one was built in 1956.

Rollin and I were Luther League counselors for several years. We held monthly meetings. The extra activities were similar to those we had when I was a Leaguer. When I was expecting Maureen, the Leaguers had been Christmas caroling, and were back to our home for B-B-Q, hot chocolate and gift exchange. The smell of that food! Oh, I felt terrible; I could hardly wait for them to leave so I could go into the bathroom and up-chuck! We attended conventions with them. We had some loving discussions with them at the one held in Traverse City. We felt close to these kids. Kids in League were: Don Anderson, Arlene and Arland Hultgren, Doris Burgess, Nancy Boros, Jim Lyles, Jack Swanson, Steve Anderson, Doris and Rosalie Lundquist, and others. We had a really fun Halloween night when each dressed up and we walked down main street in Sparta.

    For years we attended the Brotherhood's New Year's Eve oyster suppers and watch. Mom was active in Women's Missionary Society.

    We had many families as friends. Frank, Lillie, and Lucille Holmquist and our family were together many Sundays after church. I can remember the Mom's saying, "Let's pool our food and eat together." A picnic on the spur of the moment! (Again one must remember social activities were centered on church and neighborhoods. Gas was rationed, MPG of vehicles were lower etc. at this time.) Other families whose homes we had dinner and fellowship at and they at ours were Art and Dorothy Holmgren, Carl and Sada Johnson, Ernest and Elizabeth Wegal and others.

    We attended special programs and events at Algoma Baptist Church and considered many families there as close friends. The one I remember most is the Lundins who has been referred to herein writing a time or two!

## EARNING MONEY
## BABY SITTING AND BERRY PICKING

    I received a small allowance from the folks, when it started, I do not know.

    I know that in 1945 I was baby-sitting; if before that I'm not sure. I babysat Lester and Gladys Crystal's children. This was not a weekly job. Les was in the service.

If he was home on leave, I sat. If Gladys went shopping or to a family get-together, I did too.

One little girl I sat for was Sherry, at the Bow Tie Tavern on Alpine Avenue and 10 Mile Road. Mother had done the business' bookwork and they mentioned needing a baby sitter that would not come into the bar area. I could handle that! I'd work some Saturday nights, some Sunday afternoons. One favorite thing we did was to walk a few yards to the creek crossing under 10 Mile Road. We'd throw stones into the water. We also colored and read books and played games.

The family I sat a lot for was Frank and Frances Vanderhyde. They had two older boys, Frank and Bob who they didn't 'tie-down' to sit the two younger boys Dick and Dave. They lived west on Fonger around Mud Lake curve. They went out quite a bit and it was nice to earn that dollar or $1.25 a night.

One summer I sat several days a week, from maybe ten in the morning until four in the afternoon. During these hours, many days we opened stacks and stacks of out dated cans of Carnation evaporated milk (there was a Carnation Milk Company in Sparta, just east of the railroad tracks on East Gardner Street). We'd puncture these cans and pour the milk into pails. This milk was fed to the pigs being raised by Vanderhydes.

The Vanderhydes moved to Martindale Street on the east side of Sparta. I continued to 'sit' for them. They had horses but I didn't ride them much. Once, while there, I rode one south on Martindale. Down by the railroad tracks we turned around and started back on the east side of the road. Fairplains Cemetery is there. There was a large tree on its west boundary. I reined the horse to go left striving to avoid the tree's low hanging branch. It seems the horse wasn't bit-reined but neck-reined. And therefore it swung abruptly to the right. It may have been quite a sight; a branch caught me and down I went. Off into the cemetery the horse continued, more on a trot than before! It almost made me think that the horse was thinking, "Got rid of you!" To this day I have evidence of this fall; a little knob on my left ring finger!

While living on Martindale, Mrs. Vanderhyde told me she was expecting another child. My statement, "Well, if it's another boy, I'll still 'sit' for you." Tommy arrived and I cared for him too as I baby-sat. It was fun to watch him grow.

Then they moved to Pine Island Drive (North of 13 Mile Road where the Spartan Farms are now). It was while here that Mary Kay was born. I took care of Mary a few times but was not sitting much then.

I can remember picking strawberries, when quite young, with Barb and Imo. This was at Holdens and the berries were in the field at Fonger Road and Algoma Avenue. I picked strawberries in 1945 and 1946 at Wilma Montgomery's. I really enjoyed picking and could pick quite rapidly. I picked 16 quarts from 7:00-9:30 one morning. Other times I picked 31 - 50- 24 and 23 quarts all with various times longer than two and one-half hours. At Wilma's I think I earned two or three cents per quart for picking.

I picked raspberries at Jack Pennington's on Pennington Road and on acreage on Algoma Avenue a couple of years. It was not my favorite job even though I picked quite rapidly and figured I earned quite well.

## EARLY SPARTA - OUR HOME TOWN

We considered Sparta our home town. We went there to have the grain ground for the cattle and chickens. Other purchases were made in the various stores too.

Remembrances of the town are varied; I shall mention some of them. The village blacksmith's shop was located north of Division on North Union Street, on the east side. One could look into his shop and see the hot fire and him at work. The local farmers depended on him for many repairs on farm related tools and for other blacksmith services. He also probably made new tools. I know my dad went there and I was awed to see the red hot

Ivan LaVine and his daughter Sonja Helmus look at a postcard with a picture of downtown Sparta that LaVine mailed to a cousin in San Diego in 1922. A Sparta resident found the card in an antique shop, and it has returned to LaVine 75 years later.

## POSTCARD FROM THE EDGE
### Card returns, three-quarters of a century later

**Sparta**

By Kathy Bush
The Grand Rapids Press

Ivan LaVine was just 17 when he mailed a postcard to his cousin in San Diego. The date was March 20, 1922. It never occurred to him that he would see it again.

"It showed the main downtown corner and the flag pole," recalled LaVine, now 92. "The bank was on one corner, Brock's Hardware was next to it, and you can see Cnaussen's Bakery across the street."

LaVine got to test his memory last month when the postcard he sent to his cousin in 1922 unexpectedly came back to him, apparently after some experiences of its own.

Sparta residents LaVern and Sharon

see POSTCARD, page 2

iron (of what he was repairing) and how it was shaped by hammering it on the anvil ('Uncle' Claus Hawkinson was an early buggy maker in Grand Rapids and he used these tools). Later years where the blacksmith's shop had been, there was Sparta Frozen Foods. This was a grocery store, and they also rented lockers for frozen foods. Rosells rented one for several years.

Elsie Montgomery remembers in the center of the intersection of Division Avenue and Union Street that there was a flagpole. Traffic just went on the side of it... it's funny because in March of 1997 there was an article in the newspaper about the travels of a post card. This post card came back to the sender and it showed very clearly this flagpole in the intersection in Sparta. The flagpole sat atop a World War I monument honoring the veterans.

There were two drinking fountains for pedestrians to use. One of these was on the northeast corner of Division Avenue and Union Street, in front of (then) the Sparta State Bank. The second one was on the south side of Division Street near People's State Bank where the Village Offices are now. On the northwest corner of Division and Union was a small park. It had a band shell (shelter) in its northwest corner. I can remember hearing some music played from this area, probably on Saturday nights in the summer. In the late 1940's or early 1950's Bill Morgan and his dad (Harold) tore down the band "stand." They removed nails from the lumber, and cleaned cement off the cement blocks and off the lumber. They used these materials to build the first part of their 24'x26' home at 964 11 Mile Road.

## Sparta's History

The first settlers arrived in the Sparta area in 1844. The Township of Sparta was formally organized in 1846, the year we have honored as our birthdate in centennial, quasquicentennial and sesquicentennial celebrations.

Jonathan Nash came to the area in 1846 and was the first settler in what was to become the Village of Sparta. He first called the settlement Nashville, and built a sawmill on Lick Creek, whose name was changed to Nash Creek. As there already was a Nashville in Michigan, the state legislature suggested the name Sparta. Mr. Nash was the first postmaster and the first village president. He had the village platted in 1867. Sparta was finally incorporated as a village in 1883.

The first railroad to reach Sparta was the north-south Grand Rapids, Newaygo and Lake Shore Railroad in 1872. Farmers brought cattle and hogs to stockyards along this track to be shipped to Chicago slaughterhouses. The first east-west railroad, the Toledo, Saginaw and Muskegon, came through in 1888. Its station is now our Railroad Museum, the only Sparta structure on the State Register of Historical Sites. The railroads contributed a great deal to the progress and prosperity of the Village of Sparta and to Sparta Township.

The fertile land in the area attracted more and more settlers, most of whom were farmers. In 1873 the principle products were wheat, corn and other grains, potatoes, hay, wool and maple sugar, with fruit and vegetables playing a minor role in area farming. Dairy farming became, and still is, a major agricultural activity in the area.

By the turn of the last century, many German and Swedish immigrants were farming in the area. They turned to growing fruit, mainly apples and peaches. In the early part of the century fruit was hauled by horse and wagon to Grand Rapids markets. Eventually, apple storage facilities were built and technological improvements such as Controlled Atmosphere storages were made. Now there are several important packing houses and other fruit related businesses in the area. Much of Sparta's present identity is centered on the apple.

Sparta's first major industry was the Welch Folding Bed Company, begun in 1884. One long lasting industry, and in many ways the most important industry in Sparta's history, is the Sparta (piston ring) foundry. Begun in 1921, the foundry remains the industrial backbone of the Sparta area.

The Handy Wacks (waxpaper) Company came to Sparta in 1936, and is still a major industry in the community. Post WWII companies include Spartan Graphics, Spartan Distributors, General Formulations, Continental Identification Products, Pak-Sak, and, more recently, Hart Industries. These and other companies sustain and nourish Sparta's prosperity and growth.

In addition to local employers, many area residents commuting to the Grand Rapids area contribute to the local economy and to the quality of life in this community. The population of the Village of Sparta is now approaching 4000, and of Sparta Township, about 8,000.

Today, of course, along with the agricultural and industrial base, the Sparta community has developed excellent services in banking, merchandising, insurance, construction and publishing, in pharmacies, hardware, groceries and restaurants, in parks and in its own airport. Excellent schools, a variety of churches, and several service organizations and museums are important parts of our community. Offering easy access to a major metropolitan area and the finer of aspects of small town life, Sparta truly is a great place to grow.

    The Post Office was a wooden building midway in the block on Division between Union and Washington on the north side. There were the two aforementioned banks, many grocery stores: A&P, Kroger, A&G, Burgett's Grocery/Putman's Dry Goods, Red and White, and Finches; one drug store, Brocks; two hardware stores, Roger's and Johnson Brothers; and then there was a small soda and confectionery shop, Bick's, this was the meeting place of the young folks. All of these (plus others, I'm sure) were on Division (also known as Main Street). There was one more neighborhood grocery store, Badgerow's on the corner of Gardner Street and State Street. On the southeast corner of Union and Division was the Johnson-Smith building, this was a dry goods, clothing store. Later on, that corner is where the Ben Franklin Store and Walstroms were. Then north on Union, on the west side, was the Fire Station and Pinckney Paint Store. At the fire station there was a public restroom. Further north on Union on the east side was the Library, a creamery and yet further north was the school; it then housed elementary and high school students. Then at the end of Union was another train depot, it is now a railroad museum. The Sparta Lumber and Fuel Company was just east of the railroad tracks on the south side of Division. There were two mills (elevators). Wilson's, the one we went to, east of the tracks and then there was Schut and Bettes, just west of the tracks both on the north side of Division. Coal, (for fuel) was sold at Sparta Lumber and Wilson's (later Emelander's and now Sparta Elevator, though Lois Emelander Lillibridge runs it). Going to the south on Elm Street was Johnson Hardware's farm equipment storage building. Also on South Elm was Forest Field's; seeds and beans were bought and sorted there, it was near the railroad depot. On this street too, was a Standard Oil Bulk area and still further south were stock ramps for the shipping of cattle to Chicago or Detroit. Industries of the village were Carnation Milk Company, Extensole Furniture Company, The Sparta Foundry- Division of Muskegon Piston Ring Company, and The Handy Wax Corporation. There could have been others too. All of the above were during many and various years. Changes have taken place throughout all the years far too numerous to mention. In the 1980's and 1990's many new industries have been established and there are many changes in the downtown area. Medical doctors were Bull,

DeYoung, Fochtman, and Eary. Dentists were Miller, Bromley, and Sutter.

There was a flag pole in the middle of the main intersection of Sparta, commemorating World War I veterans. It didn't slow down the traffic of the time, horses and buggies and model-T Fords, but it has since been removed to make way for today's fast-moving vehicles.

## HIGH SCHOOL

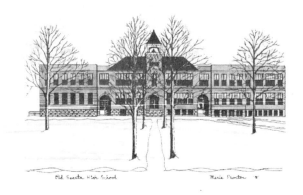

My secondary education I received at Sparta High School.

Imogene was working at Sparta Foundry, a division of Muskegon Piston Ring Company. She worked in the office eight to five. I, with some other neighbor kids, rode to school with her. We dropped her off at work and went on to school. Likewise, in the afternoon, school dismissed and then we waited for her (school dismissed later in the day, than now in 1993). There was no bus service to Sparta Schools until about 1945 or 1946 and then only one west of town. We rode in private cars. Frank Hall drove, and also later Keith. The neighbor kids paid a small sum to ride. I remember Ruth Truax, Joyce Barnes and Evelyn Straus riding with us.

Elsie Montgomery rode to her job at a grocery store with us. This was during the year's 1943-47, World War II. She was a war bride living with Forrest and Belle, her in-laws. (More regarding war in another section.)

The High School structure was a two-story building at North Union Street, Alma and Grove, in Sparta. One entered the main doors on the west side of the school. They faced Union. A little way in, the stairs ascended one flight to the administration office; after that landing one more flight took us to the second floor of classrooms. The first floor was classrooms too.

The second floor also had the large assembly room on the northwest corner. In this room we assembled, during our 'free hours,' to study. We sat in this room alphabetically. Reed, Reyburn and Rosell were near one another. The students sat from south to north, with the freshmen on the south, sophomores next, then juniors, and finally the seniors near the windows overlooking Alma Street.

There was an emergency fire shoot (slide) going out from the southeast area of the assembly room. If the alarm sounded the person in the row closest to it would open the small square door and one would duck one's head and shove off facing east. It turned to the left and we landed, out of the tube, facing north.

This is just a happy note of interest. In 1944 there was a special day at the Leo and Katherine Straus home. Twin girls arrived on April 30th. How excited I was, as was of course, sister Evelyn, and other friends. The twins were named Arlene and Eileen.

There was an experience in the large assembly room that I will always remember: I then, as throughout most of my years, was quite a gum chewer. I also had the bad habit of cracking it. This was not only a cracking while chewing but also the inward snap-snap-snap (like bubble gum) only inside the mouth. One day while unconsciously doing this, there was a tap on my shoulder. Mr. Fred Humeston, the Agriculture teacher and assembly monitor that period, stood to my left. I looked up at him and he said, "Are you making that aggravating noise? You had better remove the gum." I did!

The subjects I took were, with the plan of entering nurses training. I'm sure I was much more adept to math, than to chemistry. Chemistry, however, I did 'pass' with a D. I can't remember any special, favorite teacher. English and American literature were taught by 'Aunt' Bea Ferneau. She was a very plain appearing lady and an excellent teacher (in her latter years she lived next door to Roy and Jo Baughan; she died in about 1990). Chemistry was taught by V.Y. Tuttle (Vivian Yvonne, I guess that's why he used initials!) Miss Rie was our business training, typing and bookkeeping teacher (she also was our class advisor). Miss Rie is still living (1993) in the Sparta Area and has attended some of our class reunions. In typing class, I did some of 'Fuzzie' Kober's typing for him, was that cheating?

Mr. James Gardner was the principal. He taught history. I enjoyed his classes. Mr. Wm. DeHart was Superintendent of the school and taught government. I remember one thing he quoted several times: "Your freedom only extends until you infringe upon the freedom of another" (I used that motto many times during my bus driving years). I held much respect for these two gentlemen. I'm not certain if O. T. Baleyeat was Superintendent my freshman year or not. He was before Mr. DeHart.

In my sophomore year I lost my billfold (10 days) so I had to order a duplicate drivers license and also a Class-A gas ration book. It seems it was turned into Miss Burham the Home Economics teacher the first day I'd lost it. I'd reported it lost; she must have had it in her desk drawer. Can't say I was very happy about that!

Sparta High School Orchestra 1946-47

    We had a band, orchestra and chorus, all directed by Mr. Jack Davis (he'd come from Big Rapids). He was great! The band grew; uniforms were purchased (they may have been used ones). I played violin in orchestra. I'd taken violin lessons from Mr. Davis. Joyce and I rode our bikes on gravel (Pine Island Drive and 13 Mile Road) to Sparta in the summer for these lessons. Quite a sight balancing, that old wooden violin case on the handle bars! I sang in the chorus. The chorus had at least seventy-five to eighty members at one time. I still remember many of the songs. We had concerts at Christmas and in the spring. I had a few solo parts in chorus (no, never on the violin; I just never seemed to get into the swing of that).

    Sports of the day were basketball, football and baseball. Girls only had a basketball team. The football field floodlights were installed while I was in high school, down on Baleyeat Field on Olmsted Street. Wow, that was quite the feat! How exciting! Prior to that, football games had been played right after school hours and a few on Saturday.

    Pat Norton (Hubert) was a great basketball player for the girl's team. I'm sure there were others too. I went to many of the games, both girls and boys. These were in the gym after supper. We drove back into Sparta to attend them.

My High School Graduation

The High School at that time probably had no more than 200-250 students. Our class graduated fifty-five. Barbara Bull was valedictorian and Dean Allen, salutatorian.

During my high school years Joyce Barnes' mom and dad were divorced. Her mom, she and Doyle moved into Sparta. I remember going to pick her up almost every day. I'd drop Imo off at work, then take the other riders to school and go to her home. We remained close friends during these years. Evelyn Straus, grade school friend, was with us less. I also chummed around with Emily Bradford, Garnet Wiltenburg, Betty Gunneson and Jean Hansen.

High School had an annual picnic at Hess Lake. It was fun to go there because there was a water toboggan slide, into the lake, what a splash! We also could pay to use the roller skating rink at this site. One year I took the car and drove some kids to it. I took the car though, without permission and then I lied about it. This was a bad experience. Carl Fonger had told his folks about the picnic and somehow mentioned I'd driven. Then in conversation my folks heard it too. My punishment (beside Daddy pulling my hair!) was to call the people I'd said I'd baby-sit for on the weekend and *explain* that I was grounded and could not sit, and *why*. I was grounded for two weeks! Horrible thought! What if I didn't sit for two weeks, would I still have the sitting jobs, or would they find someone else permanently? I did learn.

Another of my escapades, April 12, 1945, I skipped school. Cousin Audley Bloom, a couple of others kids and I went to Grand Rapids. That was the day President Franklin Delanor Roosevelt died. I'd gotten home from school and saw Mom walking from the south on the gravel road. My thoughts went wild! Had she tried calling school to give me a message? Ugh! What if, if, if? Well, apparently she'd been down to visit Lottie Fonger. I don't think my folks ever knew about this until I told them years later (You must remember Rosells didn't have a phone permanently installed in their house until the new white house at 1274 Fonger Road. I think I heard Mom say, they did have one temporarily before each of her babies were born. Many neighbors, through the years, used the phone at Fonger's Store).

## 1947 Prices

| | | |
|---|---|---|
| Average Income | $ | 2,854.00 |
| New Car | $ | 1,290.00 |
| Loaf of Bread | $ | 0.13 |
| Gallon of Gas | $ | 0.15 |
| Pound of Coffee | $ | 0.55 |
| Gold per Ounce | $ | 35.00 |
| New House | $ | 6,650.00 |

## SELLING 35 ACRES-BUILDING A NEW HOUSE

9852 Pine Island Dr.

It was the summer between my junior and senior year in high school when Mom and Dad decided to sell the 35 acres. This was the home that we three girls were born and raised in. The farm was sold June 8, 1946 to Anton (Brut) and Betty Mieras. They'd looked at it on Sunday, June second. We would move to the old rectangular house (it had been a cheese factory years before) on Fonger while building a new house to the west of it.

We continued to use the milk house facility. It was summer, so milking was done at the pasture 'milking place' farm. We'd bring the milk to the milk house to be cooled and picked up to go to the creamery.

We got to know Betty and Brut well. They had no children. When we heard they were expecting a baby it was a joyous day. Brut continued to work at Gullmeyer and farmed too.

We moved to the old house on Fonger. I remember the steps to the upstairs were just to the right of the back door. What a flight of stairs, different widths, different heights, not easy to climb but Imo and I did it.

The southwest room, where the stairs were, was the back room. It had a utility type faucet and an old one-section sink. The kitchen and dining room was a section across the house from west to east. The folks used a little bedroom in the southeast corner. The living room was in the northeast corner, quite small. We used the dining room more than the living room. Another tiny bedroom was in the northwest corner (no bathroom).

We lived in this house in 1947-48-49, when Imogene and I worked at Helms.

One day at work I was sick. Imo took me to the doctor and I was prescribed Sulfa. I guess I took them a day or two. I broke out in welts of hives. I was allergic! Oh, I remember how they felt. They itched, crawled, and I felt so badly. I didn't want to itch so I bodily wiggled and wiggled! Mom suggested I pull the shades down in the living room and northwest bedroom and disrobe. This I did and I just danced and danced, wiggling all the time just to move the skin. Finally, I was so tired I slept. No more Sulfa for me.

July 1948, Dad started to build the white house (1274 Fonger-now 1270). Imogene and I helped a lot. We hauled gravel and poured cement footings. Cement was mixed with a hand turned cement mixer and stones were put in the trench as cement was poured in. The gravel was hauled with the tractor and the wagon. We dug it from a small pit on 11 Mile Road and Nestor Avenue, on Bob Fonger's acreage. Also, from a pit south of the Pine Island Drive bridge on the west side of the road.

    The materials for the house were purchased from Comstock Park Lumber and Campbell Lumber both in Comstock Park. A man, Mr. Carpenter advised Dad regarding the floor plan. He said to enclose the screened in porch and make it a permanent room. This was the den room, which went off the living room through the French doors. He also advised to eliminate the fireplace and make it a closet.

    The family worked together erecting the house: floor joists, floor, studding, ceiling joists, rafters, sheathing, siding, roofing, and electrical. The gable had Dad puzzled and I know he asked someone how to do it best (Ken Johnson or Jim Lunger). Nate helped quite often and Rollin some. Ken Johnson, from Mamrelund Lutheran, was a builder. Dad hired him to build the cupboards in the kitchen and bathroom. Rogers Hardware of Sparta did the plumbing.

1274 Fonger St.

    I was thrilled to move into the house we'd worked hard to build. We moved into it in July 1949. This was the first time that Rosell's had a telephone permanently in their home. We were on a four party line. This meant that four households all used the same Bell Telephone line. One side of the line had two rings for one household and then a household also had a long and short ring. The other side of this party line had the same rings for 2 other households. Each side only heard 2 household's rings.

People on our party line were Harry and Ellen Dufort, Bob and Gwen Dufort, Brut and Betty Mieras, our phone number was: TU-76633. Many years later probably early 1970 we requested a private line and our number was 887-7836. (Many years before the four party line there were eight parties on a line with four on each side)

On Thanksgiving night, I remember it turned cold; the pipes that were not completely covered froze. These were between the well pit and the house.

## WORLD WAR II -THOUGHTS AND MEMORIES

I have a vivid memory of the radio announcement December 7, 1941. Yes, Pearl Harbor was attacked by Japan. We'd been to Sunday School and church and were at Frank and Lillie Holmquist's farm home on 13 Mile Road, west of Sparta. It came as a news flash report on the radio; sad quietness fell upon us, as we were awestruck!

We listened to the news, reporting the war activities daily, on the local radio station. We did not have a television then, nor did any of the other families.

As I already mentioned in the High School area, Elsie Mead Montgomery rode with us to Sparta for work in the grocery store. She remained with Ethan's (Buster's) parents while he served in the military.

Nathan was at Fort Custer, Battle Creek, Michigan, for a while. He came home on weekend passes. I did go to Fort Custer one time when Barb visited him. He was stationed in California at the time they planned to marry.

Barb and Nathan left for California right after their wedding, August 21, 1942. They lived in Fresno, California, and Nathan was stationed in Pomona. Barb had a Civil Service Job, dispatching servicemen's travel by rail in the U. S. I wrote to Barb and Nate often while they were there, this is when I acquired the nickname 'Gumdrop' sister. Nathan went overseas and Barbara came home, after a few months. I remember her receiving his letters. The one that intrigued me most was the one that told her where he was. The military censored the letters. He stated, "You know where my sister lives? Take off the first two letters." Well, Nate's sister lived near Toledo; thus he was at Ledo. It was in Burma and he was near or on the Ledo Road.

When Barb came home she worked in Grand Rapids at Kirkoph Electric. She boarded at Aunt Jennie's during the week. I remember taking her and Lorraine Dufort to Grand Rapids every Monday morning and sometimes picking them up on Friday night. Lorraine boarded at Olga Hine's, I think. I remember having flat tires on more than one trip to or from Grand Rapids and changing them myself, as did most everyone!

Nate was discharged from the Army in 1945. They moved to Boon Road, Spring Lake, Michigan. Barb had purchased this house while Nate was in India; his parents had known the house was for sale.

The Luther League had paper and scrap metal drives as a money raiser. This was done by Leaguers going by car to homes and collecting it. It was then loaded on farm trucks to be taken to the place it would be sold. Recycling was important during those war years! The Leaguers also wrote to the fellows in service from the church or neighborhood. Care packages were also sent to them!

Neighbors did many things together. They always knew when a local boy's draft card was 'called up' and when a service man was home on leave. I know we were all concerned when Bob Dufort was called. He left for army duty June 20, 1943.

There was rationing. Sugar was one commodity. Ration books were distributed with stamps to use when making a purchase. Ours locally were passed out at Chalmers School. Mother and Mrs. Barnes worked as volunteers for this on February 23, 1943 and at other times.

We had no school that one-half day. Sugar rationing ended June 6, 1947 at noon!

Meat rationing was done by stamps too. The number of stamps allotted was determined by the number of persons in the household. We had our own chickens, beef and pork so we had sufficient, plus. Sometimes, at the A. & P. Store on West Leonard Street in Grand Rapids (after the egg delivery), Dad would trade some meat ration stamps with the city housewives for sugar stamps. Mom canned quarts upon quarts of fruit so we needed more sugar.

Gas was rationed too! Farmers were allotted gas for farm use and then for their cars too. We had a Class-A book; it had coupons to tear out upon receiving gasoline. There were Class-B-C and maybe D books. I cannot remember that we ever were really short of gas. We were cautious about trips not needed. Tires also were in short supply.

We bought the dairy feed at the Grand Rapids Growers. During the war years this grain came in printed, colored material sacks (not the usual burlap type sack). One tried to purchase bags that had the same print and pattern. The ladies made dresses, shirts, and aprons of this material. There were many patterns to choose from.

WARTIME and POWs= Yes, beginning September 1, 1944 Sparta had a camp of POWs located in a field to the east of Martindale and Gardner (houses now). There were 400 German soldiers camped here. They worked days in the orchards of the area; there was a bumper crop of peaches and apples that year as well as in 1945. A few U.S. soldiers guarded them as they were transferred from camp to work sites. The farmers came in to pick up their allotted number at 7:00 a.m. The guards remained with them during the day etc. The orchardists were happy to have the POW workers as many locals were in the service or had gone to factories to work. Many orchard owners were German emigrants or of German decent and could fluently speak German. Therefore the ones who spoke German loved to talk with them and also served as translators. They treated the POWs well and I understand some lasting friendships were made too. As we waited after school for Imogene to get out of work, (at the Sparta Foundry) truckloads (4-5-6) would pass. We waved at them and their U.S. guards; they waved back.

DATES in History: June 6, 1944 D-DAY- The day the Allies started the invasion in France against the Nazis. All church bells rang including the LIBERTY BELL. Churches held services all over the nation; Allies advanced quite well.

May 8, 1945 V.E. Day- Victory in Europe. The Nazi surrendered (unconditionally) to the Allies. Parades and church services were held. Parades may have been only people from schools, churches or neighbors going down streets or roads, waving various size flags that they had, and with or without a band!

August 14, 1945 V.J. Day-Not really V.J. Day but Japan surrendered to the Allies. Lot of celebrations, *big time* in Grand Rapids. We went to church. *Gas rationing* went off!

October 24, 1946 some local prices:
Butter 98 cents a lb.
Lard 47 cents a lb.
Eggs 78 cents doz. ($1.00 in Chicago, and no meat in stores)

Rollin was in the service, though not when we dated or were married. He was in the Military Police. The day that President Roosevelt's body traveled through Atlanta, Georgia he was in the Honor Guard. He was stationed near Gadsten, Alabama. When he was stationed in Cape Cod, Massachusetts, he guarded about twenty-five German

P.O.W.'s. They worked clearing woods that had been hit by a tornado.

After World War II it was hard to get a new car. The factories had to convert back to making industrial things. Imogene and I really needed a different car. We had talked to Stub Colby in Sparta, about one, but dealers were on an allotment and Colby's Garage (that was a dealership for Plymouth and Dodge) was small and in a small town. He could make no promise but would let us know.

On October 20, 1948 we looked for a used car in Grand Rapids. After looking, we went to Sparta to check with Stub. Wow-dee-dowdy, he had a new Dodge for us.

We went to work early the next day and left early to go to the bank. We then went and paid for it. Saturday we got the title and license. Boy, what a nice thrill! The car was so pretty. The color was a special metallic blue, chrome rings, an eight-tube radio, and a dual heater (accessory group # 3 included white sidewalls, clock and directional signals). Undercoating and seat covers we added. The Grand Total cost including insurance was $2,324.66. Remember that was 1948!

## MOTHER WORKED

My mother did bookkeeping-accounting work for years. She worked a day or two a month for thirty plus years at Johnson Brothers Ford in Sparta.

I was quite young during part of these years. Oh, how I anticipated the treat she'd bring home on the day she was paid. She'd bring home a long john, a bismark, or a frosted donut from the bakery. What a treat!

She also through the years (via word of mouth) had employment 'doing books' for Finches Grocery, Paul Miller Construction, Kent City Ford, The Bow Tie Tavern, Pinckney's Paint Store and later one-half days for years at Walstroms.

Paul Miller's company constructed roads and airports. He gave his private airport to the village of Sparta 50 years ago. On December 5, 2001 the Sparta Municipal Airport was renamed in his honor; "Paul C. Miller Airport." Mr. Miller lived to be 100 years old.

At that time he was a resident of Freedom Village, Holland, MI.

I drove Mom to some of the accounts. One day I was taking her to the Bow Tie Tavern (10 Mile and Alpine Avenue) and on 10 Mile I slowed down to look for a train, when I saw one coming from the south, I stopped, panic stricken. If Mom hadn't yelled, "GO, GO, GO!" I'm sure the train would have hit us; I'm thankful Mom Y-E-L-L-E-D!

Walstroms was a small Department Store. Dad took her into Sparta and went to pick her up at noon each day. Mother, as stated before, never learned to drive.

She was at Walstroms several years. I know it was when Marti and Bruce were babies and little. She'd bring a pair of socks or a small item home to them now and then. When I'd ask, "How much?" She'd say, "You didn't order it, it's my treat!"

During those years many times I drove her in or went after her. She enjoyed the kids stopping in at her work. Mr. Walstrom couldn't get over Martha's vocabulary at 18 months old.

Mother also did many individuals' income tax reports. Some came to our house with their information; sometimes she went to their homes. Some people I remember were: Ed and Elsie Erickson, Ernie and Elizabeth Wegal, Fergusons, Aftons, Edith Ingersol, Roy and Ruth Lundin, Bill and Bea Bloom, and others.

## DATING -ENTERTAINMENT

I dated Lowell Johnson and Don Bjork, from Mamrelund a few times. We went to shows. I also dated a few guys from high school, but not steady.

I dated Gordon McIntyre from the neighborhood. We doubled with his sister Phyllis and Carl Fonger. We went to Grange dances, suppers and meetings as did other neighborhood kids. The four of us went to many movies on double dates. There were theaters in all the local towns. (Sparta, Cedar Springs, and Rockford) and of course in Grand Rapids. One thing I remember when dating Gordon we'd sing and harmonize. One song was, "If You Call Everybody Darling." We also went together to the local ball fields and skating. Jim Ringelberg, and we four, was among those attending a Youth Grange camp near Traverse City about 1948. Quite a group went from Kent County. Gerald Kitson from Grattan Grange was a counselor and a Mrs. Garber from Chesaning on the east side of the state was mine.

Kent County Youth Grange at Camp

My folks were members of Algoma Grange for years. Memories of my youth recall fun times at the Grange. I became a Grange member as did many other young people. The County Grange formed a Degree Team of these youth. There were levels of membership, local, county, state and national.

It was Tuesday, April 26, 1949 that the County Degree Team went to Banner Grange in Ionia County to do an installation. We met at Gerald Kitson's, and pooled rides. Evelyn Straus (Williams) and I rode with the Roger brothers from Alpine Grange. They had a new Nash car. On the way home the lights shorted out, what a time. Rollin Lamphear was riding back to Kitson's with us. He held a flashlight out the side window and cast a beam on the side of the road. We were glad to get back to Kitson's (Belding Road near Ramsdell Drive) and to our own vehicle.

We lingered a bit and just jabbered about this experience. Then Rollin asked if I'd go to a dance at Egypt Grange with him on Friday night. We started dating April 29, 1949. Then on Saturday night we went to my Grange. The following Saturday night we went to his sister Gladys and Carroll's. His sister Avis (who also was a Youth Granger) and her boyfriend Bob VanAtta were there too. Then, Sunday he asked me to his home for dinner. He'd told me his mom made great chicken dinners; he was right.

I remember thinking Rollin certainly had brown eyes. I'd seen Avis a lot in Youth Grange and she did, and when we Algoma youths went to square dances at Egypt Valley Grange I'd seen his mom and she had brown eyes. Well, I learned he didn't but I kept dating him anyway. Rollin was always late for a date!

Three Granges in the county held dances on a regular basis on Friday or Saturday nights. During our dating years (and the Kent County Youth Grange years) many of the young people attended them. At Egypt Valley Grange, Rollin's parents as well as many of their generation of friends always attended. This is how farm families became so "closely knit." They exchanged farm work and enjoyed activities together.

We were friends of course with Evelyn Straus, Wayne Williams, Shirley Gross, Ken Anderson, Mary Smith, Glen Hale, Bernie Smith, Dick Corstnange, Gene Post, Leona Straus, Merrill Post, Mildred Straus, as well as

Suzie and George Keech, Westley and Phyllis Hessler. As you may note many of these married, as we did.

We double dated with Avis and Bob and also some with Gene and Leona.

Rollin was farming the eighty acres with his dad on Two Mile Road and McCabe Avenue. Two households could not be supported on this, so at one point we broke up. I think I told him if we were to marry his income needed to be more than the farm offered.

I remember his mom called my mom, very disappointed. I never knew much of the conversation but I do know Rollin stayed out very late (early) the next weekend and she was not happy about that!

I guess Rollin must have felt he should see about another job. Herald and Carrie Rodamer were friends of Rollin's folks. Herald was a distributor of Salerno (and other brands of) cookies. Rollin got a job delivering cookies on a route and was paid by check. He worked there until January of 1953.

We were engaged January 7, 1951 and planned a fall wedding.

1288 Fonger St.

My folks and we discussed the size of a house we should build. We decided a small one. Then, when our family grew we could buy the house (1274 Fonger) and the acreage. My parents would then have a life lease on the small house.

We started building this little house east of 1274 Fonger Road (1288 Fonger Road). It was 24x28 with a 6x8 front entryway and closet. We hauled our own gravel (from the same areas as we did for the folks' house in 1948) and poured our cement footings. Cement was made in the hand turned mixer but now it had an electric motor attached. Many smaller stones were thrown into the loose cement here too.

My dad helped often (living next door) as did Nathan. Then there was Cliff Dayton Jr. the next door neighbor boy. He was ten years old and he was our 'Go-Fer'. He also hammered roof nails at shingling time. He did a good job and was a very happy boy. In adulthood now, he has kiddingly said, "That is probably what led me into construction work."

Rollin's dad did the plumbing and helped when he could otherwise. Ralph Gold built the kitchen and bathroom cupboards.

I kept a detailed ledger throughout the whole building process, (which I retain to this day). The total cost for building materials was $3,716.92. Also listed in this ledger was the $5,000 we borrowed and the repayment with interest. The furnishings (less wedding gifts of lamps and table etc.) cost was $2,133.27.

## WEDDINGS - ROSELL GIRLS

Nathan was due for a furlough from his California base. Plans were made for an August 21, 1942 wedding. Barb was busy! I was 12 years old and so excited.

Ellen Dufort gave a bridal shower for Barb. Many people attended, the Bloom relatives and most, if not all, of the neighbors. (There is a snapshot of it, almost a historical treasure now, so many of those attending it, are no longer with us; 1993).

The wedding invitations were hand written by Barbara. She had a pretty wedding dress and she was a smiling, happy bride. The wedding ceremony was at Mamrelund Lutheran Church. The church was decorated nicely; gladiolas were in baskets and looked pretty in the front and on the altar.

Imogene was her maid of honor. Her bridesmaids were Alice Ruster and Ethel Mary Lamoreaux (Ebers). Best man was Gordon Wilkinson, ushers were Roger Bloom and Hank Fries, Dick Holmes was the ring bearer, and Jeanne Wilkinson was the flower girl. Aunt Irene Dieckman sang,

Barb's Bridal Shower

and Frank and Lillie Holmquist were master and mistress of ceremonies.

The reception was held in the church parlors (basement). Mom and others made the food for the reception with the exception of the wedding cake. It was festive and unlike most weddings of today. Simple!

Oh, how great, I now had a brother! He was a tease. (Still is!)

It was May 28, 1949 that Imogene received her diamond from Maynard Klein. Plans for their wedding and building of their house began. The wedding date was set for November the twenty-fifth. One of her showers was at Barb's.

The wedding was at Mamrelund Lutheran Church. The flowers were white, and in white baskets from Ostman's Floral in Sparta.

I was her maid of honor, Ida Klein (McDougal), and Lucille Holmquist (Swanson) were her bridesmaids. Nancy Klein and Enid Klein were flowergirls and Dan Wilkinson was the ring bearer. Best man was Kenneth Klein; ushers were Royal Klein and Bob Dufort. Master and mistress of ceremonies were Aunt Helen and Uncle Scott Holmes.

It too was a pretty wedding, with a smiling, happy bride.

Mrs. Millie Mosher made her dress and the dresses of the attendants. Ours had cap sleeves; we wore gauntlets and a headband. Mine was a pretty magenta color. Ida's and Lucille's were teal (I had my dress cut to street length, and I remember wearing it to a lovely party, at Blythfield Country Club. I went to the party with Mr. and Mrs. Trofast).

This wedding was the day after Thanksgiving, 1949. We had Thanksgiving dinner at Cousin Ellen Dufort's. In the afternoon the ladies made open-face sandwiches for Imogene's reception.

The reception was held in the church parlors and other food probably included cake, ice cream, nuts, mints and coffee.

THEN in 1951 - Rollin and I were planning our wedding. I received my diamond January 7, 1951. I was

working at Wolverine Appliance Distributing Company at the time and it was Mr. DeSaterlee who noticed it at once!

I had several bridal showers. Cousin Ellen gave the shower for the Bloom relation, Frances Vanderhyde gave the neighbors, can't remember who gave the Lamphear side or the Lindhout side (was it Gladys, Avis, Mom Lamphear, one of aunts, or some cousins, now that is a terrible memory... heh?) and Mrs. Grimes, from W.A.D.C., gave a luncheon at a place in Eastmanville.

I asked Rollin's mom if she would make my wedding dress. She was thrilled and commented, "My daughters didn't even have me make theirs!"

I had Cousin Judy as my maid of honor who wore green. Bridesmaids wore yellow and they were Evelyn Straus (Williams) and Mary Couturier (Colby). Connie Wilkinson (Poulin) at two and one-half years was my flower girl (these gals made or had their dresses made). Donald Tuttle, about three years old, was our ring bearer. It seems Donny peeked through one of the usher's legs to see how the guests were doing. Cute, as Rosemond Bernard mentions it often. Her husband Tom and she took our pictures. Connie, at rehearsal thought it very silly that she threw the rose pedals in the aisle and then had to pick them up again! She too has mentioned this as her memory of it.

Rollin had his friend Ed Mueller as best man; brother-in-law, Bob VanAtta, and my cousin Dick Holmes, were ushers. My dad's cousin, Henry Bloom, sang. Master and mistress of ceremonies were my dad's cousins, Harry and Ellen Dufort.

Our reception was held in the church parlors. Food included ice cream, cake, nuts, mints, and coffee. Imogene and Avis served coffee. My dad's cousin, Ellen Klefbohm, cut the cake. Assisting about the room during the reception were my older Camp Fire Girls, Jane and Mary Ellen Post, Carol Jean VandenBrock, Evelyn Darling, Sue Ringelberg, and Helen Couturier.

Nathan and Barb drove us to our car. A car or two followed us from church but we lost them. Our car was in the garage of Oswald and Agnes Hansen (in Sparta). We changed our clothes in a bedroom of their home and proceeded to the garage. What a surprise! They had our car meticulously decorated!

Our honeymoon was to Niagara Falls, New York and Canada. We

traveled M-21 and with steamers blowing and the 'Just Married' sign in back; we picked up another car that just tooted and tooted, as much as to say "Best Wishes." We stayed in a hotel in Ionia our wedding night.

We traveled on to Niagara the next day. We enjoyed the lights on the falls at night. We took walks and sat in the park and shopped some. The falls were something to behold a real natural wonder!

We returned to our jobs and to building our house. We lived at my mom and dad's until October 31, 1952 when our house was completed.

A memory which I don't know where to put, so I'll put it here as it pertains to my mom and to at least two of us girls. We many times would leave our purses at some one's home or elsewhere, and have to go back to get it. This became a standing joke, and we chuckled many times when it did happen.

## EMPLOYMENT
## HELMS-GRAND RAPIDS BRASS-W.A.D.C.
## (BEFORE MY MARRIAGE)

My first employment came easily. It was nice to have a sister whose work capabilities had her former boss seeking her to come to work where he now was!

Russell Gillette, a Sparta resident, had worked at Sparta Foundry with Imogene. He had taken employment with a firm, Helms Industrial Development Company in Grand Rapids. He was office manager there and came to our home one night. He asked Imogene if she would consider coming to work for him at Helms. Imogene said, "Yes."

I had just said to Mom, "I wonder if he could use more help, I'll be graduating from high school in a few weeks."

Mom answered, "Go ask him." I did and I too became an employee of HIDC.

The office was small and one of the requirements was no smoking. (A smoke-free office, way back then!) The girls' names were Floreine Saunders, my sister Imogene, Maxine Swartz, and me, Irene. How about that for the 'ENEs'? Also through the years there was a Margaret Paris, Mary Jane Feutz, Mildred VanDeCar and Delores Lewis, and others.

Margaret Paris, Imogene Klien, UK, Mary Jane Feutz; myeslf and Mildred VanDeCar; and Floreine Saunders

Imogene did accounts payable and subbed on payroll when necessary. Floreine was secretary to Mr. Lawrence Helms (owner/president) and to Russ. I did invoicing and accounts receivable. I don't recall what the other girl's jobs were. Delores Lewis worked for Mr. Ketchum, the purchasing agent.

The factory made Grille Guards for new cars. The post war cars were just becoming more plentiful on the market. The company had only one competitor VanAuken out of Detroit.

There was the office and one plant at 2145 Edgewood Avenue NE and about three or four other plants at various places in Grand Rapids. I remember one was on Lexington Avenue NW and another was on Ottawa Avenue NE. Truckers many times had problems knowing where to deliver goods because the shipping orders didn't state the correct address.

There were salesmen that covered most of the country east of the Mississippi River. Mr. Tobin was in New York State and the East, Jim Place was a salesman possibly in Iowa etc. I'm sure every car dealer in every town of Iowa was a customer. I billed invoices to so many small towns there.

Meryl Paulson and myself

I worked here June 1947 through January 1948 and then I quit to enter nurses training at Augustana Lutheran Hospital in Chicago, Illinois. I became so homesick I quit. My roommate was Meryl Paulson (Perlstrom) and I still correspond with her.

At about the time I quit nurses training, Grandpa Dieckman had a heart attack and I stayed at his home in Cicero and cared for him a few days. Aunt Irene was working at Western Electric. One day I was lighting their gas oven, to make grandpa some custard, and it didn't light as it should, *poof*, my head hair and arm hair really singed, was I glad Grandpa couldn't see me!

I came back home and again asked Russell Gillette if he needed help. He said I could begin the next week. God is good.

I began almost as if I'd never left. A man, Chuck Hilton, was hired while I was gone. Many times he wanted to instruct me as to filing, pricing, etc. Then one day

Floreine said to him, "She's worked here six months, she knows her job."

It was still rough to purchase steel and the purchasing agent Ules Ketchum had to call U.S. Steel and Bethlehem Steel frequently. Imogene and I can humorously remember how his voice would increase in volume as he persuaded the companies to put him down for an order. We wondered how his blood pressure was! Delores was his secretary and Girl Friday. She had the steel inventory on a Rolodex file and at his beckon command gave it to him. (He's still living. He and his wife celebrated their 65th wedding anniversary in 1996. ~His obituary from the Grand Rapids Press stated that he died at age 92 and that he had been married for 72 years.)

    Mr. Helms, president and owner of the company was a Sand Lake, Michigan, boy. Factory employees were several of his relatives and others were friends. His name was Laurence and if someone called him on the phone, asking for Larry, one was to say, "Do you mean Laurence Helms?" Or, we were to just say; "He's not in."

    An example of his kindness was shown in a letter dictated to Floreine. In short the letter went to an elderly man in Sand Lake. It read, "You may not remember me, but when I was quite young, I came to your store to return pop bottles. Looking back now, you gave me a dollar, which may have been out of your generosity. I now have a business and I'd like you to accept this $20.00 check as a token of 'interest' on that dollar I received many years ago." This left an impression on us gals.

    Claude and Laila Lamphear lived next door to the office and they cleaned the office once or twice a week. I remember going to their home one afternoon after I'd fainted. I had a severe case of tonsillitis and I had a fever. I had taken a drink of cold water and down I went. Laila took me and let me lay on her bed. I slept!

    Imogene took me at 4:30 P.M., right to Dr. Fotchman and I was put on Sulfa and bed rest from four to seven days. Tonsillitis, in a big way, and how long had I had that fever? This was the time that I had the hives and realized I was allergic to sulfa, so they switched me to penicillin.

    I know one time as we worked on a Saturday morning Claude kiddingly said, "You know girls, I've only a couple of unmarried nephews, you girls dating?" It was a couple of weeks after Rollin and I started dating that I told his Uncle and Aunt. They were so surprised! (This Uncle Claude made the rolling pin that I've used all these years. It was made of maple wood and he showed me a flaw in it where a fence staple had been).

At Helms I learned to operate a small business bookkeeping machine called the Centsimatic and later a large Burroughs. I feel I had a real opportunity to learn at Helms. The Burroughs had 'bar-sets' and did the extending of invoice pricing, etc. One also typed and tabulated right on the machine the unit price and machine worked the extended price. Of course, computers have this machine so obsolete; yet in the late 1940's it was great!

In January 1948 I received a $2.50 a week raise, this brought my weekly gross pay to $37.50.

There was a girl's baseball team in Grand Rapids, *THE CHICKS*. This was part of the All-American Baseball League in 1943. Mr. Helms had several season tickets to their games. At various times we girls were given a couple of tickets so we got see the games. They were exciting to watch and we really had some great seats. In the Grand Rapids

Press (May '05), one of the Grand Rapids Chicks, Dolly Konwinski, threw out the ceremonial first pitch in a Washington Nationals-Chicago Cubs major-league game.

In 1949 Mr. Helms sold the Grille Guard business to a concern in Pennsylvania. I was laid off December 16, 1949. Imogene was being married in November and did not intend to continue to work.

Mr. Helms' company then began manufacturing Helm-Scenes. These were scenic scenes, animals, etc. framed and lighted from the rear. The business was just starting and only Floreine and Mildred stayed as office personnel.

The company built a new building on the west side of Plainfield Avenue, between Four Mile Road and Woodworth Avenue. Presently (1993) it is part of the Meijer Thrifty Acres Building. Meijer has expanded the square footage a great deal. Fast forward to 2010, Meijer's Building was demolished and a new Meijer's store was built west of where Helms had been. At the time Helms built, the area was 'way out' in just the urban, residential area. The residents signed a petition to not have the building constructed. Hasn't it changed since 1949 on Plainfield Avenue? The area is now all businesses.

GRAND RAPIDS BRASS= I applied here for a Burroughs machine operator job. The Burroughs office knew I might be interested and advised me of the opening.

I had an appointment for an interview with the office manager. I was nervous to say the least. It was the first interview I'd ever had. I waited in the street floor entry. The receptionist had said the office manager would be down shortly. Wow, what a surprise when this tall man appeared. I knew him. He had gone to church at Mamrelund Lutheran when I was a child. He introduced himself as Mr. Trofast. I said my name, Irene Rosell. He asked, "Relation of Malcolm?"

"Yes, I'm his daughter." I'm sure I was hired as much because of Dad's reputation as I was being recommended by Burroughs.

Just as a side note here. When I was young and saw Mr. and Mrs. Paul C. Trofast and their little girl come down the aisle at Mamrelund I felt badly. Both he and she seemed to look so stately and firm, no smiles. I learned however, that Mr. Trofast was in every way kind, considerate and knowledgeable. We also started delivering eggs to Mrs. Trofast on Eleanor Street NE, and she too proved to be so friendly and sweet. Now in 1996 only she survives. The daughter died of cancer at a younger age. She was the mom of two boys. Mr. has died too.

I worked under a Mrs. Florence Brawn at Grand Rapids Brass. She was much older, and was having a hard time adjusting from hand posting to the Burroughs machine. I know too, that she was suffering from shingles, which didn't help her feel comfortable. She quit her position and I was there to do the invoicing and accounts receivable.

Grand Rapids Brass chrome plated faucets, etc. Some of their accounts were Sears, Kroeler, Delta, etc. These were plumbing wholesalers or dealers.

Lorraine Dufort and I exchanged driving to Grand Rapids in the years of '48 through '50. Once we got stuck in a snow drift south of 9 Mile (House Rd.) and Post Dr. A milk truck driver (picking up milk from farmers) pulled us through the long, large drift.

Also coming up Pine Island Dr. hill from West River Dr. was very slippery, and often caused cars to be unable to make it up the hill, due to lack of momentum. When this happened, they had to back down the hill again to West River, and hopefully have the momentum to make it to the top during their second attempt.

WOLVERINE APPLIANCE DISTRIBUTING CO= Mr. Trofast left G. R. Brass to take the office manager position at an Appliance Distributorship. The accounts receivables were in a horrid state. He called to see if I'd be interested in a job there. I was, and I started there August 1, 1950.

This office was located in the old Berkey and Gay Furniture Building (called the B & G Building,) at 940 Monroe Avenue.

Postings of accounts receivables were done in long hand at first, but very soon they purchased a Centsimatic machine.

They had floor plan accounts. This was when dealers paid 10% of the order and a bank paid the balance of an invoice. The dealer paid us monthly. We then paid the bank, the amounts due monthly for all the floor plan accounts. These accounts were in such an upheaval that it was two or three months before I actually got it balanced.

This distributorship handled Admiral and Magic Chef Appliances. The area of sales took in all of West Michigan. There were several service men in the parts and service department.

Pat Dykstra (Beauchamp) was the Home Economist. She gave demonstrations, etc. at Public Shows and helped private homemakers with some problems. Others in the office were Jackie Leaf, secretary to Mr. Strong-owner; Dot Fauble, Marie Grimes, Margie Byrnes, and Mary Couturier (Colby) worked a summer and a couple months one fall. A Mr. DeSaterlee worked here too.

Rollin and I were married when I worked here. In May prior to Martha's birth I quit.

## CAMP FIRE GIRLS

In 1948 I began being a Camp Fire Girls' leader with Evelyn Straus as assistant. The group started with mainly girls who were children of, or friends of Grangers. Names are: Sue Ringelberg, Jane and Mary Ellen Post, Arlene Tewsley, Evelyn Darling, Sally Gundry, Mary and Helen Couturier, Carol VandenBrock and Shirley Denton. It seemed to keep growing and growing so we had three Ranks of Camp Fire Girls. Some girls who joined later were June and Carol Bristol, Estella and Ellen Bitely, Joyce Powell, Bev Powell, Dixie and Bonnie Dayton, Carolyn Dorman, some Harrison girls, Mary Remmelts, Gloria Parks, Virginia Dakens, Bev and Betty Babylon, Ruth Knox, Gail Crystal, and Dorothy Smith.

We did activities as a group, which I hope made memories for all. We gave programs at Algoma Grange; one I remember was on the United Nations. One Christmas we acted out the nativity play at the Grange and then at the Michigan Veterans Facility on Monroe Avenue in Grand Rapids. We had our own props: manger, straw, spot light, costumes, song sheets, etc. The play went well both times we gave it. I'm sure we all left with a feeling of giving yet a feeling of having received. We went caroling to older people and shut-ins and gave them cookies at Christmas. We then went to a home and had hot chocolate and cookies.

We attended and participated in several Pow-Wows within the Kent County Council, which we enjoyed.

Another activity that the Camp Fire Girls sponsored was a benefit program at the Algoma Grange. Polio was prevalent in 1948-1949-1950. Lois Stream, a girl from Mamrelund Lutheran Church had polio that left her paralyzed from her waist down. She had been in the hospital in an 'iron lung' for some time. She talked to the Grangers, and the girls; then answered questions. Then we held a box social and all the proceeds went to the March of Dimes in honor of Lois.

A box social: The ladies and girls decorate cardboard boxes. Many varied items were used for this: sequins, ribbons, lace, paper doilies, crepe paper, flowers etc. Some were so pretty. Then a delicious lunch is put into it. This usually consisted of a couple sandwiches, a fruit, and sweets (pie, cake, cookies, cream puffs and candy). A man would be auctioneer and they were sold to the highest bidder. This bidder and the person who made the box shared the lunch together. Some fellows sometimes bought more than one.

In May of 1951 we made and then maintained a Roadside Park to the south of the cement bridge on Pine Island Drive. It was on the west wide of the road on the riverbank. The Kent County Parks Commission furnished a table and made a sign, "This Park Maintained by the Ioptya Camp Fire Girls." It hung from chains from a cross bar between two posts. We planted iris on the south side of the area. We cleared weeds, underbrush, stones, etc. in the area we would mow. Girls took turns mowing it as needed. The table was thrown into the river a couple of times by pranksters.

In probably 1949, 1950, and 1953, we rented a cottage for a week. One year it was at Hess Lake and two years at Bill's Lake. This was a great experience! It was so successful because parents were so willing to help. Edith Couturier (Mary and Helen's mom) made out all the menus and figured the portions needed to fill them. Then a committee of three or four girls, with a parent, shopped for it all. One thing we ran out of, and sort of laughed about, was toilet tissue.

It cost the girls a dollar amount to go this week; this

Upper left: Peg Babylon (a helper), with one of the girls; Upper right: Helen Couturier; Lower left: myself; Lower right: Arlene Tewsly, Shirley Denton, Helen Couturier, and Mary Post

probably was cottage rent and supplies divided by the number who went. Looking back now, it seems like quite a big undertaking.

The group was divvied into smaller groups to make meals, set table, and serve meals, clear table, wash dishes, general tasks, and activities. These alternated by days; therefore each had a chance to do all.

We made Ho-Bo stoves; these were coffee cans cut, with air intake at the bottom and smoke escape near the top. We made burners (for heat) with tuna fish cans; these we filled with tightly rolled corrugated cardboard. Then we poured melted paraffin wax into them. When these were lighted, the heat of the burner really could be intense. We cooked hamburgers, hot dogs, and even fried eggs on them. The food was laid on the top of the coffee can. Of course no camp out is complete without those ever loved *s'mores*; made probably more than one night.

Hikes were taken for nature items. Scavenger hunts for the same and for fun was a well liked activity. Singing around a campfire and of course story telling was expected at least a night or four. Then we went swimming more than once a day, a real treat for farm girls. This was before the *pool* age.

One fascinating activity was our mock wedding. Wild flowers and weeds were gathered and arranged into bridal bouquets. The bride and bridesmaids' dresses were elegantly, tied, pinned or gathered, fashioned from nighties, blouses and skirts. They were fun to make but more funny to see. The groom and attendants wore a pair of slacks and blouse with a tie made from bandanna scarves. This wedding took much thought and preparation. The receptions' food was Kool-Aid and cookies. Fun! Fun! Fun!

Parents who stayed the week or part of it were Gladys Remmelts, Peg Babylon, and Winnie Bristol

(Winnie had her younger daughters, Mary and Susie, with her; I think they slept in their station wagon).

One night's experience I must mention. All was quiet and even the other parent and myself were settled in. In the quiet of the night, probably 11:30 or so, there was a knock, knock, knock, at the back door. I sat up, so did the parent; we listened, another knock, knock, knock. We looked at one another as some girls stirred. We motioned we'd be quiet and tiptoe to the door. We really wondered "should we?" Together we did; another knock, knock, knock, at the door. We finally, carefully opened the door and there was a Collie dog and as it wagged its tail it had gone knock, knock, knock! What a relief! We chuckled as we tip-toed back to bed. The girls whispered, "Who was it?" We had to admit what it was, and we who were awake all had a good chuckle. During those years one did not have the doubts of going to the door, as we do now.

At Hess Lake, we had great fun, due to a tree having a strong, large, limb hanging over the water. I don't think it was used for jumping into the water. I do remember almost every girl climbing the tree and 'scootching' out onto the limb to pose for a glamorous snapshot.

In 1953 we were at Bill's Lake. This was the year Martha Kay went with me, she was ten or eleven months old. She was well cared for by fourteen girls ages ten to sixteen. Can you imagine?

The meetings alternated among the girls' homes. I held many at my moms' home on Fonger Road while I was single and the first year of my marriage. When meetings were at a local point, many of the girls walked home, though it was dark, it was safe. Some were picked up by their parents. Many times Rollin and I transported several home.

This group was about the only rural gathering other than 4-H for the girls.

## BABIES-WHAT A JOY

In January 1952 I was sure I was expecting a baby. I went to Dr. T. DeYoung, in Sparta. He was a real, country type doctor. I never had a pelvic examination or a blood test. He did, however, state that the most important thing a baby needs is love, even if material things are at a minimum.

All of the families welcomed the news and I continued to work at W.A.D.C. There was a man in the service department by the name of Ralph Terpstra. He, as a father, interestingly told me of his happiness as his children arrived (at a later date Rollin's Aunt Esther married his brother John).

The only discomfort in my early pregnancy was 'pulpy' membrane of an orange and lettuce; sometimes they made me up-chuck.

I had two or three baby showers. Such fun!

At about 4:30 A.M. on August 16, I felt the baby could be born today. I remember lying on the davenport for a couple hours. I watched the trees across the street blow as I timed the contractions.

Mother was working at Walstroms, in Sparta, so she called Galena Hall to come and spend the day with me (she lived on the corner of Pine Island Drive and 11 Mile Road). We had 'neighbored' quite a bit through the years. It was a blessing to have her there.

She called Dr. DeYoung but he was on a two week vacation. He really hadn't expected my baby until in September. At about 2:00 P.M., Mrs. Hall called Dr. Bull and Fochtman's office, and I went in for an examination. Dr. Fochtman said, yes but it will be a while yet and gave me instructions regarding the hospital etc. I went home and later to St. Mary's Hospital in Grand Rapids: Martha Kay was born at 4:04 P.M. (1952)

Martha was a small baby. She weighed five pounds, nine ounces and was eighteen inches long. What a precious little thing! She scratched her face in the hospital so little mitts were tied on her hands.

Before the arrival of all our children I busied myself composing poems announcing each of their births. I cut out pictures from baby shower paper which I pasted to the outside of notepaper. I printed the verse on the inside. Martha's follows:

My name is Martha Kay,
At Lamphear's home I'll stay.
August 16th was my birth date,
Five pounds, four ounces was my weight.
4:04 P.M. was the arrival time,
Mommy and I are doing fine.
Must mention: Dad survived too,
And that <u>we three</u> all hope to see you.

Many relatives and friends came to visit us at the hospital and at home. Mrs. Hall stayed during the day with me for a week. How wonderful it was to be a mom even when she suffered with colic, and cried **all day** long, with those *bitty* legs pulling up. It seemed she'd get so tired but it went on until into her 11th week.

My mother worked mornings and Dad would pick her up at noon. Her first question to him was, "How's baby?"

His reply could have been a recording; "She's still crying and crying." Martha did not cry during the night, only once until 2:00 A.M. and once awoke and cried at 2:30 A.M.

Rollin, baby and I would go to Grandma and Grandpa "Boots" (after their dog) almost every Sunday. Grandma Lamphear recalled many times, at later dates, "I'd take the baby and just hoped I could quiet and comfort her but she just cried on! I felt so sorry for her mama."

Rollin's cousin Alice Brown Bonner (and Tom) had a baby boy, Rex Allen, the same day as Martha's birth. Leona Straus Post (and Gene) had a boy, Leonard on August 18. We compared children frequently as we visited in each other's homes.

Bonners lived on Plainfield Avenue, (where the businesses north of North Kent Mall are now) and later on Grand River Drive to the east. We had picnics and dinners at the homes. On summer nights we'd just drop by, kids played, we gabbed. We kept in touch through the later years but visiting was not as frequent. (Alice died in 1985 of cancer. Tom soon after went to a nursing home, and died in 1993). Rex and wife now manage the apartments on 10 Mile Road east of Northland Drive in Rockford. Carl, the younger boy, and his family live in the north end of Grand Rapids, as of 1993.

Gene, Leona and we visited a lot too. We adults sometimes played set back or Pedro. At Posts one night, Leona had made pop corn. A large bowl had been left in the living room. We retired to the kitchen to play cards. We checked on Lenny and Martha and found them munching on pop corn as if there was a time limit to devour it, the large bowl was considerably lower. We laughed and laughed! We also commented that if they are uncomfortable tonight we will know why. This was in January of 1954; they were sixteen and one half months old.

Martha grew and we enjoyed her. She walked at about twelve to thirteen months and was talking very plainly at eighteen months. We kiddingly commented, "She may have no hair but she can talk!" She started Sunday School at twenty one months, due to talking so well. A couple of words were " 'pill my milk" and "Put on my 'no' suit."

A LITTLE WORK BACKGROUND= Rollin worked for Herald Rodarmer until January 23, 1953. He started working at Sparta Foundry, February 9, 1953, but worked there only a short time. He then had a job at Truck Equipment for a short time. Here, he and many were laid off on March 26, 1954. Rollin had employment then at Miller-Zeilstra Lumber Company in Grand Rapids, on Michigan Street between Diamond Avenue and Eastern. He worked 10 and 1/2 years here and then took employment in Sparta with the Kent County Road Commission (this would be an eight hour day and better for his diabetic condition). He worked at the KCRC until retirement in 1990, twenty-seven and one half years.

Our second baby was on the way and we had no insurance. Rollin had been laid off at Truck Equipment and changed employers and I was already pregnant. September 27, 1954, at about 5:30 A.M., I was up to use the bathroom. I went back to sleep a bit and awoke with labor pains. Rollin asked my mom to call Dr. Fochtman (we did not have a phone in our house) and we were off, at 6:30 A.M., to Stedman's Maternity Home on River Street in Sparta. Mrs. Stedman had been very sick all night; Mr. Stedman met us; told us we had better go to Grand Rapids or Muskegon, his wife was too sick. He looked at me and said to Rollin, "Take her in; I'll go get my daughter." Dr. Fochtman arrived and baby was born at 7:10 A.M. The water, they claim, must have broken at the time of my 5:30 bathroom visit. Bruce Thomas weighed eight pounds, eight ounces, and was twenty-three inches long! I'd had to slow-down labor and his little head was squooshed down, his little eyelashes were up under the lids for a long time. He now joined his sister Martha still with very little hair.

Bruce's Announcement
I'm a bundle of love, who arrived at their door,
Increasing their family to the number four.
The first weeks I'll eat, and sleep, and cry,
And watch the world with a wondering eye.
Lamphear's home is where I'll stay,
September 27th, was my birth day.
I weighed eight ounces and eight pounds,
As yet I make but very few sounds.
7:10 A.M. is when I came,
And Bruce Thomas is my name.

Just a comment... We chuckle many times now, about our "little doll house bedroom." A 12x12 square room! Furniture: a double bed, two seven year cribs, a couple of dressers, and a cedar chest and **oooppps;** that's the closet door, please, don't cover it with furniture!

When Bruce was small and it would lightning, he called it, "Hot Thunder," other interpretations were: "Tamana Man" (This referred to Bob York who sold bananas at 10 Mile and Pine Island Drive for 10 pounds for $1.00, he got them from, maybe A & P, or where ever he worked and sold them for many years at this corner. Another was "Cin-na-na-min for cinnamon."

1958 was another time of expecting a new baby. The time was early July and I'd picked string beans and readied them for the freezer. After supper Rollin went up to Algoma Grange Hall to paint with others, the outside of the building. I went out to the strawberry patch to pick some of the last tasty berries. I got five quarts, then I went in and ironed a few items, but no more, labor pains had begun.

Dad went up to Grange to get Rollin. I packed my bag and took a quick warm bath. Off we went at 9:15 P.M. Mother called Dr. Fochtman, then Dr. Eary to tell him that we were on the way to the hospital. Dr. Eary was unhappy that I'd gone directly to the hospital and not to the office first for an exam (Dr. Fochtman had told me prior, to go directly to the hospital).

I went to the hospital for precautionary reasons, instead of a maternity home. I am RH negative (type O) and Rollin is RH positive (type A).

Dr. Eary checked me for dilation and told the nurse to prep me. He was going for coffee. Well, just seconds later, the water broke; nurses rushed to the hallway and called Dr. Eary back. Baby, Maureen Sue, arrived at 10:05 P.M. Not much time wasted and she was fine (no transfusion needed). She weighed seven pounds even, and was nineteen and one half inches long.

### Maureen's Announcement
While the clock on the wall kept track of the time,
'Twas five after ten (P.M.), the arrival was mine.
The scales were ready, my weight to record,
Seven pounds no ounces, is what I heard scored.
I've a brother named Bruce, a sis Martha Kay,
And I proudly announce, July 8 my birth day!
My dad's name is Rollin; my mom's is Irene,
My second is Sue, my first is Maureen.

Martha remembers me packing my case to go.
Martha and Bruce were excited with baby. Grandmas, grandpas, aunts, uncles and their families, other relatives, and friends came to welcome our bundle of joy.

Some of Maureen's words were, "Trissmas" for Christmas, and she called Betty Mieras, first Aunt Bobbee, then Beetie and finally Betsy.

When she was small and someone called her "Mo" or anything except her name, she'd emphatically announce; "My name's not 'Mo,' it's Maureen Sue."

I had been quite ill; flu, cough, and so fatigued! I drove my bus runs and came home and slept; again and again, day after day.

Toward the end of my recuperation I felt I had symptoms of being pregnant and I was. I quit driving bus with a leave of absence in June of 1967.

Funny and humorous things I remember about this. I dreaded telling my mom when she came home from Florida. When I did though, her comment was, "Well, now all we have to think about is, if it'll be a boy or girl and just think **tent** dresses are in; no one will know for awhile." Wow!

Then at Shirley Montgomery and Dick Grice's wedding I did wear a tent dress. As we walked to the church entrance Tootie Mead Fast walked with us and commented, "These **tent** dresses, if I didn't know better, I'd say you may be pregnant!" Oh hum; she didn't know or even suspect!

Heidi made her appearance November 20, 1967 at St. Mary's Hospital, Grand Rapids. I'd planned to have Gwen Dufort give me a home permanent that morning. However, after I'd fed the couple of cattle their hay in the barnyard, I called her to say, "This is the day." I took a quick sponge bath, packed my bag, called Rollin at work (to meet me at Dr. Fochtman's office) and I called the doctor. I then drove in to his office in Sparta.

Rollin met me. The doctor examined me and commented to Rollin, "Don't break the law, but don't waste any time going to the hospital!" We got to the hospital about 9:30 A.M. and Heidi arrived at 10:03 A.M. The scales recorded eight pounds, eight ounces as her weight, and she was twenty-one and one half inches long.

Heidi's Announcement
I'm tickled pink and proud as can be,
To announce my arrival as a "leaf" to their "tree."
The hearts I'll win of the Lamphear "tree,"
They've chosen my name to be Heidi Marie.

Eight pounds, eight ounces was this "leaf's" weight,
10:03 A.M. was my "sprout" date.
Other "leaves" on the tree include Marti, Bruce, and Maureen,
While the "parent branches" are Rollin and Irene.
(November 20, 1967)

We had many visitors at the hospital and also at home.

Aunt Imogene and Carmen came to the hospital to bring Heidi and me home. Carmen enjoyed seeing the tiny baby.

There were happy siblings ready to help me at any time. Then I received a call from Bill Bloom wondering if I was ready to sub-drive for eight weeks. I had my six week check up and was on the road again, after Christmas break. Gwen came to our home and cared for Heidi in the A.M. and again in the P.M.

A couple of the things that Heidi said, that I remember are: "Spoil my feelings" for hurt my feelings. Then, "I'll go to bed at ten-certies," regardless of what time it really was. When she was ready to leave someone's home she'd say, "I'll see you 'hum-time'." Also, a word that we discouraged using was 'stupid,' instead we asked the children to say 'silly rabbit'.

FAMILY ACTIVITIES WITH FRIENDS AND FAMILY

We went on picnics with Leona and Gene Post, Merrill and Milllie Post, and Wayne and Evie Williams.

The kids played; we adults visited. We went to each other's homes and played cards as the kids played.

We did the same with Ken and Shirley Anderson and boys as often as we could. On New Year's Eve for years they came to our home, we played cards and had a big lunch at midnight. On the 4th of July we went to their place. We went to the annual fireworks at the Ada Ball Field. Bruce really had sensitive ears. He covered his ears at the first boom! It was a family fun time.

Many things we did with Barb, Nate and kids at both of the homes. Kids fished in the river, skated on the river, and swam in the river. They also had a pony to ride and a go-cart to ride in. We all went to the Grand Haven Coast Guard Festival and watched the U.S. Air Force Thunderbird Jets perform. Nate took us in his boat, two years, across the river to the end of the airport, wow, what a spot!

Once, Ruth Ann and Bruce came in, proud as could be, to tell us they had just given the baby Cocker Spaniel puppies a bath. Oh, oh, they were only a couple of days old, far too young for baths.

Our children stayed overnight at each other's homes. One time when Martha was at Connie's, she fell out of bed and cut her chin on the Conch shell night light. Connie fixed it; she put peroxide on it and a band aid. Marti has a scar as a memory.

We enjoyed times with Maynard, Imogene and kids. Our kids enjoyed seeing the cattle and asking their names, etc. We had some picnics at Lake Michigan. The kids spent a few days, vacationing there some summers. I know they thought the way Aunt Imo cut the noon sandwiches into shapes; like houses, kites, and animals, was just the greatest!

We visited back and forth with Avis and Bob, in the early years, when the kids were small. Sometimes I would take a pot-roast for supper, made in the pressure cooker and something else and we'd combine our meal. Rollin was working then, at Miller and Zeilstra, and exchanged rides weekly with Roy Lundin. I'd go to Avis' earlier in the afternoon and Bob would pick Rollin up on his way home from work. This gave the children more time to play.

We went to Gladys and Carroll's. It was usually on a Saturday night. We played cards and the kids played. One weekend when they helped with a Boy Scout outing we stayed with the remaining children, at their home.

Birthday parties (dinners) usually included the Rosell clan, Grandma and Grandpa Lamphear, Cousins Ellen and Harry and later Mieras' and Bob Duforts. In the later years there were two parties, one for the older and one for the younger generations.

SIXTH BIRTHDAY = Each of the children had a kid's birthday party on their sixth, in addition to the family one. They had all their class mates and also some of the neighbor children who may have been a bit older or younger.

The usual type games for a kid's party were played. Of course one I remember was fishing with a magnet and picking up paper clips. 'Twas a good one! The prize went to the one with the most paper clips. At, I think Maureen's, we had cup cakes with each guests name on, and one candle in each. Gift time was so fun for the honor guest.

Bruce's 6$^{th}$ Birthday

## VARIOUS THINGS TO RECALL

When the children were small, and I was out doors weeding or picking vegetables or berries, they were out with me. They were either in the old wooden, spindled playpen or in the bed of the pickup truck. They probably played right on the ground too. I had toys in the areas for them to play with.

In the summer of 1957 we moved (exchanged houses) into the white house 1274 Fonger Road. Mom and Dad moved into our bungalow. A promise made to Martha that she and Bruce would have a bedroom by the time she started school. She was four and one half years old; couldn't have cut it much closer, heh?

They had the southwest bedroom with bunk beds and a dresser. The balance of the house was bigger too. We were thrilled.

The house had a 'pull down' attic stairway into the upstairs that just had 1x8 and 1x16 pieces of lumber over the floor joists. I did hang clothes up there in the winter until we finished it into a large bedroom; probably in 1960-1961. It still had the pull down stairway in 1977 at the time of the fire.

In the summer of 1960, Maureen Sue was about two years old. Betty Mieras, Maureen and I had been shopping. I probably drove, because I dropped Betty off with her packages, and visited awhile in her house. I was home only a little while when the phone rang, and Brut asked, "Did you leave something here?"

I answered, "Not that I know of." I'd looked in the bags I'd brought home and I had everything.

He said, "It's blue and white!"

"Ohhh," I exclaimed, "do you mean I left Maureen?" She was wearing a blue skort with a white sailor top.

I don't think I'll ever live it down, because when Brut was still living he didn't let me, and now Mark Baughan doesn't!

Brut had been out in the back yard working on the tractor's tire or something and Maureen had been watching him (by the maple tree and stones). I just drove off and left her there. Poor kid!

Throughout the years on the farm we had outdoor-barn cats. The mother cats would always let us enjoy the kittens. We were disappointed when one would occasionally hide them and then they'd *hisssssssss* at us as we tried to reach them.

There were many cats during the years, and sometimes one or two had kittens in the early spring. We kept most of the kittens because it seems that they would be found dead after a car ran over them (or when I was a kid they were stepped upon or laid upon by a horse or cow). One year in particular, there were three kittens in one morning that died under a car wheel on the 'U' of the drive on Fonger. One or two of the kids recall cats being "in" the fan-belt area of a car, when the car was started one would hear a meowwww, and know immediately what had happened. One of these cats really looked in bad shape but we put it in a box with some soft rags, and low and behold later it was out and about. It limped, but it survived for many years. Then it again was caught in the fan belt but this time it did not survive. We had through all the years a cat or a kitten that would crawl up into the wheel well of the car and ride for some distance before falling off or we hearing it's meow, and rescue it. Kittens were the pets of our kids; many times I would look out the window and see the kittens being loved. Many times kittens' eyes needed washing out with Boric Acid. I always felt the pasted shut eyes were caused by the dust etc. of the barn area.

One of the last mother cats we had was at 9400 Pine Island. She was a calico, and marked very distinctively. Her head had a black and orange checker board pattern and Betty Mieras said we should name her Checkers. I wish I knew how many litters of kittens she had. I know there was a year or two that she had three litters... but always two. We were always anxious to see if there were any calicos; these were always in demand by people who wanted cats. She was a great mother and a special pet.

There was a very special cat that I remember well. I was letting the students out on the east side of the high school, and was watching many cars as they dodged and straddled a little kitten. I approached the stop sign but before it I stopped and emptied the waste basket. I got out and rescued the little frightened kitten. I put it into the wastebasket and continued as usual. Heidi rode the first run with me, so she held the wastebasket until the elementary route was to Fonger and Pine Island. Then I told her to take the kitten to Grandma and Grandpa Rosell's, and meet me again at the corner (I went down Fonger to Division and back). She hurried and did this.

Grandma and Grandpa kept the cat for a while, and then Marti and Ron had it.

They had the front paws de-clawed. When Ron seemed to have more trouble with his breathing they offered the cat back to the Grandparents. They took it again and enjoyed Cisco cat for many years. Cisco was a lot of company for Grandma after Grandpa passed away.

Marti was in college and she had the opportunity to get a nice young trained dog. Would we like it? We thought it was a good idea as Heidi could then have a pet. It was brought home, and it really wasn't trained, but it was a nice puppy. It nipped at everything, and thus she was named Nipper.

We all really enjoyed watching her grow. She was mostly Wired Haired Terrier. A very fast running pup and always challenging any or all of us, to a race.

When she wanted to come into the utility room, she would run three or four steps and then leap up onto the screen door. When we'd go down to the pond she also had a unique way of running. She'd run a few steps and then leap high enough as if to look over the weeds etc, in the lane. In reality she looked like a young antelope on the run.

If a kitten or cat sneaked into the house, we always tossed them into the utility room, and on outdoors. Soooo, Nipper received the same toss from Heidi, when she was in the house one day. Poor Nipper, she yelped, and whimpered so. We took her to the vet; she had a broken leg and he put a splint on it. Wouldn't you think that would slow a four legged animal down? Not Nipper girl, she still could outrun all of us!

Nipper was the mother of two litters of pups, which we gave away to good homes.

We had her for eleven and one half years. We were very attached to her as she was a great dog. She lay in front of the garage door one afternoon when Rollin came home from work, she had died.

As I've gone through many photos of the grandchildren, many include kittens or cats. When the kids were sick, Rollin and I would take the kittens down to VanHorns so that the children could love and play with them.

Bruce and Linda had a cat "Snowball" for many years she adopted them as her family.

The Baughans had a gray cat, Panther, in Florida. It was quite an active cat; she could jump onto the sill of the porch screen from a great distance. She calmed down quite a bit as time went on. She moved to Ohio with them and also to Washington. She died in WA after several years of being a good hunter in the fields around their home.

Corrissa, Christa, Brenna and Janelle

Neither VanHorns nor

Harts had cats/kittens so ours always had loving from those kids.

The Lamphear and VanHorn granddaughters stayed overnight together on a few occasions. I had a clothes hamper full of old dress-up clothes. Some of these had been their great grandma Rosell's. On one afternoon, I couldn't resist taking their picture!

## TORNADO

Stephanie Hartzell, with tears streaming down her face, looks over what had been her brand new home on the corner of 11 Mile and Summit Street. There is nothing left of the toil of her parents, Mr. and Mrs. Paul Bourdo, and their dream of the home they had planned for many years.

In 1956 there was a tornado April 3rd that leveled Gladys and Carroll Tuttle's home at 1059 Nixon Street, Grand Rapids. It was one of the worst on record. The path of destruction was very long. The damage was of great magnitude and there were many injuries and 17 deaths. There were only a few minutes of warning; some didn't hear it.

Carroll had the family and a visitor go to the basement and he watched outdoors until he too took cover.

Cathy Tuttle (VerHage) was hospitalized after a cement block, or something hit her. She had a broken back.

Rollin got to work (Miller Zeilstra) on April 4th O.K., the morning after the tornado. It was while he was at work that morning that he was informed that Tuttle's home was gone. The lumber yards were busy supplying plastic for coverings and of course plywood sheets etc. Rollin worked some overtime nights, making deliveries. He helped as much as he could evenings and Saturdays at the Tuttles. I sent down casseroles and desserts. Karen and Donny spent a few days and nights with us. It was such a tragic scene to see these miles and miles of destruction after the tornado. Yet it truly made one realize God's in control.

NOTE= A previous tornado in Flint, Michigan hit June 8, 1953. It too was devastating and it killed 116 people.

The tornado watch and warning system was then put into effect. We prepared items to take to the 'tornado-shelter' and we were taught how to react should one hit.

Our house had no basement so we used the well pit for our shelter. We mainly put items into it; we only went into it once, maybe. The 'tornado suitcase' always went out, a jug of water, a flashlight, a hatchet, a small ax, and some jackets, were some of the other items. In the suitcase we had packed the home movies, precious photos, extra change, cash and favorite items or toys, it was heavy!

When I drove bus and school let out for a tornado watch, then, Marti and Bruce were home first. They would put the items into the well pit. We, however, usually went to Mieras' or Dufort's as they had basements.

Rollin's stomach was a barometer. If the weather conditions were right, for a tornado watch; he was having 'dry heaves' even before a watch was announced. One day he was loading a truck at Miller and Zeilstras and had the dry heaves. A fellow worker was loading it with him and Rollin said, "I'll bet there will be a tornado watch." Sure enough, when they went into the office area, they were told of a watch. The fellow worker commented, "We knew, Rollin's stomach warned us!"

## STRAWBERRIES

We had a nice strawberry patch between our house and the chicken coop in 1958. The crop was abundant and Martha kept picking at intervals throughout the day until 2:00 P.M. She picked a 16 quart case. What an accomplishment at six years old!

## WORK
## SOIL CONSERVATION AND ALGOMA TOWNSHIP SCHOOL
## AND OTHER PART-TIME JOBS
## (AFTER MY MARRIAGE)

### KENT
### SOIL CONSERVATION DISTRICTS
Rockford, Michigan

In 1956 Ken Anderson asked if I would like a job requiring about a half day a week. I'd be clerk for the District Directors of the Kent Soil Conservation Districts. The small office was located in Rockford for several years.

I typed soil descriptions of farm lands and colored aerial view maps. Farmers could look at a legend and tell what type of soil they had according to the colors on the map. As time went on I received more hours of work. I attended the monthly meetings, took minutes and did correspondence.

The office director-conservationist at first was Dick Drullinger and later Lester Marks. The conservationists working in the fields with soil and water conservation practices were Jim Emery, Eino Niematalo, Jim Squires, and Don Kline. Marv Schafer was a conservation aid.

Some of the Directors that served while I worked there were: (and their Township) Irv Rogers, Caledonia; Ralph Johnson, Cannon; E.L. Phelps, Courtland; Ken Anderson, Ada; Milton Wylie, Tyrone; John Spangenbrug, Sparta; Harry Yeiter, Bowne or Gaines; Chuck Hilton and Lloyd Hill of Alpine; Charles Roberts, Sparta; also others through the years of 1956-1969 or 1970.

When the office was in Rockford I met Bev Emery and the kids. We had coffee and gab-fests at times during those years.

Mom took care of the children while I worked. Bruce was about 18 months old at the time I began this job. I remember him standing, crying his heart out as I drove out the driveway. Mom said I wasn't to Fonger Road and Grange Avenue and he was just fine.

The office later moved to new offices on Plainfield Avenue just north of the expressway. I used to work between bus runs in the later years but also took soils maps and descriptions home to work on (I was working on soils maps; with my foot in a cast on a chair, when the announcement of John F. Kennedy's assassination was made).

HOUSEWORK= I did house-cleaning for Hazel Pennington (Pine Island Drive and 14 Mile Road), one day a week when Marti and Bruce were little too.

POTATOES= Richard and Marcella Jewell, neighbors on 12 Mile Road east of Algoma Avenue, were potato farmers. They hired many neighbors to pick up the potatoes. Potatoes were picked up by hand and put into wooden bushel crates. Betty Mieras and I picked up for him a couple of years before I started driving bus. Gwen Dufort and I picked them up after I had bus runs. I remember hurrying and scurrying to get to the field and then picking up potatoes as fast as possible. Then getting home in time for a quickie shower and back on a bus route. We were paid 5 cents (maybe ten cents) a crate. My goal was to get enough so I'd earn $5.00. One got very dirty, the soil was a sandy loam and as one tossed the potatoes into the crate, fine dust could fly (in fall I also pruned the raspberry cane from the summer bearing canes).

APPLES= It was probably in the 1970's that Ed and Bea Longcore on Peach Ridge north of 12 Mile Road had apples to be picked. They could use some help, so Rollin and I offered to pick when we could (a few nights and several Saturdays). I'd never picked apples. It was a challenge to climb up the ladder and lean out to get those within reach. We had sacks/bags with a strap around our neck to put them into. When the sack was full, we'd go down the ladder and empty the apples into a large wooden crate. The ladder was moved to another position when the apples were picked until a tree was bare of fruit. Rollin and I both enjoyed doing this. We really didn't pick for pay; however, I know Longcores paid us something. Through several years, we also received apples from them for winters' use. They were dear friends from Mamrelund Lutheran Church.

ALGOMA TOWNSHIP SCHOOL= I don't know what year Brut Mieras asked me if I'd like to do the Algoma Township Schools' book work, I did them for a few years. Brut was president of the school board.

I did this work at Mieras' home, at night in the dining room. Maybe it was only three nights a month more or less. I made out teacher and bus driver payroll, sent in the state reports, posted receivables and payables, and kept a running balance for the board's information.

BUSTER MONTGOMERY owned a gas station and auto repair shop in Kent City. I did state and federal monthly reports for the business for a few years. Two things I remember him saying were: "If a mistake is made...we will correct it." and "If you notice my net income is down, just know that I've had it happen before...one just tightens the belt a couple of notches. It only takes me a couple of weeks to get used to it."

## KIDS' EARLY SCHOOL DAYS

Martha started kindergarten class at Algoma Baptist Church, due to Algoma Township Schools not having enough class rooms. Mrs. Elna Harvey was her teacher, Ruth Lundin's sister-in-law.

In 1st, 2nd, and 3rd grades she attended Chalmers, a two room school (On the corner Pine Island Drive and Fonger Road; now a township fire barn). The south room of this building is where I had attended K-8th.

Bruce began kindergarten at Edgerton school (no longer there; I think a mobile home park driveway may be about where it stood). This school was one of several in the Algoma Township unit. He too then attended Chalmers School for his lower grades.

They both went to Algoma Central, (4th, 5th, 6th, and later just 4th and 5th) Sparta Jr. High and Sparta High Schools. Marti graduated in 1970 and Bruce in 1972.

When Bruce was in about the 1st grade, he had a rough time. I'd look out and see Martha walking him home from school. It seems he had been sleeping one night as we drove home from Grand Rapids and the car ran over a frozen dead rabbit. He awoke and wondered what we'd hit. Whether he'd been dreaming and if all was tied into a misinterpreted scene we don't know, but that's when the episode began. We had to show him that all the windows and doors were locked each night. We had to reassure him things were all right. He put in some frustrating days and nights... his tummy was a bundle of nerves... we even got medicine from the Doctor.

During these years we had a big mixed breed dog named Prince. If Prince was loose he would go to Chalmers School. I would get a call from the teacher to come get him.

Maureen's schooling began at Chalmers School with Miss Mary Ward as her kindergarten teacher (later married, then Mrs. Crawford). Other teachers were: Mrs. H. Burch, Mrs. Irene Stoliker, and Mrs. Mag Brown. These teachers also had taught Bruce and possibly Marti. She went through second grade here; Algoma Central for third and fourth and when Sparta Middle School opened her fifth grade was there as well as sixth, seventh and eighth. Secondary school was Sparta High School. Graduated in 1976.

During Maureen's seventh grade year she had a Miss Carla Holmgren (later Mrs. Jack Frasier) as a home room teacher. This class came to our home for a party (pictures on VHS tapes).

In high school (or was it middle school?) Maureen received the "Betty Crocker" award. The name seemed to indicate "Homemaking" as the subject of the test, and I thought it was. Many years later, I saw the test for this award, and it included so many varied fields. These fields were electrical, home making, plumbing, judicial, politics as well as others. It surely put the winning of this award into a different perspective.

The field day, during the kids' years at Chalmers and Algoma Central was an annual event; it included basketball throws, the baseball distance throw, the high jump, the 3 legged race, the broad jump and some relays. Ribbons, made by the parents were given out. Blue, 1st; Red, 2nd; White, 3rd; the parents put a lot of time into making these and they were very nice. Money projects at Algoma Central were the Friday hot-dog sales. Mothers would volunteer to cook the hot dogs, and set up the table in the hall for a cafeteria-type choose-your-own topping and then clean up. This was a good project and the kids looked forward to Fridays. Many items for instructional learning were purchased because of this project.

There was a PTC group that was actually very active, especially at Algoma Central School. One must remember these were still neighborhood schools. Pot-luck suppers, harvest sales, monthly meetings, and the great Field Day which the parents planned and supervised, plus, the annual family picnic were the major activities of the organization.

Heidi's school years started in the village of Sparta. She attended Central Elementary of the Sparta Area Schools. Her kindergarten teacher was Mrs. Sharon Reister. She then attended Algoma Central (our 4 room country school) for grades: first, Miss Bonnie Freeman (Mrs. Meyers); second, Mrs. Pat Eldridge; third, Mr. Raymond Gress and fourth, Mrs. Mag Brown.

Miss Freeman had her introduce Charlie Meyers, her fiancé, to the whole class. I remember she was disgusted many times with Mr. Gress, one time was when he told her she couldn't smile in class... it seems that is when she started to 'hate school'. Mrs. Brown made an unhappy day for Heidi, when she threw away a papier mache "Bust of Laura Ingalls" after Heidi forgot to take it home.

## MARTI IN PLAYS

In 1959 Marti had a large speaking part in a play for the Mother-Daughter banquet. Mrs. Doris Swedberg (pastor's wife) was gifted in writing and directing the plays. Many of the church girls and ladies had parts in this play. Marti did a great job of memorizing her lines and acting her part. The next year she again was in a play, but didn't have as large a speaking part. Then in 1961 she gave the toast to the mothers at a Mother's/Daughter's banquet. She was involved in plays later in her life too.

## MIS-HAPS
## STITCHES= HOSPITALS

Marti had a 'lazy eye' as a toddler. We took her to a Dr. VanLaar for an examination. He told us it would correct itself with some exercises. We were to lift her up by both arms, by both legs, by one arm and one leg, and alternate them. This was apparently to strengthen the eyes. Either it corrected itself, or the exercises helped.

Marti had the Conch cut mentioned earlier, when she fell out of bed and Connie put peroxide and a band-aid on it.

She did have her tonsils removed April 27, 1965 by Dr. Richard Burton.

Bruce had so many bouts with tonsillitis his first and second year of school. He missed many days. In the first grade he had his tonsils out in Dr. Fochtman and Eary's office. From that time on he missed almost no school; except to go to Uncle Scott Holmes for orthodontic work. Both he and Marti had orthodontic work done during Jr. and High school days. When we wanted to pay Uncle Scott with $$$, he'd say with a big smile, "I do my daily work with patients for my livelihood---Nieces, nephews and very close loved ones, I do for pleasure." So we gave him fresh vegetables and fruits from the garden when in season and canned fruits, pickles and frozen meats to show our appreciation.

Bruce went to a boys group, Boys Brigade, at Algoma Baptist Church. Many of his friends were from there. They played the game Bombardo many times. One evening he fell and broke his wrist. It was his 'growing' bone. He had three different casts on this wrist, before it was fully healed. He had these on from April 5, 1970 through October 19, 1970. Bruce was in Charlene Mieras and Dan Piell's wedding during that time. The weekend of the wedding he did have the cast off, for that time only!

Then came January 9, 1971. Snowmobiling was such fun. He was out with Tom Koert and another one or two riders. I was on an extra bus trip with the basketball team to Lowell. (Betty Mieras drove too, and it was the only time Rollin and Brut went with us on a trip). We arrived home to the phone ringing. Agnes Koert told us Bruce was injured. He'd been taken to Drs. Fochtman and Eary. We immediately went there, no one was there. We went then, to Dick and Agnes,' and he had been brought back there.

He had been to the doctors and had a 'bruise cut' that required 14 stitches above his lip. While at Dr. Fochtman's, doctor chuckled and said, "Gosh Bruce, I just got your arm fixed... now this!"

This accident happened on the Camp Lake Golf Course (corner of North Division and Broman Road). There's a slight flow of water from a pond on the west side of the course; like a creek. It was frozen over; two other 'biles' had crossed, ice broke and when Bruce was to go over, the skis caught under the ice and he flipped. The bruise was from where his chin had hit the steer bar.

Maureen was quite the 'emergency' girl of the four kids.

June 26, 1966 we went on a picnic with Bob, Gwen and the kids. We were at Pioneer Park, (Muskegon) and in Lake Michigan, bathing. Maureen had stepped on something, apparently glass. She came out of the water crying and with blood coming from her foot.

We were down a high sand dune from where our car was parked. We wrapped the foot in a smaller towel and up the sand dune I went. I carried her and it seemed I'd go one step up and slide back two. We stopped at the Park

Ranger's quarters on the way out of the park. They let me wash the cut under the sink faucet and gave us three wash cloths that could more easily be held about or on the cut. We called Dr. Fochtman when we arrived in Sparta (from a pay phone on Main Street). He wasn't on call so we called Dr. Eary. He met us at once at their office and sewed her cut.

    She had hernia surgery June 5, 1967 at St. Mary's Hospital. During her recovery, I was near her and breathed some of the air she exhaled, boy did I become woozy. I didn't want to faint because I was pregnant.

    Swimming lessons were offered at the West Side YMCA on Leonard Street, in Grand Rapids. This was in 1967 and Maureen was in the grade that could sign up. They went by school bus from Sparta to the pool. While Marti and I were on the egg route, (July 18, 1967) a call came to our home from one of the adult sponsors. They asked my dad who our doctor was. Then they said they would call when the bus left Grand Rapids and take her directly to Dr. Fochtman's office. Dad planned to be there for Maureen when the bus arrived. Dad then called an egg customer where he thought we'd be for the time it was. We called home as requested and then we hurried faster on the route. I got to the doctor's office in time for her. Maureen had stitches for a cut on her head.

    She also had a broken 'tail' bone after sliding down a pool slide and hitting the bottom of the pool. Dr. Oates and Johnston gave her four adjustments.

    When she was dating Mark they had a car roll-over accident. This happened on Pine Island Drive, south of 11 Mile Road. They drove the car home, to our house. We went back to see where it happened. NOTE: Officers had been called to a roll-over, pin in. They came, found nothing, nothing except a receipt with Mark's name on. They went up to his home; his folks knew nothing, the officers called our home from there. Rohn Crystal was one officer. He gave Mark a lecture but no ticket.

We had a house fire on January 19, 1977. While escaping through the front picture window, she cut her shoulder. She received four stitches and was treated for smoke inhalation.

Heidi was in the second grade when she broke her arm. I'd warned the kids not to put the swing seat up on the chains. I'd often say, "You could fall and break an arm from there." Well, the swing was not hooked-up. She did break an arm; she was at Anita Lovell's.

I was on the way home from the bus runs and I saw this vehicle coming toward me flashing its headlights. It was Rollin with Heidi; I knew her arm was broken due to its curve. I took her to Dr. Fochtman-Eary's and they told me to go to the emergency room.

X-rays were taken and the technician took her in to put the cast on her arm. She was so brave. She never cried! It was set and when she came out, I was going to pull her sleeve down, oops! I said, "How are we going to... oh, when we get home we'll just cut down the sleeve's seam."

She just burst out crying and through sobs she said, "This is my favorite body suit." It was green with sleeves of white eyelet embroidery. The body suit had been a Christmas gift from Marti.

Heidi went again to the emergency room with a sprained ankle from jumping on the trampoline. However, I know of no other injuries from jumping on our trampoline. The trampoline we bought in the late 1970's. It has been used very much by our kids, their friends and now other neighbor kids and our grandchildren.-1993.

FAMILY MEMORIES OF SPECIAL EVENTS

In December of 1959, before Christmas, Grandpa Knapp Lamphear needed to go to the hospital for hemorrhoid surgery (the Ferguson Hospital was renowned for rectal care and plastic surgeries. It is no longer there as a hospital, 1996). Rollin and I, Maureen, 18 months old, and Bruce, five years, went to stay with Grandma. We took the crib for Maureen and we took Bruce out of school. Marti stayed with her Grandma and Grandpa Rosell and went to school. We helped grandma with chicken chores and took her to visit Grandpa. They had an egg route; we surely knew the 'ropes' for preparing eggs for delivery, and we took her on their egg route.

The first week of January, at Grandma Lamphear's, Bruce came down with the Chicken Pox. Then after returning to our home, the other two kids had them too. This was followed by the Red Measles and the Mumps... each of the kids had them and I was 'in' from January through May. Bruce had the least poxes, Maureen had the measles very bad, but she had very little swelling with the mumps (if the others hadn't had them we'd have said she had slightly swollen glands and a mild fever).

The McDonald fast foods opened in 1955, and as a treat we would go there for a hamburg with the kids. Wow, what fun to go with the kids to a restaurant. The hamburgs were thirty-nine cents each. There were no drive-thru windows, and we went in and sat in a booth to eat our meal.

It was during the years that I was doing Algoma Township Schools' books, that Betty and Brut and we became closer friends (must mention here that Betty is Rollin's second cousin). In the years following we were together a lot.

Charlene and Marti, Steve and Bruce were to each other's home to play several times a week. We had so many 'shows' put on by the kids at night.

An experience that broke Bruce's heart was: Steve and he were out with my dad in the field. Dad was husking corn, throwing the ears into the bed of the pickup truck. The boys climbed from the truck bed, up onto the roof of the cab and were sliding down the windshield and down the hood to the ground. Grandpa Rosell told them not to. They continued. Bruce came in crying; I asked, "What's wrong?" He told me of their sliding and grandpa telling them not to and I exclaimed, "It couldn't be that bad, Steve's not crying!"

Bruce replied, "Well, you'd cry too, if your grandpa *clunked* your heads together!" (I'm sure feelings were hurt the greater amount.)

Standing is Steve Mieras, bent over is Bruce, and Marti is crouching.

Other highlight activities together were early morning breakfasts on holidays. We would get up and go to High Roll Away, Newaygo; Tamarack Park on M-82 (west of Howard City) or to Meyers Lake. Then the fun came. The fire was built and the coffee pot was put on to perk, bacon and sausage were fried and then came eggs; all cooked over the open fire. What an aroma in the early morning!

A trip in 1963 over Teacher's Institute in October is a memory. (Teacher's Institute was a two day meeting of teachers, state wide, during which they could view new books, material, techniques, and in general, be able to take new ideas back to the home school. It will be referred to a couple of more times!) We had the 1963 car and the little Shasta trailer. The Mieras' had a station wagon and a tent. We stopped at Zeb and Marian Fowler's, on the west side of the east bay, in the Traverse City area. Marian was Betty's aunt and Rollin's first cousin. The next morning we went for a walk up into the cherry orchards and back through a wooded area of maples. They were so colorful. We have pictures of the sun filtering through the trees as some hiked down the hill among the trees.

We then went on into the Upper Peninsula. We camped at Brimley State Park. The water was turned off for the season. The kids went down to Lake Superior for the water and we boiled it. The kids had fun walking the trails.

We visited Kitch-iti-Kipi, (Big Springs). We all enjoyed riding the cable raft back and forth over this clear, deep pond and spring. The fish were such a fascination to all; one could see into such depths and follow them for yards. There was no one there but us, it was so peaceful! Here again, one must remember that, at that time it wasn't as commercialized as now, nor were there as many tourists, and we were there at an off season.

It was on this trip that Maureen sang so often, "See My Pony, Jet Black Pony"; Uncle Brut may have encouraged it too! For many years he counted it as a memory.

We celebrated birthdays at the homes. An annual event from about 1960 and following was the Kent County 4-H Fair in Lowell. This fell near Martha's birthday. The two families went together at about four o'clock in the afternoon. We viewed the animals, sewing, insects, and canning exhibits... so well done. Next we went on the rides on the Midway. One time Mick and Martha were on the Ferris wheel and I guess they got at least double the dose.

On a Sunday night near a birthday of Martha's, Mieras' were down. The boys turned the back yard flood light on to go outdoors and play. They came back in, saying they heard something *buzzing* like a June Bug, but they hadn't seen any; too late in the season. Brut and Rollin went out and sure enough, there was a snake coiled up close to or under the flowering current bush. It was a Massasauga Rattle Snake. They killed it with a ball bat. Upon measuring it we found it to be 27 inches, with five rattles. Its belly was so big; a decision was made to dissect it. So Brut, in a white shirt, did just that. A whole mouse was taken out. We have movies (now VCR) of it.

Carrie Rosell

In about 1964 Betty and I took the kids' play wagon and hiked to the back of their 40 acres and dug up some small dogwood trees. We tugged the wagon over roots and uneven ground but were so happy to have got some to transplant in our yards. Brut got home from work and chuckled as he commented there's some right back of the tractor garage! Oh well! One of the dogwoods I planted on the south east corner of the gray house. It did well and a picture of it, in full bloom, with Mom standing there is a favorite of mine.

Prior to 1962, Betty and I tried to take the kids swimming at Meyers Lake in the summer; though not on a regular basis, it was fun when we could.

We had a farm pond dug July 3-5 of 1962; it was fed by several cold underground springs. Our kids really enjoyed the daily swims. They learned to swim quite well and to dive too. The guys built a little diving board on the south side of the pond.

Mieras' kids and ours (with a few others) put on water shows. They were doing this even when some were in High School, some were younger. How they all played and enjoyed the pond together. We have movies (VCR) of the show on Maureen's fifth birthday. Charlene Mieras had made a BIG SIGN "Happy Birthday" and secured it to the page wire fence. They had made tickets and gave them out as relatives came to observe. They had lawn chairs down for the seating! The show was very good!

Other neighbor kids who enjoyed a refreshing afternoon swimming in the pond during various years were: Shirley and Larry Montgomery; Marlynn and Jeff Dufort; Marcia Larsen; Sue and Mary Gunnett; Deb, Terri, and Cindy Benson; Mark, Sherri, and Teresa Manson, and others.

At one point there were recipe cards in a box and kids pulled their name card and put it in the front area of the box; upon going home they re-filed it to proper name area.

Many beans were snipped and cut, down by the pond by Gwen Dufort, Betty Mieras and myself. This was done at the time our kids were learning to swim and fewer kids may have been there.

We put some small fish in the pond, Bluegills, Sun Fish, and Perch. They grew well and we had fun fishing for them and the meals were great. There was one huge bluegill, (we called him Grand Daddy) that would come and get a worm out of the hand as we dangled it. Yes, the pond was used and enjoyed.

When Heidi was eight months and until she was somewhat older, she would be at the pond in her stroller. I remember one time, the brake was not set and she leaned forward (or for whatever reason); it went rolling into the pond. She landed face and tummy in the water with the stroller on top of her. I'm sure I was there, probably settled into snipping or cutting beans for the freezer. Needless to say, there were some fast movements to get her out.

More recently, (the 1980's and 1990's) the VanHorn, Lamphear, Baughan, and Hart, (grandchildren) have fished in the pond. Janelle had the misfortune of having a hook attack her instead of going into the water. (Scary, huh, honey?) These same children, in the winter, did some skating on their boots, or skates. Aaron and some of his friends, one or two winters, played hockey there. Bethany caught her first fish with Grandpa from the north bank of the pond. Derick Baughan claims the pretty, large rock on the north side of the pond.

Stawberries plants iced over

The pond water was also used for irrigation and frost protection. We had asparagus and strawberries down on the north side of the pond. Early spring temperatures were four degrees lower at the pond than up at the house. Mornings at 4:30 or 5:00, if the temperature was 38°, plus or minus, off we'd go to start the irrigation pump. What a beautiful sight by 7:00 A.M. with the ice on the strawberry blossoms and a cross work pattern on the page wire fence. The irrigation system helped to produce beautiful large strawberries. It also irrigated the garden back of the gray house; sweet corn, beans, raspberries etc.

Heidi enjoyed the out-of-doors all year. She'd be outdoors when the snow was so deep. At an early age she loved her swing set. A memory in 1970 is; she was outdoors in her bath robe and a hat with ear lappers, otherwise bare, swinging; the ear lappers lapping and the robe swinging open. It was cute because it was so innocent. She showed her 'ever loved' swing set to everyone who came to our home!

Her friends were local girls. Cindy Ring and Denise Stryker were pals before going to school. Kindergarten and after, included Tammy Bliss, Anita Lovell, Wendy

Norquist, Tammy VanZyll, and Brenda Ricketts. These kids played back and forth at each other's homes.

Heidi remembers the time Rollin, my dad and she were crossing (the old narrow) North Park Street Bridge. They were in the pickup and the side view mirror hit the bridge. Glass shattered and came through the open window. It was brushed off Dad's clothing when they arrived home. Later, however, Dad found a piece of glass in his belly button. She thought it had gone through his system and come out. Much later she realized that it'd gone down the inside of his shirt and he found it in his belly button.

We camped often with Bob and Gwen. Sometimes just the four adults camped and fished at Lake 26 (or Marion Lake) north of Ellsworth. We have some silly, happy memories of it. The families also camped at Tubbs Lake, Pickerel Lake, and Sand Lake (up north). Memories, memories! One time at Tubbs Lake we watched some baby Killdeer in a sand area, with the mother favoring her broken leg, protecting her young. Interesting how nature has its own patterns of defense.

Olga Hine, Bob and Gwen Dufort, myself and Rollin

Silly tricks played on one another, pebbles thrown on roof, cold utensils in the bed, short sheeted beds and red light flashing! Always good and fun meals, some of them over camp fires. The kids fished with adults at times.

Sometimes they went rowing in the boat and otherwise played well together. We visited Harold and Olga Hine one time when just the four of us went. They had a cottage at Torch Lake. We all still laugh about how Rollin shook dreadfully, due to the cold temperature of the lake, as we tried to go swimming. Cousin Olga served us a delicious dinner and it was the first time I had a sweet cherry pie.

We purchased two lots north of White Cloud with Bob and Gwen, Chuck and Maxine Meek (Gwen's brother). We three families had many memorable weekends with our kids up there.

One year Brut and Betty spent some time with Rollin and me there. We saw a family of Baltimore Orioles. They captured our attention for many hours. Something we had never seen before, baby orioles. Otherwise we just relaxed; went for a ride, and played cards

One weekend before Maureen and Mark were married, Rollin, Heidi, Maureen, Mark, and I went camping there. Mark was to sleep in the truck's cap. During the night we had a terrific downpour, with lots of lightning and thunder. Rollin called Mark to come in and sleep in the dinette area, which he did. In the morning, when we awoke and looked outdoors, the whole lot was flooded with probably four to six inches of water. Mark had his motorcycle with, and he and the girls had so much fun riding through this water. It was at that time too, that Mark, Maureen, and I went out shining deer. We traveled quite a distance from the lot, on many gravel, dirt roads, counting several pair of eyes (most of these roads were used by loggers). We were on one road and it was very narrow. The brush on the sides of the road was brushing against the truck. We were on the top of a hill and looked down a very steep incline. We decided not to take the chance of going down it. We did not know where it would go, or worse, if it were a dead end road; could we get back up it with the dirt and chatter bumps! We backed up quite a distance before we could turn around. It was difficult backing up because we could not see many feet behind us with the back-up lights, and the brush interfered with using the spotlight. We have not used the lots for several years now, but they did serve us for several weekends as the kids were growing up.

During an energy crisis in the late 1970's and early 1980's each family tried in their own way to conserve energy. We did this by using "the den" as a bedroom for Maureen at 1274 Fonger in the late 1970's. At that time we had semi-truck loads of logs hauled to us. We'd saw these  into "chunk" size and then with an ax or log splitter split them into the size needed for the furnace. This was a lot of work for Rollin and me. We also did this after we moved to 9400 Pine Island in 1981 (next paragraph tells about the "move"). We had a small woodstove in the basement. The proper fans, working through the air ducts brought heat to the whole house. We often chuckled about-sawing logs, splitting logs, stacking into rows to dry (outdoors), and then transferring to stacks in the basement, into woodstove, then back outside with the ashes...was this an experience? Heidi remembers that the crack in the concrete on the north end of the driveway's apron was caused by the one semi load which drove over it to the unloading spot.

Mark accepted a job in Florida, after being laid off many months. Needless to say they needed to sell their home at 9400 Pine Island. Rollin and I exclaimed, "If we can sell ours, we'll buy yours!" A classified ad was placed in the Grand Rapids Press for Saturday, Sunday, and

Monday. Friday while Maureen was cutting a client's hair, she mentioned that her parents' home was up for sale. The client asked where it was located because her brother may be interested. So that evening Ron and Kathy Wolters came to look through the house. After showing the house, Rollin and I went to take care of the Van Horn children. As we entered the kitchen, Marti said that the Wolters called to say, "We want first chance at the house, don't sell it over the weekend." Papers were signed the next week. We consequently moved our belongings to our "new" house later in April. Our belongings were packed and stacked on a hay rack wagon pulled by our tractor. As we drove down Pine Island, various friends and neighbors passed us in their cars. Janet Vanderhyde is a friend that will not forget her thought, "They look like the *Beverly Hillbillies!*" (This had been a prime time TV show from 1962-1971).

## GRANDMA ROSELL
## TRAIN RIDE

Grandma Rosell (my mother) took her grandchildren to or from Chicago by train.

Marti was taken with Connie and Doug in June 1958. They visited the Museum of Science and Industry and Sears Tower and possibly other places of interest. Some of them may have gone to Brookfield Zoo. They also visited some relatives. Grandma many times, in later years, said little Marti had to 'keep up' with them, walking, etc. But she never complained. They stayed at Bertha Brahm's, (Birdie) with whom Aunt Irene boarded. They had a nice time. I know they came home by train.

Bruce went by train with Carmen and Ruth Ann. They too visited places of interest and relatives. Grandma said they giggled, and giggled, and giggled at Birdie's home. She often said boys giggle as much as girls and in this case Bruce and Ruth probably giggled more than

Carmen. She probably quit, when Gram asked them to. They came home via car with Aunt Irene.

Maureen and Shirley were taken by car to Chicago. They visited The Brookfield Zoo, The Art Institute, and The Prudential Building. They stayed at Birdie's too. They came home by train.

By the time Heidi was old enough to go; Grandma was not able to take her because of poor health.

## GET TOGETHERS
## EXTENDED FAMILIES

AUNT JENNIE had her birthday coffee, each year in the afternoon, at her home. Her friends came as did the Bloom ladies, Aunt Helen, Mom, and us. The dining room table was laden with coffeecakes, cookies, rolls, and a birthday cake or two. The coffee was brewed by boiling in the granite enameled pot that day. They broke an egg into it to settle the grounds!

I can't say Aunt Jennie ever received very many gifts, as such, but rather monetary remembrances. She used her own meager income frugally but these added gifts made her life a bit more enjoyable.

"Aunt" Jennie Hawkinson

On April 4, 1956 (the day after the tornado) was one of her parties. It was this day that I'm sure Bruce lost a little sterling silver baby ring. We never found it, though I searched the yard and house of Aunt Jennie's.

Aunt Jennie had to give up her home after falls that left bone fractures. Her recovery time was spent at Sunshine Hospital (Fuller Avenue where Kent Community Hospital is now-1993). She then moved to Luther Home, at that time it was on Division Avenue just north of Burton

Street. For as long as I can remember, Aunt Jennie's hands were very crippled (deformed) by arthritis. She endured much pain.

I then had an annual birthday luncheon for her at my home 1274 Fonger Road. Mother made a delicious chicken noodle casserole, Cousin Ellen made rolls, Imo, Barb and I made salads and cakes. The Bloom ladies (including younger ones now) and our family ladies came to this. It was a joyous time and served somewhat as a spring reunion of the cousins.

Betty Mieras and I had the windows washed inside and out for this occasion; what a great incentive and goal!

LINDHOUT= I went to the Lindhout (Nellie Lindhout Lamphear) family's' Christmas party the first time while dating Rollin. Wow, what a lot of people! I tried to remember families and who went with whom. I did a pretty good job, because soon I knew them as well if not better, than Rollin. Grandma had five sisters and one brother who attended with their families (Mae, Sadie, Katie, Esther, Ruth, and Bob).

The parties were held for years. The first ones I attended were at a school house on the corner of Ball Avenue and Michigan Street in Grand Rapids. Then they were held at Franklin Park's shelter house. There was a gift exchange, gal-gal; and guy-guy type. The kids all had fun, there was room to play and be active.

The year Bruce was a baby; Grandpa Martin Lindhout had six of his daughters and himself holding six babies and one toddler, (his great-grandchildren). He had many older great-grandchildren but these were the little ones! Grandpa died before the next party.

The lunch was a potluck. Grandma Nellie always was requested to bring ground roast beef sandwiches. One of her sisters always brought date pin-wheel cookies;

favorite of many. The table was abundantly supplied with festive and favorite foods.

It was December 11, 1960 and we'd just returned from a Lindhout party. We received a phone call. The caller said Fonger's store was on fire. We could hardly believe it; we'd just gone around the corner and had noticed nothing. Rollin immediately changed his clothes, donned warm outer ones and went to the store. The volunteer firemen and neighbor men were there all night.

The weather was frigid, seems as if it were below zero! I was home and made coffee all night for people to take down to the fighters. I also scrubbed my kitchen floor

during that night or was it in the morning by then! Rollin's family was coming for his birthday on the 12th. Fonger's never rebuilt. Ringelberg's built a store and station on the SE corner of Fonger Road and Pine Island Drive in 1962, Fonger's had been on the NW corner.

LAMPHEAR REUNION= The Lamphear Reunion was always held in the summer. The majority of the years it was held at Egypt Valley Grange, located on the corner of Knapp Avenue and Egypt Valley Road. Later after the older generation had passed on we had it one or two years at Townsend Park and a year or two at Alice and Tom Bonner's. It was held the first Sunday following Labor Day.

This too was a very large gathering in the first years I attended. It was a Sunday noon potluck and as at most reunions, food was very abundant and tasty. Visiting with one another was the activity of the day. I did become more acquainted with Rollin's aunts, uncles and cousins. There were some cousins who were near his age, but many of the second cousins were too. I will mention here that Rollin had about fifty first cousins (both sides) and I have three!

BLOOM = (Malcolm Rosell's cousins)
Henry and Dena (Rosell) Bloom's children were my dad's first cousins. They were:
- Olivia (Olive) Bloom married Ralph Gold, Ernest Nix and Charles Olson.
- Adolph Bloom married an Anna Soepbore
- Marcus Bloom married Mary Bennett
- Ellen Bloom married Harry Dufort
- Olga Bloom married Harold Hine
- Henry Bloom married Norinne Nagel
- Margaret Bloom married Wendell Grummet
- Roger Bloom married Alyce Spolestra

The Bloom Christmas party seems to have been an annual tradition forever... and memories are abundant.

It was first held at the Algoma Grange Hall, 13 Mile Road and Grange Avenue, but I can't remember ever going there. We first attended when it was held at Rockford Community Cabin, Rockford, Michigan, when Martha and Bruce were little. Our Rosell family; Barb, Nate and family; Imogene, Maynard and family; Mom and Dad; Rollin, myself and children, attended for years.

The siblings, their children and grandchildren got together, for several years, on a Sunday the first part of December; now it's the first Sunday in December. (1993)

In addition to Dad's family, others attending were Aunt Helen's, plus some cousins on Uncle Henry's side.

Attendance was exceptionable; I considered the Bloom family, as a family remaining very close through the years.

    This was a noon pot-luck and the abundance on the dinner tables was something to behold, the taste was great too! As people arrived and as preparations were being completed the cousins and friends visited.

    After the dinner, the tables were taken down and there was a program. The group for years had a committee that encouraged the young children to speak a short piece (pieces were even sent to parents if they had none of their own) or a special talent could be presented. Baton twirling, singing, dancing, instrumentals and even karate were included through the various years. There were some years when some adults also had humorous songs or a reading.

    Upon the conclusion of the program the group joined in Christmas carols and winter songs. As they sang, "Here Comes Santa Claus," who would appear but the jolly white bearded elf himself. What excitement and merriment! Santa gave the children a gift from under a decorated tree and also a candy cane. The children came and sat on his lap, some were frightened. It was fun to watch the expressions on their faces. Sometimes Jolly Santa even gave a loving hug, or sat gently upon an 'oldsters' lap. How the kids giggled!

    Prior to the above program a short business meeting was held. Cards were signed for those who weren't in attendance due to illness or wintering in the south. An introduction of new babies, new in-laws, and friends in attendance was at this time too.

    The clan grew and the party moved to the Sparta Civic Center. There were times 150 to nearly 200 attended.

    Though, in more recent years, my mother (Carrie) went to the gathering with Bob and Gwen Dufort; we as a Rosell clan have not. This for years was due to church or school programs or other family parties. I hope to attend some in the future. If this hope doesn't come to pass; I still have happy memories.

The Blooms had a picnic, annually in the summer, years ago. The ones I remember were at Long Lake Park, a County Park off of 17 Mile Road. One large picture we have shows many of the relatives.

I must mention here too, that any Bloom shower (bridal or baby) was a delight to attend. Those ladies always were reminiscing, or playing a fun game, with vim-vip and vigor. They made laughter ring with merriment.

## BUS DRIVING YEARS

Betty Mieras and I helped Marvin Field do school cleaning at the four room Algoma Central School and the two room Chalmers School. This we did in summer and at Christmas break.

Rollin surprised me with this mailbox.

In August of 1964 I was talking to Dick Koert (a Sparta Area School bus driver) and he told me that Bill Bloom, Sparta School's Transportation Supervisor needed a bus driver. Dick thought I should apply. I did. I was to sub-drive for eight weeks on Bunch VanDenHout's run west of Sparta. He had a broken leg and expected to be laid up for these weeks (this Bunch was the same man that gave me my first driver's license road test). This run was west of town, in the area of Mamrelund Lutheran Church.

This route was quite a challenge; three VanOfflen boys, two Decker boys, two Wilk boys, and three Simon boys, wow! I wrote a letter to Bill on what I thought was my last day on that route. I parked the bus in the bus yard on Olmsted Street near Baleyeat Field. I got into my car. There was a note stating to come to the high school office and talk with Bill, ugh! He told me that Bunch wasn't coming back. The run was mine if I'd like it. I took it. The buses only ran one run then; so we had K-12 riding the same bus. It was interesting!

April 1, 1965, Bill called me at home about 1:30 P.M. to say Bob Luby had quit, could I take his run. I must start at Chalmers School; go around the horn of Fonger Road, Nestor Avenue, 11 Mile Road, Grange Avenue, and Fonger Road and up to Algoma Central School, get those kids and take them all home. This run was just elementary, servicing the two outlying schools in the Sparta School District, with a big enrollment of students in the area. So I began driving a run which I had for many years. This was a run right around my home. Later the elementary schools began later than the middle and high schools so there were double runs in the morning and night.

In 1967 I was expecting a baby. I was thinking about quitting, but Bill encouraged me to take a leave of absence. Baby was born November 20, 1967 and I was back driving a bus January 6, 1968.

I came back at this time to sub on the Camp Lake Run, as the driver had had surgery. When these weeks were done Lu Merritt said she really would just as soon not drive full time for a while. I had my run back until retirement in December of 1991.

Heidi started riding my school bus in the afternoons in September of 1968. Gwen continued to care for her in the mornings and if Heidi was taking a nap in the afternoon, she again came to our home.

The following years she rode my bus in the A.M.s too. Betty and I stopped at the C and B Restaurant each morning between the runs. We bought hot chocolate. They had it ready as we approached the counter. Mr. Floyd Schut, a Sparta business man, many times gave Heidi a penny. I can't remember if there was a gum ball machine there for her to use it in, or if she put it in her bank.

I worked in the transportation office from September 1974 to June 1981.

Extra Trips, they were any trip other than your regular runs. I went on many of these; band, choir, sports, senior citizens, etc. I drove about three years to the National Cherry Festival in Traverse City, Michigan. The band under the direction of Robert Stiles participated in various competitions. They did well. We watched their competition as well as the long, interesting parades. The students and we were housed in area schools. The bus drivers had a classroom by themselves. All attending brought sleeping bags. We drivers brought cots, to lay the bags on! We ate most of our meals at North Western College and bought a few pizzas or McDonald's on occasion. This festival was attended by thousands of tourists. One year the Anheuser Busch Clydesdale Horses were in the parade and we parked the buses near the air conditioned horse trailers and watched them being unloaded. President Ford was an honored guest in the parade one year; we only caught a glimpse of him because it took so long for us to park our buses. One year Heidi went with me and Amy Ysseldyke went with Sharon. A couple of late afternoons when we returned to the school we drove the buses out in back and did 'do-nuts,' and went between trees. This I know made a lasting impression on many of the kids, including Heidi! Another highlight this year was the demonstration from the U.S. Air Force "Thunderbirds." We viewed this show from the west side of the west bay. We parked the busses on the side of the road. We had long, but enjoyable days. Fun, fun! Memories!

Kindergarten Orientation, I was in charge of for years. This was when parents and children were told the 'do's and don'ts' of crossing to and from the bus stop and various hints and advice for following bus rules while riding a bus.

During the years Allen Hosmer on the elementary route (lived on Fonger) brought many green chrysalises (cocoons) on the bus in their own containers. He told me that they were Monarch Butterflies ready to hatch. In the afternoon, I waited a short time at Algoma Central to have the children board. He came out first, with a cocoon for me to gently hold as a Monarch emerged. What a thrill! In all my years of out-of-doors and enjoying nature this was a first.

One Halloween night, when the Algoma volunteer fireman gave hay rides and cider and donuts to the local kids, I dressed up and attended. Rollin drove me to the first house west of the firebarn and I walked in from the west. I dressed in Rollin's brown insulated underwear and used a stuffed nylon stocking for a tail and another nylon stocking over my head/face. I made ears out of brown construction paper. I was transformed into a cat. Many of the kids from my bus route were there. My! What excitement... who was the cat? I remember Steve Zwyghuizen was probably about a third grader, dashing around me wondering who I was. I took him up and threw him over my shoulder meowing, and meowing. I put him down and went on my way to the Ringelberg's store across Pine Island and visited them. I left them and went to Lottie Fonger's house. When I entered her home, the kids came running up Fonger to catch me. I got into her house. I lay down on the floor on a rug in front of her couch. The kids knocked and she played along so well, she opened the door and just said, "Oh, my cat, she's just laying on the rug purring!" The kids left. I stayed at Lottie's long enough for them to be on the hayride and not see me walk home.

SPARTA'S FIRE= As bus drivers drove into Sparta on Tuesday, December 3, 1974; we all noticed a huge cloud of dark smoke. A fire started in Johnson Ford dealership and service. It was located just north of the main street corners, 32 N. Union. They felt that the fire started when gasoline ignited about 9 o'clock a.m. (This is the same business that my mother, Carrie Rosell, did bookkeeping for years.) Eight fire departments fought the blaze. It was said that the smoke could be seen from Grand Rapids, 15 miles away. It spread onto East Division to Keck's shoes, Momber's Drugs, Finch Meat and Grocery, a Western Auto Outlet, and Rob's Roost Restaurant. It was really a huge fire and changed Sparta business area's main street. Johnson Bros. never rebuilt and the area is now a parking lot. Momber's expanded using Finch's area.

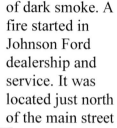

THE APPLE SAGA= I was to take Betty Mieras some apples (on my way into the bus run) an ingredient in "Morning Glory Muffins." I'd told her I would leave them in a bag at her mailbox. I stopped and stepped out of my truck to put the apples at the box. I slipped (so very quickly) on black ice and was on my back in the roadway of Pine Island Drive. Betty was at her living room window looking out and wondered, "Why is she backing across the road to the west?" Then she realized that the truck was just going. God protected me, and the truck was not in line with my body. It passed me and was stopped by some brush on the west side of the road. No other vehicles were traveling the road right then (What a surprise!) I got up and walked very carefully and left the apples in her mailbox. Then I crossed the road to the truck and drove it out of the ditch and was again off to my bus runs. Thanks be to God for his protection.

In January 1986, while driving bus into Sparta I stopped at the railroad tracks. While the door was open a couple of ladies, out for their morning walk, stepped a bit closer and told me about the space shuttle Challenger disaster.

One afternoon when I came home from the bus run I was so surprised. I entered the kitchen and on the counter was a yellow mailbox. The mailbox was mounted on a child's flatbed toy truck. The cab of the toy truck had been painted yellow too. It was decked out complete with red flashers (for crossing), and red running lights. The mailbox portion was painted with black squares representing the door and windows. My bus number, #20, was also painted on the front. Coincidentally, Rollin gave it to me on my 20$^{th}$ anniversary of driving bus for Sparta Area Schools. Rollin and Terry Richardson made it during their breaks at the county garage. We used it for many years…even after I retired, but one night it was vandalized by someone. It was battered and bent to the extent that I told Rollin not to fix it.

During my years of driving, a fellow driver died, Amy Brady.

During these years; three tragic deaths; students, involving school buses.

During these years; Bill Bloom died.

During the time I drove with, for short or long periods of times, 40-45 drivers.

During this time I wrote tributes to Amy Brady, Bill Bloom, retiree Joyce Chipman, and my own bus students, and in April 1993, to retiree Pat Hubert. I have many more memories but that would be another book!

## IRENE'S TRIBUTE TO BUS DRIVING!!!

Take time... and read this... right now!!!
All of you, Bus Guys and Gals,
I want you to know this first;
Since we are transportation pals.

I shall be hanging up the keys (12/31/91)
To bus twenty, or any other;
And... I'm actually very excited;
I'm not kidding you, sister, brother!

For one year and one half,
The decision's been in the making;
Now I can stay home and
Enjoy more leisure time; baking!

I've worked many years for this,
Many, many hours for sure;
But others have expressed
Enjoyment in retirement, with allure!

You, my friends, I will miss,
And all those students too.
On foggy, wintry, windy days,
I'll surely be thinking of you!

I'll enjoy a second cup of coffee,
While sitting, watching my T.V.
On some of those blustery days,
I'll bet you may even envy me!

It's been a real challenge,
Always, safety first and foremost;
Driving a bus, as driver,
Never let's one's mind coast!

The care of lives entrusted
To me, spelled "Responsibility";
Therefore, I put forth in all
I did the best of my ability!

Yet, driving carried with it,
A privilege and much joy;
Of caring, sharing, and being a friend,
To most every girl and boy.

I have many great memories,
Of all the years gone past;
Hope to write some down soon;
Some of them will last!

Kids with such cute sayings,
And also actions sweet;
Their clothes so very pretty,
Their hair combed, oh... so neat!

Of course, there are those few,
I would have to honestly admit;
Challenged me b e c a u s e...
They just "Could not sit!"

I've loved all these kids,
Through all of their school years,
And kept close watch of them;
With help of various mirrors!

They'd hit, kick, and throw things,
And then sometimes, I'd shout;
Many times then, there'd be
A few show off "Their pout!"

I've fixed so many zippers,
Colorful lunch boxes too;
Wiped many, many noses and
Tied oh, so many-a-shoe!

Must also mention the "Ugh" days,
The kids who had the "Flu"
Would "Up-chuck," yes all over;
And I'd clean up "This Phewwww!"

I've told them "Ad-lib" stories,
Also taught them various songs;
Disciplined them with love,
Explained rights and wrongs!

As these kids grew up and...
Now are parents too,
They've commented with love,
"Wish we had the patience of you."

I look back upon the years,
And wish and wonder why;
I didn't keep a list of names
Of kids who "me passed by."

I look back at pictures,
Some dating way back when;
Wonder, who and where they are,
Others, I "bump into" now and then!

I've gone to many graduations,
To showers and weddings too;
Then even welcomed a bundle
Dressed in pink or blue!

Friends, I've made of families,
Otherwise I'd not have known;
But tell me, "Is it older age";
Or have the years, "Just flown"?

That baby brought to the bus stop,
New sister/brother of little Sue,
Grew up in, "Was it 4-5 weeks"?
Gosh; now she/he is riding too!!!!

Then, too I must mention
Natures' beauty day by day;
The bright moon of fall mornings;
Shed a brilliance... such a ray!

The dew upon the spider's web,
The sunrises' early hew;
Are pictures I'll never erase;
And hope that you don't too!

The bursting of green leaves,
The early flowers of spring;
The birds back from the South;
Robins, geese, blackbirds - Red Wing!

The array of beautiful colors,
On local trees in fall;
Are just some of the fringe benefits,
And God's created them all!

Yes, I'll miss many people,
Many of natures' wonders too;
But I'll remember each and every day,
To pray a special prayer for you!
(December 9, 1991)

Below is a poem from a newspaper article, author unknown, date unknown.

What Is a School Bus Driver? A school bus driver is a person who smiles in the morning and smiles in the evening and eats Rolaids in between.

A school bus driver gets there when nobody else can, finds houses that don't exist and children with no names.

School bus drivers have eyes in the back of their heads and hear every word, even in sign language.

School bus drivers are immune to noise.

A school bus driver's favorite words (besides "good morning" and "good night") are "sit down."

Sometimes a school bus driver gets tired, but seldom gets mad, and always, most faithfully, gets there.

## TREASURER- ALGOMA TOWNSHIP

I was asked by the Township Board members to consider running for Treasurer of the Township. I ran in the primary against, Jim Ebenstein, Republican, and Luella Bitely, Democrat. I then ran in the general election against Luella Bitely, and won.

I was treasurer of Algoma Township for the years 1978-1983. Frank Vanderhyde was Supervisor, Martha Henning was Clerk, Don Bates was assessor, Bob Ysseldyke and Lambert (Carl) Friske were Trustees.

Rollin and Heidi were a great help. The township did not have computers then.

Martha, Frank and I all did our work in our homes. The two of them were great to work with. I can still hear Martha saying, "No problem!"

The land owners came to our house to pay their taxes (December 1 -February 14). We also issued yearly dog licenses. The busiest day was Friday, as the treasurer was to be available that day. Mortgage companies and title search companies called all the time to see if taxes were paid on certain parcels. Many calls were taken by Rollin or Heidi and they looked up the information and gave it to the caller. If they couldn't do this, a message was left for me so that I could and then return the call. There were distribution dates for the taxes to be paid to the schools, county, and township (Algoma Township had Cedar Springs, Rockford, and Sparta as schools, and also Kent Intermediate Schools). This distribution I did, with Rollin's help, by hand posting. During the last two years that I was treasurer, computer cards were pulled, taken to Grand Rapids to be run, and compared to my totals. It was nice meeting all these people with varied personalities and attitudes. We knew the ones who would want to check the tax roll, those who saved and paid in cash, some was *musty* smelling money. Most were very friendly and kind. I'm happy for the experience of being township treasurer. It was because of a second tax collection in the summer that I resigned. I was still driving school bus and I wanted my summers free for a more relaxed time.

After I no longer was treasurer; I did work at some township tasks. I did take census in 1987. While at one home, I had the misfortune of having a dog bite me. It took months to heal. The owners understood. They paid the doctor bills and the dressings for it. I have also worked on several primary, general, and special elections. It's always good to see the faces of many residents that I would not see otherwise. I resigned from the Election Board in January of 1996.

## THE HOUSE FIRE

January 19, 1977, the day started out as usual. I remember Wayne Bronkema had to be urged by his dad and encouraged by me to get on the bus. Heidi had gotten on at the Fire Barn.

I was going up Algoma Avenue hill, north of 12 Mile Road, when I met an Algoma Township fire volunteer traveling south with his car's red light activated. I commented, "We pray that all will be well, wherever the fireman goes!"

The kids were getting off the bus at Algoma Central School, and Mr. Ray Gress, a teacher there, came and stood by the side of the bus door. All the students for Algoma had disembarked and only White School's resource room students remained.

Mr. Gress then stepped onto the first step and said, "Irene, did you know your house is on fire? The man said all is O.K. though!" Wow, all is O.K., but my house is burning!

I asked him to call Bill Bloom, to tell him

163

I was dropping down to my house then I'd take the resource room kids to White School.

I'd only passed the house three miles and four stops before. I'd seen nothing, but, had I really looked? The firemen said it was contained to inside until it received oxygen; due to them coming in with hoses; then the flames came out the windows.

Many cars were on Fonger Road. I had to park to the east of the gray house and walk to the white one. Firemen said, "We've got it under control, you may go in." "Where's Maureen?" I asked. Frank Vanderhyde then told me that Frank and Reva Huey had taken her to Drs. Fochtman and Eary. Maureen came back from the doctor's. They treated her for shock, smoke inhalation, and a laceration just down her back on her right shoulder; received four stitches. She received this cut jumping through the north living room window. Maureen would have to return to the doctor a couple of times to have her lungs checked. Rollin came home too, as he had been called.

Frank Vanderhyde offered to drive the bus, but I told him he couldn't, because he didn't have certification to drive students in a bus, but he surely could ride with me. When we got into the bus garage, I hurried in to talk to Bill Bloom. I didn't say "Hi," or "Good Morning" to Paul Strickwerda (a fellow driver) and he commented, "Where you going, to a fire!"

Wow, that did it! I just began to cry and answered, "Yes, my house has had a fire." He felt so badly, but I knew he said it innocently.

It was a cold wintry day. The insurance agent came, as well as the adjuster. Plywood came immediately to cover the broken windows, all by 10:30 A.M.

We learned from the fallen kitchen clock, that it was 8:20 A.M. when it fell (the batteries had fallen out at that time). The heat was so intense in the kitchen that the globe had fallen off the light fixture and the bulb was like a tear drop (glass melts at about 1500°).

Maureen first heard cracklings and subconsciously thought it was bacon frying. She then smelled smoke and wondered if the bacon was burning. Then came wakefulness and it was smoke and it wasn't breakfast! She left the northwest den room (used as bedroom due to the energy crisis at that time) and went into the smoke filled living room. She tried the front door, it wouldn't open; it was warped. She then took the large decorative candle and hit the front window hard; the inside panes broke. The 3/4" plate glass storm window did not. She took a dinette chair and thrust it through the broken pane; also breaking the storm window. She jumped out into the snow and ran to Linda and Bill Bronkema's. She yelled, "Our house is on fire, our house is on fire!"

Linda asked, "Whose house, whose house?" Linda did not recognize Maureen. She was panic stricken, somewhat sooty, and just plain unrecognizable. Linda called the fire department and then Bill at the store, so he could unlock the fire station for the firemen and save a little time.

There were firemen at the station when Bill arrived; they were getting ready to leave for our fire. They, with township supervisor Frank Vanderhyde, were meeting with the State Fire Marshal's Commissioner to check equipment and the safety codes for the Township policies. The tones rang Alpine Fire Station with the comment, "You got a fire almost next door at 1274 Fonger Road."

The firemen at the station looked at each other and said, "That's not Alpine; Fonger Road is Algoma's," and off they went. Again God is so good. These men were already at the station. These men did not have to enter their cars and drive from home to the station... oh the minutes that were saved!

Norris and Ann Fox, neighbors on 11 Mile Road, offered us their travel trailer. The snow on Thursday was so deep, (the fire was on Wednesday) that the County Road Commission brought a front end loader in to clear the drive and area for the trailer. This indeed was a big favor.

I drove the bus Thursday A.M.; during the day though, the students went home due to the conditions of snow (a sub-drove). Then Friday, Monday, and Tuesday were ALL SNOW DAYS, no school!

Our snow blower had a very hard time making a path to the barn and shop-shed (where we kept the one vehicle). One had to make a shovel path a bit ahead at times to give the blower room to again do its job. When done, it was quite interesting to see this path so low with the snow banks sooooo high!

There was a huge dumpster put into the back yard right under the kitchen window. Junk was just shoveled into it. Men from The ABC Construction Company of Grand Rapids were there Thursday A.M. Consumers Power re-hooked the electric so the furnace would run. Wow! Smoke damage extensive, the kitchen was completely burned and also the upstairs (the fire gained oxygen through the pull down stairway, it acted as a draft). The kitchen/dining room door was closed so there was less oxygen from there. The smoke damage; I just couldn't get over; clothes in drawers, closets, and everywhere were yellow and smelly. Ugh! Books' pages were yellow and smelly too.

The reconstruction took until the first week in April. All of the roof rafters, except two on the east and four on the west needed to be replaced. The pull-down stairway was replaced by a regular open stairway to the upstairs with a landing. It all looked nice.

Most of the furniture was totaled out, due to smoke or water damage. This is where we took a big loss, because most everything was twenty to twenty-five years old, thus depreciated!

Relatives and neighbors were all so kind. Kenneth Norman and his son Al, along with Julie, Al's little girl, were the first people to come and see us after the firemen had left. They had words of encouragement as they'd had a fire. Contributions came in the first day. Many meals were brought in by relatives, neighbors, parents of kids and bus drivers. Mamrelund Lutheran Church and

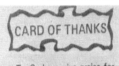

CARD OF THANKS

To God we give praise for our daughter's life and safety. We are also thankful to our neighbors who cared for her under such unusual circumstances.
To the volunteer firemen of Algoma Twsp. our sincere thanks for doing a great job!
To our many other neighbors, friends and relatives accept our sincere thanks. Your acts of kindness, love and concern at the time of our house fire have truly been appreciated.
Rollin & Irene Lamphear
5p

Algoma Baptist Church gave us checks. The Algoma Sunshine Circle ladies gave us a quilt that they had made. The transportation department gave me a surprise shower, some teachers, aides and office personnel also gave gifts. The neighborhood gave a shower at the fire station for any who would like to come. Some there that surprised me were Reha Lamphear Byrd and Bonnie Byrd Dukakus (her hubby John was one of firemen), also Don and Teresa (Sawicki) Wahlfield. She had taken my position at Wolverine Appliance Distributing Company when I quit working there. The gifts at both showers whether items or money were appreciated.

 While housed in Fox's trailer, Rollin had a couple of insulin reactions. Heidi got the chicken pox; she then stayed with Grandpa and Grandma Rosell, in their house. I've thought too, how we banked the sides of the trailer with snow for insulation purposes. With so much snow around it, and the trailer's furnace; we were cozy. We surely went through the fuel oil for the house as the construction workers worked on the roof. It was cold outside!

 I spent so many, many, many hours inventorying things lost in the fire. Information needed: the date purchased, cost, cost now, quantity and then the cost extended. Did I ever use the various catalogs supplied to me by my neighbors!

 It too was a God-send, that the insurance on the dwelling had been raised, just three months before. That was the first change since the policy had been taken out in 1957!

 We agreed with the insurance adjuster who said on the first day, as he departed, "We can just thank God that you're not arranging a funeral, all else can be replaced."

 Maureen was planning to be married in May and she was making her own wedding dress. She had some of it done including the yoke of lace. This was so smoke damaged! She had made some of the pinafores for the attendants too. These were white eyelet and also sustained smoke damage. Since I didn't sew, I did offer to buy a wedding dress. She decided that if she could replace the lace; she would make the dress. While staying at Baughan's, she, Jo, and Cindy make the wedding dress and the dresses of some of the attendants too. Imogene soaked and re-soaked and hung the pinafores out in the sun and they did recover from the smoke stain. I'm thankful to her for doing that too.

Doug and Pat Klein were being married that year too, and their wedding invitation order (which they ordered through me) was completely water damaged. It sat in the dinette area.

The oil paintings that Dad had painted that hung in the living room and dinette were heavily smoke damaged. I would not let these go out to be cleaned. I did it myself with Dow Bathroom Spray. It did take a little of the sheen off, but otherwise it surely took the smoke off. Son-in-law, Ron VanHorn, had painted us a beautiful still-life picture. He had given it to us the Christmas of 1976; this picture had not 'aged'. Within the picture was a stark white tablecloth, with the folds so beautifully done; well, it's antique white now, and the whole picture looks as if it were several years old. Regardless, I still cherish it, it's very well painted!

An unfortunate situation came to light. I realized the antique settee and chair, which had been Aunt Martha Skareen's, had not been returned with the cleaned furniture. I did some calling and it was returned. Marti and Ron received this from Aunt Martha when we helped her move to 'the home'.

# GRANDMA ROSELL'S BIRTHDAY PARTY FOR KIDS

In 1979 mother wanted to give the neighborhood kids a party on her birthday.
Heidi and Cindy Ring helped get the peanuts hid, the clothes pins and bottle, and whatever else they used in the games.

Mom did all the calling on the phone to invite the children. They were Heidi, Cindy Ring, Tammy and Bonnie Bliss, Anita and David Lovell, LuAnn, Wayne and Leona Bronkema, Lynn and Kari Piell, and Steven Blish.

Oh, mother enjoyed these little ones so much. She watched as they played the games and was excited to see their happiness. This was in July, so it also gave a special day for the kids to be together.

We had punch, ice cream, and cake for refreshments. Every one enjoyed it, just because!

## SUMMER CAMPOUT

The summers of 1985 and 1986 the Wilkinson and Lamphear families had a couple of weekend camping trips. We went to Sandy Beach (Croton-Hardy Dam area). We went boating, the kids went swimming, and the camp fires were kept going most of the day and far into the night for all to enjoy. The five or six units, parked on about four spots in positions that left an area inside for the fire and tables.

The meals were combined and **yummy.** One noon meal, we had spinach salad made by Barb, it was finished by Connie and me using straws, was that dressing ever tasty!

For family gatherings I usually made Baked Beans.

BAKED BEANS- cover until last hour
2 # navy beans (soaked and then cook until they begin to crack)
These next four ingredients add to the beans and stir.
1 # bacon cut into one inch pieces
2 1/2 C white sugar
1 Onion (I blend in blender)
Salt and pepper

Bake in 200 -250° oven for ten to twelve hours; stir once.

## HAY RIDES- EXTENDED FAMILY

In March of 1984 Maureen and family were here from Florida, we had an extended Rosell family hayride at Dufort's. Those that could come came, those that did not care to go on the ride stayed at our home. It was a fun experience for all, especially the younger kids.

December 15, 1984 the extended Rosell family again gathered for an evening hay or sleigh ride at Dufort's. Those who didn't care to go on the ride again stayed at our home.

After the ride we had a supper-lunch and visited. As we visited we heard a commotion in the front of the house. Upon going to the door, Rollin saw Santa; he had a bag of treats for

Janelle, Travis, Santa (Mark Vanderhyde) with Levi Deters on his lap, Ethan Deters, and Nate Poulin.
Far left background: Scott Holmes

the little ones. His smile and chuckle prompted smiles on both the young and adults. His Elf Johnny was so happy too, as he helped Santa hand out small gifts to the kids. Then he helped arrange the children on Great Grandma Rosell's lap and around her for pictures. Aunt Helen and Uncle Scott joined in this evening of merriment.

    Thanks to Heidi, Rollin, and myself it was a great surprise for all! We had fun just keeping the secret from all. Thanks to Mark Vanderhyde and John Rusilowski for an evening so well performed. We appreciated it more than they will ever know.

## KIDS
## JOBS -ETC. THROUGH THE YEARS

    MARTI was a baby-sitter, and she also did house work and ironing at Marge DeMutes.

    As soon as Marti had her driver's license she had a part time waitress job at Finger's Restaurant on Plainfield Avenue. She worked nights and summers.

    She went right after school and often worked very late. In the winter especially, I know I worried about her driving home. Winter snow and wind on certain nights were treacherous for driving on Algoma Avenue's hills north of 10 Mile Road as well as any roads.

    She worked at Greenridge Country Club as a waitress in summers during her college years. It was here that Marti met Homer Saxton, an elderly man, with no blood family left. He was a handy man at Greenridge and received room and board there. He watched the parking area as the waitresses left to go to the cars.

    I think Homer adopted us. He would drop in often. He was always happy to eat with us regardless of what was on the menu! He began to bring his violin, and enjoyed playing it for us. If I were honest about it, the playing, reminded me of my scratchy playing of yesteryear. I'm sure

Homer in earlier years may have played his well. It was just such good therapy for him to have it out after many years that we just let him play.

He gave Marti an inlayed wooden table that his parents had received as a wedding gift. It's a sorry world though, because Marti used it as a prop at a play she directed at Cedar Springs High School, and it was stolen.

We kept in touch with Homer even as he was in the nursing home area of Kelsey Memorial Hospital in Lakeview, Michigan. He died and they had no reason to let us know. We went to visit him a week or two later and the lady at the desk seemed confused when we asked for his room. She called a nurse who asked if we were friends, and then she told us he had died. Rollin and I were both in tears on the way out of the hospital; we left only with memories of Homer. We even wondered about his funeral, etc.

In Kalamazoo while in college Marti worked at TurMiKi Restaurant.

She attended Western Michigan University and roomed the first year with Kristi Badgerow (Fochtman), a friend from High School. She then rented an apartment with three girls. Two remained with her for the balance of her time there, Kathy Couchman and Phillis Cox. Betty and Brut loaned her their bunk beds, for use in the apartment.

Marti student taught at Riverside Junior High in the north end of Grand Rapids.

BRUCE worked baby-sitting and as farm help through his earlier years. Then in 1970 he had his driver's license and he worked at Tony's Car Wash (Tony Harmon was the same fellow my dad had help as a boy on the farm). This was the first drive-thru car wash in Sparta. I guess it was good that Bruce was mechanically inclined as he did some repairs when necessary on the machine.

The summer before college he worked at Sackner Products in Grand Rapids. He worked at Discount Tire on

Plainfield Avenue, during his college years. He came home every weekend.

He attended Ferris State College in Big Rapids taking instruction in air conditioning and heating.

In October 1973 he came home one night (9:30 or so) with a deer he had shot with his bow and arrow. He was in college so, Dad will you take care of it? Guess who did most of it!

MAUREEN also baby-sat. She'd like to have worked at Finger's but Finger's now had liquor and her age was too young.

She attended the Luther League Convention in Texas in 1973 similar to the one I attended in 1947, but they went by bus and there were probably more in attendance.

During her 11th grade year (1974-75) she attended State College of Cosmetology in Grand Rapids, then located near Fulton Street, Division Avenue and Monroe Avenue. She, Cindy Baughan, Cindy Beardsley, and Kathy Gillette all attended. They exchanged rides. They paid their own fees. This arrangement was made because the 'slots' at Kent Skill Center in Grand Rapids were full. The girls doing this had to have their hours completed at S.C.C. before the next school year began in order to have credit for it. They went to S.C.C. all through the summer of 1975. Maureen then worked at Richard's Coiffeur in Sparta during her senior year.

February 26, 27, and 28th of 1976, Maureen went with Richard and others to the Chicago Trade Show in Chicago. An ice storm began. Rain, then sleet. I wondered if they'd make it home. The highway around Lake Michigan was to be respected in the winter during any storm. They made it to Sparta about 2:30 A.M. I went in to get her, what a view; the trees were thickly laden with ice, etc. almost scary. It was lightning so fast and so bright that the area was like day. The ice was not bad in the southern part of the state. They came onto it closer to home. There was no electric power for days, worst ice storm in years. Consumers Power Company replaced two million feet of power lines and seventeen hundred power poles. I remember taking the local kids out in our open fields and hiking on top of the ice crust and hearing tree limbs *snap*, due to the heavy ice.

HEIDI baby-sat too. During her Senior year she went to classes at Sparta High in the early A.M. At 10:00 she went to Kent Skills Center on College Avenue in Grand Rapids. In the afternoon from 1:00-4:00 she worked at Wolverine World Wide in Rockford. In May before, graduation, The Kent Skills Center sent her on two interviews. She took a position with Universal Forest Products on the corner of Three Mile Road and the East Beltline, in Grand Rapids.

## AFTER COLLEGE
## KIDS' MARRIAGES-WORK-FAMILIES

Marti graduated from Western Michigan University, Kalamazoo, Michigan, in 1973. Her first position in the teaching field was a 'permanent' substitute at Cedar Springs High School. Shortly after, she had a full time job there. During her years at Cedar Springs she directed some great High School plays. Some were: "The Diary of Anne Frank," "Cheaper by the Dozen," and "The Birds' Christmas Carol."

Marti met Ron through Bruce. The guys had an apartment in Paris, Michigan while they attended Ferris State College in Big Rapids. Marti had a blind date with him; they started dating in 1972.

Ron was nick named "Wolf Man." He had a beard, mustache, and longer hair. One of the things I remember thinking, if not saying to Marti was, "Well, one thing is; should you two decide to marry, at least your kids may have thicker hair!"

One thing Ron remembers is I served him some homemade dandelion wine... he thought it tasted terrible. (This reminds me, of when, as a child, I had picked dandelions for my mother to make dandelion wine. She was stronger than I, so when I had filled the Mason jar with dandelion blossoms, she always pushed it down and had me go find more to fill the space!) Also one night at supper lunch, Ron asked to have the turkey passed (meat for sandwiches) and after he enjoyed the second one we told him the meat was pickled beef tongue. (It was!) Ron and Marti were married November 17, 1973 at Mamrelund Lutheran Church, Kent City, Michigan. Ron was the son of William and Velma VanHorn.

They first lived at White Creek Estates, a mobile home park near Cedar Springs. In 1976 they lived in Sturgis, Michigan (in an apartment); Ron was working for Zales Jewelry. This town is very old and the houses were interesting to study. We went down to visit them a few times and usually had a picnic in a city park before going home. Very nice.

Aaron James was born August 20, 1977; his first home was in the trailer park, White Creek Estates. The family then bought a home 3804 Auburn Avenue NE in Grand Rapids. A short time later they moved across the street to 3825 Auburn. Janelle Leigh joined their family December 14, 1980 and on November 9, 1982 Christanna Beth greeted them. She, from a very small baby to seven years old, was in and out of the hospital frequently with asthma attacks. Her last long hospital stay was the week of April 20, 1988.

The children all go to Northview Schools, Grand Rapids, Michigan.

Soon after Janelle's birth, Marti quit teaching at Cedar Springs High School to be a full time Mom. In 1986, she applied and tried to go back into her teaching field but she was 'over qualified,' so she began teaching part time at Davenport College. Currently, she teaches full time at Davenport and is working on a Doctorate at Michigan State University (1993)

Bruce, graduated from Ferris State College in early 1974, and then began work at Trane an air conditioning-heating business in Grand Rapids. He then worked at Meijer Thrifty Acres in Lansing. He had an apartment in Grand Ledge, Michigan, and came home almost every weekend.

During this time he met and began dating Linda Farrell. Recalling an amusing circumstance involving how they began dating was: they met at the Green Apple Restaurant on 4 Mile Road near Alpine Avenue and Bruce got Linda's phone number. The next week-end, while at home, he was trying to reach her and became frustrated when he couldn't. He commented that he must have the wrong number. Dad and I questioned what her name was. He said, "Linda Farrell, but you wouldn't know her." Dad said, "I know some Farrell's, does she live on Pettis Avenue? If she does, then her parents are Pat and Kay!" As information flowed, he did locate Linda's phone number and they dated.

Linda went to Florida and Bruce was to call her after the date she said she'd return. Bruce didn't call immediately and one evening I answered the phone to hear, "You don't know me but I know Bruce and I would like to talk to him; I'm Linda Farrell." I answered, "I don't know you, but Bruce's dad knows your mom and dad. He lived across from your Grandpa Farrell's on Two Mile Road." I gave Linda Bruce's phone number in Grand Ledge.

They were married on June 19, 1976. The wedding ceremony was performed, in a pretty setting at Townsend Park, in Cannonsburg, Michigan.

Bruce transferred to Meijer Thrifty Acres, Kalamazoo, Michigan and lived in a mobile park there. Linda finished earning her degree in Special Education at Western Michigan University (thus the transfer for Bruce). They then moved to Lowell, Michigan (mobile home park). Linda taught school in Ionia County and at Lincoln School in Grand Rapids. Bruce worked for Meijer Thrifty Acres, at the Ionia and Greenville stores.

During this time, Bruce and Linda began building a house. It was off Bailey Drive, and Lincoln Lake Road near Lowell, Michigan, (on a private road Bahala). Rollin enjoyed helping, as time permitted. He placed the little Shasta trailer on the side of the house, and they could use it as a need presented itself. Rollin left as soon as he got home from work many afternoons (eating his supper on the way). He also stayed in the trailer, during his summer vacation and helped daily. I remember at the time we were shingling the roof. I was nailing fast and furiously and enjoying every minute. Until I was to get down, then I froze. There were several attempts to help me get from the roof to the ladder, as Bruce, Linda, and Dad all tried to help me down. A fond memory I have of being on the roof, is when we spotted a Scarlet Tanager, almost parallel to us in the tree tops. It is the only time I've seen one in the out-of-doors.

Corissa Lynn was born January 10, 1984, she too was a sweetie and we were happy with her arrival.

A few years later they moved to an apartment in Kalamazoo, Michigan. Bruce worked at the 'shredder' owned by the Farrells, during this time. They then moved back to Kentwood, Michigan, into an apartment. They soon ventured into their own heating and air conditioning business.

They still lived in Kentwood when Brenna Rae joined their family July 26, 1987. Shortly after, months anyway, they purchased a home at 4047-56th Street near Wilson Avenue, Grandville, Michigan. The business is located in Grandville and the girls attend Grandville Public Schools. In 1995 they purchased a building on 56th Street east of their home for the business. Prior to this they had rented space.

Maureen continued after high school to work at Richard's Coiffures.

Maureen went to high school with Mark. They both were in band. All-State was performing in Sparta and we housed two of the girls. Mark had not been chosen to be in this band, but an alternate and was called to fill in. After the performance there was a party at Steve Truax's home. Maureen went with the two girls who stayed with us. Mark was at the party and asked Maureen for a date (Did he think she was a **_WONDERFUL_** flute player?)

They were married, May 20, 1977 at Mamrelund Lutheran, Church Kent City, Michigan. Mark's parents are Roy and Jo Baughan.

They lived in a trailer park off Alpine Avenue until they had a house built at 9400 Pine Island Drive. It was built in 1978.

Travis Duane arrived a few weeks early on, April 4, 1980. We visited him at the hospital for three weeks (Aunt Erna and Judy from Jackson Hole, Wyoming were visiting us at this time). 

**9400 Pine Island Dr.**

Travis observed his first birthday at the above address. At his first birthday he had four living great grandmothers and two living great grandfathers. Then in

April of 1981, they moved to Orlando, Florida, as Mark had employment with Martin-Marietta, a company in the aerospace industry. Maureen did baby-care in the home.

Their home there was at 313 Chutney Drive. Brent Daniel was born February 18, 1983. He had Sturge-Webber Syndrome (with Hemangioma) and lived only four days (2-22-83). He is buried in Algoma Township Cemetery on Grange Avenue, Rockford, Michigan. The following year, July 29, 1984, Derick Lee joined them as a family member.

They had a house built (1984-85) and moved to 9071 Palos Verde, Orlando, Florida. In January, 1988 Mark moved to Ohio, a change of employment. They rented a farmhouse with 20 acres at 15885 Rapids Road, Burton, Ohio. Maureen and the boys stayed in Orlando; Travis finished his school year and Maureen hoped the house would sell. They joined Mark in June.

Maureen has commented at times how pleased she was when Elsie Montgomery visited her and they packed some of the kitchen stuff. Elsie has remarked that Maureen was not feeling well at the time.

Then another move came in December 1988 with a change of employment to Columbia Aluminum Company and they moved to Goldendale, Washington.

The boys attend Goldendale Public Schools. Maureen has full-time employment within the school system. (1993)

Heidi began work right after graduation at Universal Forest Products, Three Mile Road, and the East Beltline, Grand Rapids. She worked in various departments, until April 1993.

Heidi and Mike went to the same church and did things together with the active youth group. Mike really would have liked Heidi to be his girlfriend, but she **did not** like him at all. They continued to enjoy the group activities and after some time she apparently saw the qualities of Mike, that at a younger age she'd not seen! They dated steadily from April 29, 1982 and were married April 26, 1986 at Bella Vista Church, Rockford, Michigan. (Parents of Mike are Robert and Loraine Hart) Both Grandma Lamphear and Grandma Rosell attended in wheel chairs.

In October of 1985 my mother moved into Grandview Foster Care Home on Alpine Avenue, in Grand Rapids, Michigan. Heidi and Mike then, re-decorated the 'little gray house' at 1288 Fonger Road. They lived there from 1986-1992.

They began building a house in May of 1991, and moved into it; 1400 Fonger Road in February 1992.

Bethany Marie was born December 18, 1992. Heidi became a 'full time mom' in April 1993. We again had the enjoyment of welcoming a new baby into their home. Emily Jordan arrived to live with them on June 18, 1995. These two little ones have also brought me much happiness.

JUST GENERAL<br>THOSE WE LOVED-EXPERIENCES ETC.

Sometime in the summer of 1983 Betty and Brut came down in the late P.M. with a *huge* puff ball. We commented about it and took pictures of it. They'd found it in their field.

After that Brut said, "Now for the bad news, I've been laid off work." What a shock, he'd been in the employ of Gullmeyer and Livingston for over forty years.

Heidi went out with Betty and Brut and us quite often. One night on my birthday we went to Granny's Kitchen on 28th Street (no longer in business) and she ordered a grilled cheese sandwich. Brut never let her live it down, go out where you could order something special and what does she order, **grilled cheese**! Later by several years, she could kid us adults back!

When Heidi was in Jr. High and also in high school, Brut, Betty, Rollin, and I went to Fables Restaurant on Alpine Avenue, almost every Sunday night; this was after Betty and Brut had been to their church. We'd have coffee and an order of onion rings or mushrooms. They'd have their supper lunch.

One Sunday night it was snowing very hard. It was blizzard-like conditions. Some of Betty and Brut's kids had left Betty's for their homes and Betty commented, "Be careful, it's terrible weather out there, call when you get home!" Well, the kids called; then Betty and Brut called us to go to Fables. The four of us, got into their pickup cab and went slowly to Fables. Funny, no other vehicles were on the roads! There were no vehicles in Fables parking lot! We were the only patrons there! We ordered, and the workers said, "Go find a seat, we'll serve you tonight. Not too busy... as you probably noticed." We've chuckled over that many times!

TRAVELOGUES- An entertaining evening we've enjoyed for several years. The Kiwanis Club of Grand Rapids sponsored these travelogues. One favorite narrator was Don Cooper, Box 7, DeBorgia, Montana, 59830. (We talked to him prior to our Alaska trip, and he gave us a few pointers: roads, scenery, C-B usage, etc.).

We started going several years before Brut passed

away. The four of us had great seats in the Welch Auditorium, in downtown Grand Rapids. There are six programs a year, various months September-April depending on scheduling. Later it's been held at Sunshine Church on the East Beltline. In 1996-97 we decided not to attend.

OLDER NEIGHBOR= Abe DeWilde was a neighbor who lived to be 100 years old. He lived at the corner of 11 Mile Road and Grange Avenue. The last few years at the Cedar Springs Care Facility, Cedar Springs, Michigan.

Abe DeWilde, Mart and Dorothy Ringelberg

Many years earlier I know Daddy always took home made wine and goodies to him and I went with. I was always given a home-made cookie or two at this time. This was while his parents, sister and husband lived there too. His parents, and his sister Anna's husband died, then Anna and Abe continued to live there.

April first was Abe's birthday and for a few years I had a neighborhood birthday party for him. We have a nice picture of many older neighbors at the one in 1980.

He was quite old

when I drove the bus past his farm. Some afternoons I'd notice him out near a fence line, taking out an old fence, and rolling up the wire. He was sitting on a small stool or crate.

He and Anna had a sale of household belongings before they moved to the healthcare facility. Maureen bought Anna's cedar chest, library table, and a small sewing chest. I bought two small pickle/candy dishes.

Sugar shacks heat up as sap starts flowing in area maples

THE SUGAR BUSH= Two generations and now into the third, the Dufort family has been making maple syrup; an early spring project. The tapping of the trees and boiling down of the sap has always been interesting to me. It takes 40-45 gallons of maple sap to make one gallon of maple syrup. The area where the trees are tapped is called the 'Sugar Bush'.

I remember, as a teen-ager (about 1946), visiting the sugar shanty out in the woods. The steam coming out of the roof, puffy and pure white was beautiful. The taste or two of the syrup was *soooooo* sweet, and delicious! The sugar shanty was in the woods for many years. The business grew and they added on to the shanty and installed an evaporator and eventually an even bigger one.

For several years we took orders on the egg route for syrup. We also picked up large cans at Fairbanks Bakery on top of Michigan Street hill. These had covers on them and Duforts used these to collect the sap, for a few years.

The amount of wood used for the fire, to evaporate the sap is tremendous. The Dufort men have usually cut most of it from the woods prior to the syrup season.

As the years went by, when Bob and Gwen were boiling, they built a shanty up behind their house, 1409 Fonger Road. This was necessitated partly because of vandalism in the woods' area. Sad!

Our children and now the grandchildren enjoy visiting the sugar bush and shanty.

Through the years many bus loads of children also visited the sugar bush.

ANNIVERSARY DINNERS= Frank and Janet Vanderhyde's anniversary and ours are close. Two days and two years apart. The tradition of our annual dinner out, started years ago, maybe the 1970's?

We've gone to many different restaurants through the years! Several I'll mention as maybe highlights for one reason or another.

The Patchwork Quilt, near Middlebury, Indiana was one, I drove Vanderhyde's car on the return trip. The first cruise control car I'd ever driven. Patchwork Quilt was Amish. The food was great. I'm still wondering what ingredients were in some of the salads.

In Michigan we patronized the following through the years. We went to Point West located on Lake Macatawa near Holland; the wait time was to be forty-five minutes. Wow, Rollin better eat sooner! Off we went to VanRaulte's in Zeeland, "Closed for Remodeling." We went back to Grand Rapids to the Golden Eagle Room, at the airport; Rollin ate much later, than had we stayed at Point West!

Other places have been; Embers in Mt. Pleasant, The Bungalow in Big Rapids, and The Peaches Room at The Marriot Hotel when it first opened in Grand Rapids.

We did not always go the month of our anniversaries. It's been as late as near Christmas, like the year we went to Clifford Lake Inn, west of Stanton. I enjoyed the decorations of the rooms, and the little shop in the basement area. We went there a second time too.

Thornapple River Inn, in Ada is one I still chuckle about, where a couple of us ordered fish. When they were prepared they came out on the tray, heads-eyes and all. They then took them aside and de-boned and de-head them. I remember exotic mushrooms were served with this meal. Janet and I could hardly keep from laughing when we exchanged glances as the fish first came in. When the waitress came back and asked how things were. Janet said, "Just fine."

I said, "Do you really want to know?" When she'd left we again almost laughed aloud.

Then the Chesaning House in Chesaning, Michigan. We were seated and who came to say hi, but Betty Mieras and Ginger Manson who were on a day Mystery Tour and had dinner there too.

Two years, several years apart, we ate at restaurants that Frank's brothers' owned. One was up near Hardy-Croton Dam and one was in White Cloud.

Gibson's is where we went in 1993, after which Frank and Janet gave us a tour of Dave and Carol Vanderhyde's new house on Algoma Avenue. Beautiful setting, a most beautiful house!

Aaron and Rollin

HARVESTING HONEY= In the fall of 1982 Rollin and I were walking in the back field and all of a sudden there was a "sssssshh" sound. As we walked on we realized that the sound was from bees. We followed them to a tree. This tree had a hollow so we knew it was a bee tree. Before things thawed in the spring of 1983 Rollin, Aaron and I went out to harvest honey. Rollin sawed the part of the tree so we could get the comb. This was interesting. We used the large metal kitchen spoon to help get the combs out. We were almost done when a bee or five came out of hibernation. You guessed it! Aaron got stung. We drove the tractor with the utility trailer up to the house (quickly) so we could put meat tenderizing salt on the stings. After the combs were all gathered we put them into Pyrex bowls. Then the bowls went into the microwave oven and the combs were heated to extract the honey in a more liquid state. We were so excited about the fact that we "pioneered the extraction of honey from the wild." We processed three plus quarts. It was tasty.

FLOOD OF 1986= It was September 17, 1986 and a school day. Rains had been steady; ditches, creeks, and rivers were overflowing (14 inches of rain in just over 24 hours).

The buses from east of Sparta had to go north to 17 Mile Road and then west to Sparta Avenue and into the schools. The number of days we did this I don't remember, I think it was four or maybe five.

It was quite an experience deciding how one could go to Grand Rapids, Rockford, or Sparta, because the Rouge River was in command.

A date to remember before that by several years was April 1975; with a ten inch snowfall.

CHRISTMAS DECORATIONS= For years Rollin enjoyed decorating an outdoor spruce tree for Christmas enjoyment. At 1274 Fonger Road it was a little spruce in front of the porch. It grew through the years and extended above the garage ridge board. Ladders and notched clothes line poles were needed to decorate it. Many years the lights went around it spirally, latter years they came from the top to the bottom as rays.

At 9400 Pine Island Drive he thought that lights with a scallop effect would look pretty outlining the drive and turn around. This he did with stakes in the ground and the lights' wire stapled to them. Then too, the little spruce tree, (planted the day Travis Baughan came home from the hospital) on the hump was decorated. This spruce grew fast and needed more lights often.

The decorating expanded to scallops at the bottom and top area of the porch. Garland and red ribbons also were at the top.

In 1990 we entered a contest sponsored by the Sparta Chamber of Commerce for the Sparta School District area. We did the above, plus we had a spotlight on the white birch wrapped with red ribbon and big red bows. A spot light was also on the pine stump, red pump, and the barrel filled with boughs and red Poinsettias. The bay window had candles lit (indoors), which, when dark inside, glowed with cheery friendliness. Results of the contest; we took third place.

CRAFT DOLLS= The dolls, Maureen had seen and purchased in Ohio. They were wooden bodies, dressed, and placed on a wooden base. They were complimented by some items as ducks, sleds, chalk boards, kittens, etc.

We started making them in 1989 at Maureen's. Making these dolls filled some the time that previously we coffee'd, played 'Hand and Foot,' or visited with Betty and Brut. (Brut died suddenly April 21, 1988. The phone rang as I was putting on my jacket for my morning bus runs. Rollin answered it, and said, "Yes she is." He then handed me the phone. When I said, "Hello," no one was there. I asked Rollin who it was, and he said, "Betty." I asked, "What did she say?" He replied, "She said 'It's Brut! It's Brut!'" So I asked Rollin to call the bus garage and tell them that I had an emergency. I raced up to Betty's and yes, Brut had died during the night. Betty had found him on the family room floor (this was a **very** sad day in our lives).

We attended a few craft shows and sold them and other smaller items. We also sold several via 'word of mouth'. We made probably about 260 dolls. Maureen bought hats for us, from their local Variety Store in Goldendale, Washington, by the gross. It was a fun, challenging experience and Rollin and I enjoyed it. We quit in 1991 because we could no longer get proper size hats for the wooden heads.

OUTTING TO BUCKLEY= For several years Nate and Rollin have gone to Buckley, Michigan with our trailer and enjoyed! They always have such fun thinking of going and reminiscing for the next eleven months. They do their own cooking (probably I should say Nate does) and one of their meals was always Hobo Pizza. We have it several times at home if we can during the year.

Buckley is located south of Traverse City, Michigan. Buckley, to many guys, means, "The annual, Old Engine Show." The show displays small type engines, on up to large-huge steam engines and a lot of old tractors. There is a *huge* flea market on the grounds during this event. The camping area is also acres upon acres. It's full too!

When the guys are to Buckley, Barb and I have alternated going to each other's homes. One year while here we drove a whole afternoon just looking at new areas being developed. Mostly around the Rockford and Lowell areas. One year, it must've been 1989; she sewed seams and lace on material for our craft dolls. Once, while at her house we tied off a quilt that she'd worked on in Florida. In 1992 we drove up to Baldwin and visited Joyce Chipman (former bus driver). The following night Imogene, Maynard, and we went to supper at Grant Station. In general we just 'do our own thing'. In 1993 we remained at Barb's, as she'd had back surgery on August fifth. The fellows didn't go for a couple of years due to Rollin's health. In 1996 the four of us went. A highlight for Barb and me, then, was visiting Gwen Frostic's studio and sales area.

FAMILY FUN–CAMPING= One year when Christanna and Janelle were small; we took them camping up at Interlochen State Park. We had a great time. We swam some, and played table activities with a little girl from Lansing the day it rained. Aaron was at a cottage nearby with Grandpa and Grandma VanHorn and we went to visit them.

There were about three or four years that Bruce and we went camping in the fall for a weekend. We went to Brower Park. The first year Corissa went. I believe the next years Brenna was with too. He took a tent and they stayed in it during the night. We took the boat and went out fishing. Of course, we never caught any. However, a very small fish was caught one of the years by Corissa. It was fun to play at the playground and also to hike a little down by the water. Linda had always packed a nice assortment of toys and activities. I was always in my glory, as we colored or used stencils to make pictures. The camp fire was usually glowing well in the early evening and sometimes a bit longer. We ate well, always having some of the meals cooked out-of-doors.

The one thing I'm sure none of us will forget was the night when the three were in their tent and it was cold. Better judgment told Bruce to move into the trailer. So, in came the sleeping bags, the girls, and Bruce. He had to put the dinette table down to make it into a bed. Then put the "bags" on it and crawl in. Three of them in that little bed! Well, the next morning Dad and I aroused, and I glanced over and was startled! I said to Dad, "They must have come in during the night and we didn't even hear them!" It surely was fun, but it was hard to find a free weekend for both of us therefore it ended.

This may not be camping, as such, but I remember the night there were to be many falling stars. The VanHorns came out and we went into our back yard and watched in the dark of the night. We sat on lawn chairs and lay on blankets. We did view several. We built a bon-fire in the driveways' gravel turn around and roasted marshmallows too. It was fun!

Van Horn's purchased a 32' sailboat in early 1995. They've worked hard on the boat and have enjoyed the sailing of it.

A day each summer of 1995 and 1996 Rollin and I enjoyed a day of sailing with them. It is refreshing and "care-free." They talk the sailing jargon which neither Rollin nor I understand. Both Janelle and Christa can maneuver the sailing ropes and Marti, per Ron, does a great job. They delight in this activity as a family.

MICHIGAN ADVENTURELAND= We took the grandchildren to Michigan Adventureland north of Muskegon two different years. The first time it was just the two VanHorn girls and the two Lamphear girls. They had fun riding the various rides. Dad and I sat as they proceeded from one to another and we were pleased that we could take them. The next time all of them went, except baby Bethany. Again I think they all had a good time. The Baughan boys were here alone. They'd ridden back with their Baughan grandparents, and then flew back to their home, in Washington.

Aaron, Janelle, Brenna, Derick, Corrisa, and Christa

CHRISTMASES= Following 1982. Christmas Eve's, after the Rosell's no longer were getting together, varied. We went to Marti and Ron's once. Then for the years 1984, 1985, and 1986, we had a progressive supper with the gifts opened at the last stop. I'm sure we all enjoyed seeing each other's homes decorated for the holidays. Weather conditions, somehow, played a role in the safety of travel, so we abandoned the progressive part of supper. Roads were sometimes slippery and sometimes visibility wasn't good. Following that we went to Marti's and to our home, and in 1993-1994-and 1995 Heidi had the gathering. Every year the Christmas tree had an abundance of gifts under it. After a bountiful supper, the Christmas story was read from the Bible, followed some years by some instrumental selection. Then came the opening of gifts. How they all grow... the reading of the gift tags by first one, and then another and by 1995 the only ones that could not was Bethany and Emily. In 1996 I again had it at our home.

## ROLLIN'S HEALTH
## 1963-1996

October 1963= Rollin had been losing weight, was tired, had blurred vision, and when hands were held outright they trembled. He was diagnosed with an overactive thyroid. This didn't seem to surprise us, as his mom, sisters Gladys and Avis all had had double surgery for it. He was put on medication, and they would schedule him for thyroid surgery.

Rollin was employed at Miller-Zeilstra Lumber Company and made frequent trips to Lansing. He jokingly, yet with meaning, told of not finding enough trees to 'use' between Grand Rapids and Lansing.

I'd broken my foot while laundering the kids Halloween costumes. I stepped on the bottom of a duffel bag, a base of one half inch cardboard; turned my foot, heard it snap, and had a pain in the pit of my stomach. I crawled up the steps from the 'tilly' room to the kitchen, lay on the linoleum floor, and waited for Maureen to come home at noon from kindergarten. Mom had hosted church guild in the A.M. I then sent Maureen over to Mom's to tell her I needed help. Cousin Ellen Dufort was there and either she or my dad took me in to doctors (Sparta). As I was having my foot set into a cast, I asked Dr. Eary if Rollin's new medication should cause frequent urinations. He checked Rollin's chart and said, "No, have Rollin come in for a sugar test tonight."

Rollin did this and he came home. His eyes filled with tears as he said, "The doctor said, 'I don't want to alarm you but you could go to the hospital tonight or wait 'til morning'." He had to wait two days for a bed.

Rollin started drinking his coffee black right then. He had used both sugar and cream. After he'd been in the hospital a while they said his blood sugar was down to six hundred. Normal in 1983 was 90-160. We never knew what it may have been!

A few days later he learned his thyroid surgery hadn't been cancelled. They came to take him to surgery and he said, "Mistake! Right now I'm in here to have my blood sugar regulated."

His blood sugar became regulated. He learned to give himself insulin shots; the pancreas was dead not just sluggish. The dietitian met with him several times and then gave him the 'exchange list' that he was to follow. Yes, he's used them faithfully ever since. The kids were great; they knew the diet exchanges by heart. They reminded him of things if necessary. Our friends and relatives have been more than understanding. I have been, and am, proud of them all!

Rollin remembers seeing pictures on T.V. of President John Kennedy's assassination. We can't remember which day of his hospital stay it was.

He came home for a week or two before going back into the hospital for his thyroid surgery, by Dr. Henry VanDuine. The doctors were amazed at his rapid healing. He was then put on thyroid medication. We picked him up late the afternoon of December twenty-fourth and went to Barb and Nate's for Christmas Eve of the extended family.

The years following, Rollin's blood sugar was watched carefully. Those first years the tests were urine tab checks and a visit to the doctor each month, then three months then even once a year. Dr. Fochtman told us when having a cold or flu to increase the units of insulin. Dr. Fochtman always gave a call back whenever we called and left a message.

In 1974 Rollin had the first bad insulin reaction. We had planned to go to 'the lot' to camp. He was to load a few things into the back of the truck and hook up to the travel trailer.

Mother had chicken, gravy, and potatoes ready at her house. I had asparagus and mashed strawberries ready to take over.

Rollin went out to put the tandem bike and gas can into the truck before supper. He came back in and resting on the utility room steps said, "I can't do it, I just can't do it!" He was referring to the fact that he couldn't load up. He came in with my help and I told him to lie on the davenport. He tried to get up, when Mom called to say supper was ready, but could only get to a kitchen chair with my help. I put some strawberries into a small, soft Tupperware bowl and told him to eat them; I'd go get supper and bring it to him. I did. Upon my return, he was frozen with the bowl to his mouth, staring. I tried to get him to eat some mashed potatoes and gravy. He couldn't swallow, I phoned Mother's and asked Heidi to bring more gravy.

Bruce was coming home for the weekend and so, when Heidi returned to Mom's I told her if Bruce drove in to have him come to our house. He did. By then, Rollin was on the floor, his mouth rigid. I called Dr. Fochtman and he said to call the ambulance, I did! Bruce came and asked, "What can I do?"

I replied, "Call someone who will be at least as calm as I am, oh, call TOM BLISS!" He did and either

 Tom was already on his way or he told us he'd heard it on his monitor and was heading out the door. It was so good to see and know Tom was there.

Paramedics came. They gave him glucose and he went by ambulance to St. Mary's Hospital's emergency. I rode in the cab of the ambulance. He was almost O.K. by the time we were near Pine Island Drive and Post Road. He was checked over and sent home with the doctor's comment, "Go home and eat the biggest banana split you'd like."

Jo Baughan brought Maureen and Mark to the Hospital. Maureen had been there for supper. I believe Bruce came down and brought us back home.

Heidi and Grandpa and Grandma were in the back yard of the 'little gray house'. They were happy to see Rollin with us. Heidi, seven years old, said she remembers Grandma Rosell thinking she was frightened and told her they would pray to Jesus.

We had sundaes that night and thanked God for His loving care.

We did go to the lot on Saturday.

In the months June to January from the above experience, Rollin did seem to have more problems. The thyroid seemed larger so we went back to Dr. VanDuine, now in private practice only. During the months of going to Dr. VanDuine, Rollin had extreme chills and a most raspy voice... the kids hardly knew it was he on the phone and it was laughed about it as a family joke... he also had a lot of short-long breaths and held his breath in during his sleep.

In August 1974 I became most concerned so I consulted Dr. Fochtman to refer us to another doctor. He recommended Dr. John Pool an Endocrinologist. During Rollin's first appointment Dr. Pool had two post graduates who took all his case history and examined him. They said,

"Dr. Pool will examine and make the diagnosis, but off the cuff we'd say, Hypothyroid; the raspy voice, the chills, etc. are all symptoms." Dr. Pool agreed with the above. Thus we started with a great doctor. Rollin was put on sick leave by Dr. Pool, January-May 1975.

During January 1975 Rollin had many blood tests as well as others. The results were astounding: cholesterol was higher than the graph; thyroid lower than the graph; sugar was see-sawing; and he had angina pain. He was taken off thyroid medication. Rollin saw Dr. Pool two times a week for a while; tests were done regularly. Dr. Pool would discuss what to expect between each visit, and it was so!

In March, at one of the appointments, Rollin was told that when the thyroid test becomes higher (normal count) that he should consider a second surgery or a 'radioactive cocktail'. We told Dr. Pool whatever he'd advise, we'd do. We chose the latter because there would be no hospital stay nor any 'healing' needed. Dr. Pool explained that the thyroid gland attracts iodine as strongly as a magnet attracts iron. The radioactivity from the 'cocktail' would take the gland out of commission. It's like having a surgery without a scalpel.

Rollin took the radioactive cocktail and Dr. Pool explained what to expect in one week, three weeks, etc. He assured us cholesterol would drop, angina pains would subside or cease; thyroid would become more normal. He was very concerned and compassionate; letters came with reports regularly. He was almost back to normal (except for diabetes) by May 1975.

Dr. Pool retired and Dr. Tate took over his patients. Our insurance carrier changed once or twice and we changed to a family doctor again. Dr. Oren Mason keeps great tabs on Rollin with exams, tests and a caring personality.

Through the years, 1992-93 he basically had the usual doctor appointments and lab work. The ups and downs of brittle diabetes we coped with, with the blood monitoring and using our knowledge.

In October of 1994, while out to Maureen's Rollin had quite a cough. When we came home, he immediately went to the doctor. He was treated for bronchitis, then pneumonia. It seemed that all through 1995 he struggled with pneumonia, fluid under the lung, more pneumonia, etc. In late December of this year he was in the hospital a couple of times. The first week of January 1996 too. It was at this time that he had several problems. Angina, heart attack, pneumonia, and then... the doctors told us that he was a prime candidate for kidney dialysis within two to six months or a year at the most! The renal team at St. Mary's Hospital is great. The dietitians explained the new diabetic, kidney, and heart diet to us. They gave us the exchange list for it. They have been great returning calls to answer questions any time we asked.

I rushed Rollin to the hospital December eleventh of 1996 and the results of the tests indicated he must have had a heart attack.

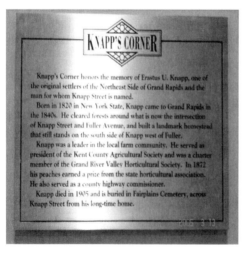

This is a bit of history; humorous too. One day Rollin and I checked at the Plainfield Meijer and Alpine Meijer for an "over the counter" medicine, and neither store had it. A new Meijer store had just opened four or five weeks before at the corner of Knapp Avenue and East Beltline. We decided to go and inquire if they had the medicine. We enter the far north door of the store. I noticed to my right, a plaque on the wall. I assumed that it may be honoring Fred Meijer, who started the grocery chain in 1934 in Greenville, Michigan. I approached it and it read "E.U. Knapp"... Wow! This plaque was honoring Rollin's great-grandfather, his grandma Lamphear's father.

## ROLLIN'S OTHER EXPERIENCES

The date I don't remember, (possibly 1986 or 87) but Rollin and Mike were trimming the Moraine Locust tree behind 1288 Fonger Road. The chain saw grabbed and Rollin's index finger was cut. I took him to St. Mary's Hospital. It was stitched up, and he was given antibiotics.

During the end of December of 1987 Rollin had a torn Achilles muscle in the left calf. He'd taken an extra long step and it went snap. He was on Workman's Compensation until February 16, 1988. He sat on the davenport with his foot elevated.

January 3, 1990 started out a year of... woes!

Rollin frequently drove the County Road Commission pickup truck to get "parts." On this day he left 44th Street (Grand Rapids) and was returning to the North Complex (Cedar Springs). He realized it was the noon hour and so as he drove he was eating a sandwich. He drove through Grand Rapids on the Expressway US 131. He should have continued North on 131 but instead he veered to the left onto I-96 and onto (in 1990) a new Exit to North M-37 (Alpine Avenue). He never stopped at the end of the exit but he crossed (careened) across all **s-i-x** lanes of traffic on M-37 (just South of Green Ridge Plaza and K-Mart). The pickup truck hit the curb hard enough that the front end of the truck jumped up on the top of the guard rail.

Law officers converged. Rollin asked, after they took him to the cruiser, if they'd get his orange juice on the seat of the pickup and his blood sugar monitor. He was taken by ambulance to Blodgett Hospital. He was checked and released to Marti. I got word via the bus radio on my second P.M. run (Elementary). Norm Ostrom, Rollin's boss came to the hospital, to check things too.

In April 1990 Rollin had a lump on his left jaw. Dr. Palm removed the cyst on Wednesday, April 25th as an outpatient of Blodgett Hospital (Successful). Rollin was told to take it easy on Thursday and to do only as he felt comfortable doing on Friday.

On Friday I had his lunch ready and on the counter; as I left for my kindergarten run at 11:15 A.M. He said he planned to sharpen the lawn mower blades and later mow the front yard; he would do the back yard on Saturday. I came by the house (about 3:00) on the high/middle school run and it looked 'dead' outside. I got to Meyers School for kindergarten pickup and called home; no answer. Central Elementary next, called; no answer. I hoped he was now outdoors.

Upon getting to Fonger Road and Pine Island Drive on the elementary run I looked very well for traffic from the north. If Rollin wasn't outdoors, I was going in! What an empty feeling, the mower had not been moved; Rollin was not outdoors. I backed the bus into the drive. I told the kids, "I'm putting you on your honor, Irene has to go in; she thinks her husband is very sick." What they didn't know was; I wondered if it were even worse!

I entered the kitchen; Rollin lay there on floor at the west end of the counter near the refrigerator; its door was open. He was rigid and staring blankly. I wanted him to acknowledge my presence, finally after four or five times of saying, "Rollin, I'm here, can you answer me."

He said, "Ahhh." Off to phone 9-1-1.

I tried getting some apple juice with a spoon into his mouth... "Swallow, swallow, swallow." Finally! Then I got some defrosted, concentrated orange juice from the refrigerator and did the same.

I called Betty Mieras; she came and sat with the kids on the bus. Someone else came, put their hand on my shoulder and said, "You're doing just fine, Irene." (I was still spooning orange juice with the swallow, swallow, swallow dialogue).

I thought the voice was that of Mike Mieras and told Rollin, "All's O.K., Mike's here, you know Betty's boy Mike." As it turned out, it was not Mike, but Algoma Township Fire Chief, Steve Johnson, oh, well! (This is the same person referred to as Mick Mieras in the prior paragraphs.)

The ambulance with paramedics from Rockford came; pumped glucose under his tongue, hooked up IV of glucose, and even asked me for sugar. Rollin was coming back well, when he was loaded into ambulance. Betty took me by car.

Transportation personnel, Bill Boros and Jaynee Hoag, brought my car out and Jaynee finished my run. Thanks, to all those concerned in transportation! Betty had stayed on the bus and released some children to their parents. Many parents stopped in, seeing the bus or hearing of it being in our yard.

Rollin 'up-chucked' in the ambulance as they entered the hospital drive; before entering the emergency room. We brought him home after he was checked. His muscles ached for a week due to him being rigid for so long.

We tried to re-construct Rollin's time after I left on my kindergarten run. It seems he remembers going out for the mail; that when he came into the house he rested, apparently at the dinette table and fell asleep. How long did he sleep? Did he fall off the chair or did he drop to the floor as he stood? His glasses were on the landing of the stairs by the hallway. He remembers 'scootching' to the 'frig' and trying to drink apple juice from a tall pitcher and just could not do it. He heard the phone ring the two times I called. He heard the bus backing into the driveway, *b-u-t*..........

We asked Bob and Gwen Dufort if they knew when the mail came. Bob said at their place about twelve fifteen. So; how long was Rollin really down? I backed the bus in at ten after four!

Again thanks be to God. Many families called, concerned, and told us we were in their prayers.

June 7, 1990 = Rollin coughed at the breakfast meal. I commented, "That sounds like it's congested."

He said, "It even kinda hurts!" I told him to call in sick and to call the doctor. He did. He met me at the roadside on my second A.M. run and said he'd leave me a note after talking to the doctor. I came home from the bus runs, and he had left a note that he was to the doctor.

Dr. Wagoner examined him; sent him to St. Mary's for x-rays, and St. Mary's said, "Take the x-rays back to your doctor." Dr. Wagoner read the x-rays; Rollin was sent to Blodgett Hospital and was admitted immediately. He had Type B pneumonia. He was given mega doses of antibiotics. He was in hospital thirteen days. (Jim Henson of the famed "Muppets" died of this, just a few weeks before this.)

March 6, 1991= I was about ready to go on the kindergarten run and Rollin came up the stairs. He'd cut his pinkie finger on the band-saw. He insisted he'd be O.K. to drive to the Med-Center on the East Belt Line and Plainfield Avenue. He was examined there and given a tetanus shot and sent to Butterworth Hospital. He called

Heidi at Universal Forest Products and she took him. Dr. Wong examined it but an associate sewed it up. Heidi took him back to the Med-Center and he drove home.

## IRENE'S HEALTH

Frequently, through the years I had *sinus*, and sinus infections. I missed time at work on occasion with the fever and severe sinus headaches. A couple of years it was bronchitis and I needed to be in bed for several days and cough, cough, cough. My ribs ached!

My 1963 broken foot episode is covered under Rollin's health. When I visited him on crutches, people at the hospital questioned, "Were you in an accident?"

In 1983 there was a calcium buildup in the shoulder area. I thought at first it might have been the result of the bus shifting so hard. However, upon having x-rays at Dr. Newman's in Rockford (chiropractor), it showed a calcium deposit. I remember the excruciating pain, if the aspirin didn't overlap, oh, how it pained! The feverish-ness of that arm area (bursitis) was extreme. Betty Mieras asked if I'd like her to help me shower, ohhhhh, music to my ears! We laughed so, as I stood in the shower, tears of pain were rolling down my face, yet both she and I were laughing. She moved my arm ever so slightly upward; it hurt so... then we'd laugh again, move again, a tiny bit and OUCH and we'd laugh again--I will not wish such pain on anyone! I am right handed; my signature on a few checks was almost unreadable.

October 1, 1993= I had a total hip replacement on the right side; Dr. Clarence Walls was the surgeon. COSTS- Dr. Walls-$4250.00, Anesthesia-$924.00, Total Hospital Bill-$12674.27. All went well. I followed instructions, no pain since, how wonderful. (Now March 1994, I am still working on coming up the stairs more properly, one foot on an individual stair!)

August 5, 1995 proved to be an exciting evening. Rollin was very ill with pneumonia. Mike Hart had told us he would mow the yard. I, however, thought I would do the front yard and then he could do the back yard. I had made a pass around the front, in front of the porch area. But for whatever reason, I wanted to trim closer to the retaining wall. Well... I went over the retaining wall and the forty eight inch, 18 horse power mower came on top of me! The motor quits, cuts power to the mower, when one leaves the seat. It was the tractor part that landed on my ankle. I kept yelling for help. The lady, Mrs. Zank, across the street was moving. Her sister-in-law heard me. She yelled to the family to get over across the street, something was wrong. Rollin heard me too, he was talking to Heidi on the portable phone. He took the phone and opened the front door and Heidi could hear me screaming, "Help me, help me"! She yelled to Mike and Loren Marsman that there was an emergency at our house and they were down in a flash. The lady across the road from Heidi was outdoors and heard Heidi yell at Mike, so was over to offer her help--she stayed with Bethany and six week old Emily. Two persons from Zank's lifted the machine off of my ankle. Then Mike, Loren, and another person from across street, pulled me out from under the machine. They were oh... so careful. The young lady from across the street got ice and put it on the ankle. Mike got his truck ready for me with cushions, etc. Then the fellows carried me to the truck, Mike rushed me to St. Mary's and Heidi and Rollin came in Heidi's car. X-rays were taken; I had an extra large break on the inside and a regular break on the outside of the left ankle. I came home with a large cast on my ankle/leg. Heidi called Betty Mieras from the hospital, to see what her schedule was. She was available. Heidi knew her dad was unable to care for himself or for me under these conditions. Betty was a God-send the whole week. Many relatives and friends were so caring. Betty, Imogene and Maynard did my string beans, and finished a recipe of watermelon rind pickles. The main meals were brought in for a whole month. What a blessing! I had many trips to therapy in Sparta during December and January.

## TRIPS

1949 JULY 16-29 - Judy Dieckman and I accompanied Aunt Irene Dieckman and Clara Behrens to Florida. I remember a detour in Georgia. It was one that went on country roads and we saw a lot of Georgia red clay. It had rained and it was really gooey! We stopped at a country store with one gas pump. There was a man sitting in front. We asked him if we were still on the detour. We were. He then continued to confirm, "Keep going, there's a straight away, then a 'forced' turn, just keep following, you'll get back on the highway O.K." We had a motel room at the Norman-Shoreman in Miami Beach. We were probably on the third to fifth floor, a beautiful view, overlooking the ocean.

Aunt Irene and Clara went to Nassau. Judy and I had fun swimming in the ocean and sun bathing and on the beach. We got a terrible sun-burn (she and I have commented on this as we've visited recently). We watched movies at the motel. We also took a tour of the

Irene Dieckman, Judy Dieckman, and Clara Bahrenes

Seminole Indian village.

The four of us drove down to the second key of the keys then back to Naples and stayed overnight. Aunt Irene wouldn't let us girls go to a movie that night!

I'm sure Judy and I had a fun time goofing-off, though I can't remember any specifics.

We went to Cypress Gardens; floral beauties were breath-taking to us (it was not as large an area as it is now-1993). We saw Bok Tower, we enjoyed the fragrance of orange blossoms for the first time, we visited the ancient mission at St. Augustine, and also Silver Springs. On our way home we enjoyed the beauty of the Great Smoky Mountains. The trip through the Mammoth Cave in Kentucky was awesome. I've always enjoyed caves!

We arrived home and the new house at 1274 Fonger Street was ready to be occupied. The folks had moved in, so I slept in the den, it was my first night to enjoy the new house.

1951 LUTHER LEAGUE CONVENTION= The summer of 1951, Lorraine Dufort, Mary Joyce Kriger, and I went to Colorado Springs to the International Luther League Convention. Lorraine drove; I assisted. We drove to Oakland, Nebraska where Reverend Gilbert Brown had gone, when he left Mamrelund. We spent the night there and picked up his daughter Katherine, who attended the convention too. We also visited Boys Town, Nebraska when we were that near to it.

There were others from Mamrelund who attended the convention and if I remember correctly, Mrs. Harold Saur, drove them.

We stayed at Peak View Motel; many of the motels were mostly filled with Luther Leaguers.

This convention also had inspirational meetings, discussions, sing-a-longs, etc. There were great youth leaders here, like at the Los Angeles, California one in 1947.

Before leaving the area we did go to the top of Pikes Peak in a touring car and to Royal Gorge and to its bottom. As we crossed the suspension bridge over the gorge it swayed. The flags on the bridge were a beautiful sight.

Upon leaving Colorado Springs we went north into the state of Wyoming. There we drove and thought, via the map, we'd come to towns to lodge in.

Well, these towns were only a gas station, garage, a tavern, and maybe a grocery store. On and on we went more little towns, and finally a bigger one. It had a hotel; rain was coming down hard, so we dashed in. No rooms available. This was about 9:00-9:30 P.M. We asked if we could just rest in the lobby and pay them

Lorraine Dufort and myself

something. Oh, no, that was not allowed.

We drove around the town a little. On a residential street, with a streetlight near, we parked. We all were resting well, if not sleeping, and there was a light flashed into the car. I'm sure no one spoke, either in or on the outside of the car, but we girls surely were on the road again in a hurry! We drove all night and it was the first time we'd witnessed twenty four hour road construction. Big floodlight bars with ten lights on, were high on poles and lit the area. We drove through miles of construction. They graded the road and we followed a truck through.

Lorraine Dufort, Carl Fonger, and myself

We visited Carl Fonger at the Rapid City, South Dakota army base. It was nice he was located for us, after we arrived on the base.

Due to the many miles driven during the one night, we arrived at Lutzen, Minnesota (where Rev. and Mrs. Brown had a cabin near Lake Superior), hours ahead of schedule. We stayed with them a bit longer, and then the three of us traveled to Michigan via Duluth, Minnesota and the Straits of Mackinac.

1954 - Mother, Marti and I went to Oak Park, Illinois. Then Aunt Irene drove us to Judy Dieckman-Bob Waughtal's wedding at Aunt Erna's in Manson, Iowa. Marti was a good traveler.

1955 COLORADO SPRINGS, COLORADO= We took my folks and Martha on a trip to Colorado Springs. Martha again traveled well. She enjoyed seeing our 'new bedroom' each night. She also would ask if we were going to eat in a 'rest-burnt.' We feel she may have associated the candles lit at the table and 'burnt.'

On our way out we visited the Black Hills. We came in on the back side of Mt. Rushmore, on a road that was under construction, there was no sign on the end where we entered... no wonder road construction equipment had to pull off the roadway to let us through. Martha had her picture taken with Blacky the Indian at Mt. Rushmore; we had a great view of the faces.

While in Colorado Springs, Cheyenne Indians were there advertising the rodeo in Cheyenne, Wyoming. The group must have had their dinner on the upper floor of the restaurant where we were having supper. They passed our table on the way to the stairs, so we viewed their beautiful native dress and head pieces. Martha was wide-eyed with wonder. It was announced that the group would be having their native dances in the early morning of the next day, so I got up and took some movies of them (now on VHS tape.)

We toured a pottery works in Colorado Springs. This was VanBriggle Pottery which made the items from native soil, and the type which had the red hue was depleting. The other color which was most popular was a turquoise. We have a lamp and maybe a piece or two bought at this time.

We traveled to Pikes Peak by tour car. Dad was very faint at the top (elevation sickness). The driver gave him smelling salts, he was better then. Martha was so concerned. We drove out to Royal Gorge and passed over the Bridge of Flags. Beautiful scenery; mountains, streams, and country.

On our return trip in the open country of Kansas, Dad was driving. Rollin and I were dozing. All of a sudden there was a *jerk*, we awoke! Dad had let his foot off the accelerator! Dad said, "I was going 90 mph **OH-OH-OH!**"

We stopped in Minden, Nebraska to visit Harold Warp's Pioneer Village, a museum, plus buildings of yesteryear. This was owned by a manufacturer of Plexiglas. We also stopped at Bethphage Mission in Axtel, Nebraska (a mission originally sponsored by Augustana Lutherans), where mentally, and physically handicapped are given good care. They had group homes for decades, for those who could live semi-supervised lives. It truly was and is a great place (now there are satellites of this mission in many states-1993).

    During the above vacation Bruce stayed with Aunt Barb.

    1956 UPPER PENINSULA= October, we went to Barb and Nate's cabin and had a fun time. I remember getting into the car with Nate so I could see the deer along the road as it became a real two track or less. I know as we 'bumped' over a bump on the two track that the 9x13 cake pan came out of the back window. Ker-plunk! We watched the deer at the salt block, hiked, etc. The car ferry ran the Straits of Mackinac. It was always fun to board and ride over the water to the opposite peninsula. This was the last time we rode it. The first car drove over the Big Mac Bridge on November 1, 1957, such a feat of engineering, what a beautiful structure!

    1957 QUEBEC-NEW YORK STATE= We, Martha, Bruce and the folks went to Quebec City, Canada. We stopped to view Niagara Falls and the Floral Clock (London, Ontario) so pretty, as usual. On to Quebec we drove along the Wellington Canal. We went to the Chamber of Commerce in Quebec City and hired a guide. He drove our car all through Old Quebec and New Quebec. In old Quebec we went down the narrowest street. Our car was the 1957 Plymouth Savoy, with those fins. Martha and Bruce enjoyed seeing the kids in the street scamper quickly out of the way.

    In a town somewhere, we saw a street sign Dufort. It really caught our eye! In one village we went to a fort and museum. We saw the changing of the guard. Dad heard here, that the Baseball Hall of Fame and a museum were in Cooperstown, New York. It was worth going to, and was not that far out of the way, so we went there. The kids really enjoyed this museum and the ride in a wagon, drawn by horses. It was The Farmer's Museum, and there were cottages where candles were being made, flax being carded, yarn being spun, bread being made, wooden barrels being made, a blacksmith at work, etc. A big barn, with an upstairs, displayed old farm machinery. A building across the street housed a Doll Museum; it displayed dolls of the years past, very enjoyable. The Baseball Hall of Fame was most interesting to Dad and Rollin.

We went on a boat tour of the Thousand Islands, in the St. Lawrence Seaway. This included a tour of the Heart Castle. The guide pointed out the shortest international bridge, where the border of the United States and Canada met. It connected a very, very small island to the larger island where a house was.

We then drove down to the Finger Lakes region to Penn Yen, New York, where we stopped at Estella and Charlie Lanphear's (Charlie was Dad Lamphear's first cousin; Charlie's dad, Franklin, and Dad Lamphear's dad, Joseph Albert were brothers). Then we visited Charlie's son, Franklin and Peggy Lanphear. We had a picnic, under a canopy, by the fish pond. Franklin and Peggy had three children, a boy of about fifteen, a girl younger, and a still younger girl about eight or nine years named Jane. Franklin had a sister too, Mrs. (Maylon) Elizabeth Wilbur. Note: many New York La**m**phear's spell their name La**n**phear.

1958 UPPER PENINSULA= Going to Barb and Nate's cabin was always fun. We went again in October. Maureen was three months old. It seems I almost left her on the davenport, as we prepared to leave. I've been reminded of that at times!

We had fun watching the beavers, we pulled apart their dams, and they'd rebuild it over night and in the morning. The flap of their tail was thunderous as they warned others of us being near! Fun! We played cards, went on hikes, picked flowers for center pieces, went on day trips to Marquette and the various falls.

1959 TRAVERSE CITY= We went camping in the trailer at Zeb and Marian Fowler's. Marian was a first cousin of Rollin's. While there Gladys and Carroll and family were too. We just had fun, playing, walking and swimming near or in the bay. The kids enjoyed it and of course we adults enjoyed visiting and the beautiful scenery which is such a part of the peninsula there. Fowler's farm was on the west side of the east bay. Later Gladys and Carroll bought a parcel from them and spent more time in the summer there.

1959 COPPER HARBOR - KEWEENAW PENINSULA= With the little Shasta trailer, Mom, Dad, Marti, Bruce, Rollin, and I took a vacation in Michigan. We traveled north to Northport on the West side of the West Bay in Traverse City, Michigan. Somewhere in that area we went through the "Lund's Gardens," this had trails which led around to the stations depicting the life of Christ. It was very nice, flowers, streams, and birds all made such a natural setting.

We went into the Upper Peninsula and visited the (Big Spring) Kitch-iti-Kipi. We camped one night at Calumet City. There, the kids and I picked thimble berries in a field. The plants and berries are similar to that of a raspberry. The beauty of Brockway Parkway was lovely. Kids and we enjoyed Fort Wilkins too. We toured a copper mine. On the way home we stopped at Marquette Prison; lovely grounds and a nice souvenir shop. We went over to Mackinac Island. We toured the Fort Museum. Grandma, Marti, Bruce, and I toured the island by horse and surrey. As we went passed the golf course a ball came *zooming,* hitting the bald head of the man in front of us. We could almost watch the goose-egg rise! (Maureen stayed with Aunt Barb at our house).

1960-VARIOUS= We visited Greenfield Village and Henry Ford Museum in Dearborn, Michigan.

We also went to visit Bob and Meryl (Paulson) Perlstrom in Lake Villa, Illinois (Meryl was my room-mate while I was in nurses training).

Maureen was a good little girl. She was being 'potty trained' and did so well.

Bob and Meryl took us to O'Hare International Airport to see planes and jets come and go. (Looking back this may be 20/20 hind sight! As we got out of the car to go to the airport Rollin whispered to me, "I'm not going; I can't see!" He stayed at the car. The meals here were not as timely as his weekly, or even his weekend ones. Now we wonder if the wait is what caused his vision problem, or too high sugar due to nibbling. This was three years prior to his diabetes diagnosis!) Anyway our visit with Bob and Meryl was nice.

1961 NEW YORK STATE WITH ROLLIN'S FOLKS= We went over Teacher's Institute in October to New York State. Rollin's folks, Martha, Bruce, Maureen, Rollin, and I traveled with the little Shasta Trailer. Maureen, Rollin, and I slept on the back davenport, Gram and Gramp slept in the dinette area, and Martha and Bruce used the canvas type hammock over the davenport... this hammock will probably be something the kids will always remember. We headquartered at Earl and Margaret Dexter's in Syracuse. (Earl was Dad Lamphear's first cousin. Dad's dad and Earl's mom were half brother and sister)

From here we visited other cousins (cousins, second and third removed). They were Sarah Seeley, Thera Wilson, and Kitty Leppert, also one by the name of John Lanphear was owner or manager of a Standard Gas station. When we visited a cemetery, we found that Franklin and

Joseph Albert's father did spell the last name Lamphear. The name of the second wife of their father was Sarah Ann. She was the mother of Franklin and Joseph Albert's two half sisters, Cora and Ida.

Gram and Gramp Lamphear stayed in the home of the Dexters. We five, stayed in the trailer. It was cold, especially one A.M. There was half an inch of ice in the bird bath.

The kids rode well and behaved in a way that Rollin and I were proud of them. (I must state, I have one big regret: I now wish I'd kept in touch with at least one of these cousins).

1962 GUYS TRIP FISHING= Rollin, Nate, Dad and Bud Wilkinson went fishing at Cedar Lake and Wabachobee Lake in Canada. The International Bridge was being built at that time. I remember at home the temperature dropped and I took the Ford tractor; used its light to help see, and covered the strawberries with straw, the next year we had irrigation!

1962 PENNSYLVANIA= This year we went to Penn State University at State College, Pennsylvania, to visit an army friend of Rollin's. We stayed at a fraternity house with them.

Joe and Marie Walton had a son Joey, and daughter Cathy. Our kids had such a good time playing together, in the big grassy yard.

Joe gave us a tour of the countryside. I remember the narrow black top roads, with the curves and hills-wow- my tummy was lost several times. We went to an area of a covered bridge (or an old mill?) and walked down an embankment.

I think this was the first time I'd eaten long thin spaghetti with sauce on it, I know it was a first for our kids! I made goulash, but never spaghetti.

1963 GUYS AGAIN TO CANADA FISHING= The guys went fishing in Canada. They had fun, took the little Shasta trailer and two boats as they had last year. They had a good catch and traveled the completed International Bridge.

In 1963 we went as a family, with Betty and Brut to the Upper Peninsula. This is already in FAMILY MEMORIES. It was in October, over Teacher's Institute (defined in 1961 New York area).

1964-1965-1966 - I cannot place where, when, or what we may have done, this may indicate that some others are misplaced or that they were camping years and not trips. Anyway, I'll leave it to one's imagination the where's, when's, and what's.

Back: Rollin, Judy (Dieckman) Smith, Ed Smith
Middle: Carrie Rosell, Marti, Erna Porth, Henry Porth, Malcolm Rosell, Bruce
Front: Brad Waughtal, Jon Waughtal, Maureen

1967 IOWA= Mother had a letter from Aunt Erna (Dieckman) Porth and Hank of Manson, Iowa. Judy, Ed (Smith) and boys were coming to visit in Iowa. She'd said it would be nice if we could come visit too. They farmed, raising lots of pigs and corn, beautiful crops and fields.

This time again, the little Shasta trailer with Mom, Dad, Marti, Bruce, Maureen, Rollin and I, traveled. We camped in Porth's side yard. I was pregnant.

Ed was Judy's new husband. It was great to be together. Judy's boys are a year older than Maureen and Maureen's age. We played baseball, volleyball, ate, and talked.

Later, we were even happier we'd visited together. That fall Hank was found dead, after having a fatal heart attack, in the field.

1968 FLORIDA= We decided to go visit Grandpa and Grandpa Rosell over April spring break. I always felt that me getting my bus route back, after subbing for eight weeks, was a 'God Send,' thus earnings were saved so we could go. We went via North Carolina so Marti could see Dutch Vandenberg at college. (A fellow she was dating). The scenery was beautiful. We drove down with Heidi sleeping in the bassinet, or on one of our laps.

Mom and Dad were delighted to see their new granddaughter.

We left Heidi with Grandma and Grandpa while we visited Cape Canaveral, later, Kennedy Space Center. It was fabulous; hard to imagine the magnitude of it all. Oh, Heidi cried at Gram's most of the day.

We also visited Busch Gardens, and went through Fairy Tale Lane. We went on a tour boat with Olga and Harold Hine, and saw alligators and other wildlife of Florida.

On the way home we stopped at Silver Springs and rode a glass bottom boat and viewed the pretty fish. At the motel Heidi got on a pony.

We arrived home to a lovely bouquet of daffodils on our kitchen table and a neat bunny rabbit cake. Compliments of Charlene and Betty Mieras. (It was Easter Sunday).

1969 UTAH= We visited Gordon and Mary Colby in Richfield, Utah, again with the Shasta. We left as soon as we could on Friday night. Bruce didn't really feel he wanted to go on this trip but we convinced him to! Marti stayed home and worked at Finger's Restaurant.

We went through Iowa in a terrible thunder and lightning storm with torrents of rain.

        The stop at Pikes Peak, Colorado Springs, Colorado was nice. We went up on the cog railroad and down in a tour-limo. While going up by rail we saw a lot of wildlife, and Bruce talked to the limo-driver all the way down. The Race to the Clouds was held on the Fourth of July. Many people camped out the night before the race. It was interesting to hear at what elevations they stayed. We went to the Garden of the Gods in this area too. Here Rollin purchased a ring. Its setting is petrified wood, which resembles a pretty fall scene. He didn't wear it for years, now in 1994, he is wearing it again.

     West out of Denver, we saw the destruction of forest fires' from some years before. Kids were awestruck at the tree trunks all standing stark bare. We stayed at Silver Plune Camp Ground just before going over Loveland Pass. We wanted to go over the pass during the cool of the next morning. It was raining hard as we pulled into camp. We just parked, prepared supper, and ate. The sun came out as we ate. Rollin and Bruce leveled the trailer, etc. The girls and I hiked, over the stream on the stones, just enjoying all of it. The sheer rock rising straight up for so many, many feet, wow, what a sight! (Since then a tunnel has been built through the mountain).

     Morning came with a lovely sunny day. The brightness on the rock was beautiful. We pulled out of the campground and traveled to the top of the pass. There we paused and the kids walked to the sign. We took a picture there and Heidi toddled on up the trail, quite a way. Bruce and Maureen went and got her. We all enjoyed watching the cars and trucks on the highway below from the height of the pass summit.

We had a great time at the Colby's. The kids went swimming at the town pool. Rollin went out with Gordy to 'mark' trees. A trip Mary, the kids and I took was to Big Rock Candy Mountain. We stopped at a Mormon Historical Site. On this day Maureen had her hand slammed in the car's door. It was on this day too, before going, that a gas station attendant felt we ladies should get new tires. What he didn't realize was, Bruce told us, "He's pulling your leg." We told the attendant we'd go back to the house and get another car, Mary's.

The two families went up to Flat Top to spend the weekend. We stayed in the Forest Ranger Station. The beauty of the meadow, flowers, and deer, these are memories. We had our first fried tacos there, fried by Mary.

The road going up to the station was a Utah state road. (Possibly Utah 70). The upper part of it was gravel and oh, so dusty, and curvy! The drops, off the road's side, were sheer down with no guard rails and no trees to prevent anyone or anything from going to the bottom. Oh, I didn't want to go down or up that road again! Upon leaving the mountain top we took a road on the other side of the mountain. It was black top with guard rails and trees.

Going back to Colby's we went to Bryce Canyon. Oh, what a sight! The stone formations I think are one of the most beautiful sights I've seen.

Colbys had planned for us to go to Zion National Park too. Due to me being frightened about going down the same way I'd come up, I said, "I'd just as soon stay at the station and enjoy." The truth was that had we gone to Zion, we would have gone down the 'other side of the mountain' on the above mentioned paved road etc.

On our way home we stopped in Iowa to visit Aunt Erna. In conversation we learned that the bad storm we'd driven through in Iowa those nights before was so severe by Aunt Erna's, that the corn was riddled down to eighteen to thirty inches high from the hail that night. It had no leaves, just the stalk (Aunt Erna lives north of the highway we took out west).

**1971 GRAND MARAIS - UPPER PENINSULA=** June- We went camping here with Bob and Gwen Dufort. We hiked, gathered stones, and just had fun. The dads fished in a couple of areas. We hiked down the AuSauble falls area which then was just a path. Little Heidi was a pretty good trooper. We drove around the area and just enjoyed. Maureen, Heidi, Marlynn, and Jeff were with us this time. Marlynn found an agate in this area, on one of their vacations.

**1971 SASKATCHEWAN, CANADA=** August- The little Shasta trailer again traveled; with Mom, Dad, Heidi, Rollin, and I. Martha and Bruce both stayed home and worked. Maureen spent one week with Deb Andrus.

We went up through the Upper Peninsula to the International Bridge. There was an accident near the Canadian side. We waited twenty minutes. We continued around Canada's Highway 17. While I was driving, outside Wawa, the car sputtered. Rollin asked what the gas gauge read. Whoops! Over a small bridge we sputtered and I pulled as far off onto the shoulder as possible. Rollin got out to walk. There were some people walking the rocks across the highway. Rollin asked them how far to Wawa, and they said ten miles. They then offered to take him in for gas. They also brought him back. What kind people! (We figure the 'hold up' for the accident was where the extra gas was used; as we idled.) As we waited, cars would pass on the roadway and the trailer just shook. Mom rested on the davenport in the trailer. Dad, Heidi, and I just got out and stood around.

Around every bend and curve there seemed to be a river or stream. Each one had a sign with its name on. I remember Heidi had Gram reading each of them.

We picked up Canada Highway 1 at Thunder Bay. Not too many years before, Thunder Bay had been serviced only by the railroad. We traveled through Ontario, Manitoba, and into Saskatchewan. In Regina we went North on Highway 2 to Stalwart.

We were going to the home of Loren and Dorothy Wilcox, who my folks knew from the J & J Mobile Park, Bradenton, Florida where they wintered.

Loren farmed sections of land. Planted mainly to wheat. One could look across acres and acres of waving wheat. Mustard, flax, and sun flowers also were main crops.

I recall when they took us on a ride that they commented about clouds of flies. Later we saw one of these clouds. There were flies on a white house too. There were so many flies, that the white paint looked like gray-black. We visited some friends of theirs, had lunch with them, and viewed their beautiful flower garden.

It was a pleasant visit. Dorothy, Loren and my folks had a nice time together. Dorothy was so *easy* to be with. We slept out in the trailer. We heard coyotes howl; Heidi listened for them.

Returning home we dropped down to U. S. Highway 2 and again enjoyed the farm country of North Dakota, and the other states. We had a good trip home.

1972 CONNECTICUT= In the fall I took some time off bus driving and went with Betty Mieras to pick up Charlene and baby Lynn and bring them home to Michigan. We left by plane from Grand Rapids, Michigan. I remember holding Betty's hand as we took off. I just knew I'd lose my stomach and scream! Not so, it was a nice take-off and also the whole flight. A gentleman in an adjacent seat told me what the lights below were, like the Boardwalk, etc. We went to Hartford (Windsor Lock) Connecticut. Mike Mieras met us there, and took us to Charlene's.

Baby Lynn was so sweet, big brown eyes. We just enjoyed one another as we got ready for the return trip.

Mike also came home, after serving in the Coast Guard, and his stuff was in a "U-Haul." We had two vehicles and I followed the u-haul when I drove. In the mountains, I recall there was 'black ice' on the roadway; I was alerted to it because the vehicle in front of me made a slight shift.

We stayed in a motel the one night and I offered to stay with Lynn, while they went for coffee or supper. I felt so badly when Lynn cried and I could not calm her (similar to Heidi with Gram Rosell when we went to Cape Canaveral in 1968). It was a neat trip. It was my first plane ride.

1973 FLORIDA= Dad and Mom had been spending winters in Florida, for about eleven years. Dad had an accident in Bradenton that totaled his Ford Maverick. We were told it was good Mom was not with him at that time; they felt the 'broadside' would have killed her.

Rollin and I left after Maureen's confirmation service; Imogene had the extended family dinner in her honor. (It was about May 20th; right now I don't recall who Heidi stayed with). We traveled all night. I can still think about being on a detour and wondering if we'd missed a sign. I remember stopping at the Tennessee Valley Authority Dam site and using the rest room there. We took turns driving the Chevrolet pickup. We arrived at the J and J Mobile Park in Bradenton, Florida the next day.

We sorted and packed what the folks wanted to take back to Michigan, because they did not plan to return the next year. Dad and Rollin really packed the pickup cap full.

Mother had a lot of back and hip pain for many years. There was no way we could ride back with four in the cab of that pickup. A neighbor took Mom and me to the airport. Dad and Rollin rode along. We had a wheel chair for mother. We transferred planes at O'Hare in Chicago. A Red Cap wheeled Mom to the concourse of the plane going to Grand Rapids. The flight over Lake Michigan was beautiful. There were several family members at the airport to meet us.

The guys came home and the folks sold their trailer Oscar Averille of Kent City, Michigan.

1973 CONNETICUT= Betty and Brut had talked of going to see Char and Dan Piell and baby Lynn. It depended some on whether the hay got in, and this depended on the weather.

It was about four or four-thirty in the afternoon that we had a call from Betty saying they would be going to Connecticut. Would we like to go too? Wow, this would again prove my mom right. Our big fault according to her was, "If one says 'go,' the other is in the car waiting!" Yes, she's right!

Well, Rollin had to get permission to use some of his vacation. But how? Walt Proctor was his boss. We knew he'd be at a local bar in Sparta. Rollin hated to think of going there to ask. Bruce said, "Dad, the only way, is to go check." Bruce went with him.

They found Walt and he said, "It would be O.K." We borrowed money from Bruce, and from my folks to use on the trip.

We were off, having packed, etc. by nine o'clock in the evening. We went by way of Pennsylvania, and stayed a night at Clearfield.

It was nice seeing little Lynn and the kids. Heidi was thrilled to play with Lynn. They lived in Ledyard, Connecticut. The countryside was quaint with its stone fences and winding, narrow roads.

We went to Mystic Seaport. Heidi really enjoyed many parts of this great museum. The whaling boat was of real interest. The old homes in some of these towns were something else. They were close together and had two and three floors. The date of when they were built was stated somewhere near the door. They had belonged to the old sea captains. We had some great sea-food on this trip.

## 1975 TRIPS TO THE DOCTOR-PROBABLY!!!

1975 MAINE= This trip was June 26-July 4, 1975. Rollin had been sick and out on sick leave January-May.

We left with Barb and Nate, and as Nate pulled out of our driveway, Rollin took my hand and said, "I never thought, a few months ago, that we'd be going on a trip." We were headed for Bar Harbor, Maine.

We stayed the first night in Clearfield, Pennsylvania. As we wound our way to the village, we could see the Mountain Laurel bushes in bloom in the wooded area. Very pretty!

We visited a pottery factory in Bennington, Vermont. I still (1994) have a two fingered mug from there; speckled brown. We stayed in this town overnight.

We toured, after hours at no charge, the Morgan Horse Farm. A nice informative tour. We stayed in Middlebury, Vermont. The whole countryside of this trip was beautiful.

A highlight in Stowe, Vermont was a gondola ride up a mountain. The view was spectacular. This is the beautiful village, in the mountains, where the VonTrapp families' lodge was located. We had lunch at their lodge, and the real *MARIA* herself, was there. She sat in the booth with us and visited. Barb told her that Ruth Ann had played the part of Maria in a production that Spring Lake community had put on. Maria told of her thoughts of how the story had brought joy, entertainment and education to so many. She was shorter than I'd expected her to be and of course quite along in years now! We bought the book <u>MARIA</u>, and she autographed it. We found out later pages one through twenty four are missing! We stayed in Littleton, Vermont.

The scenery in the White and Green Mountains were beautiful on the rural, country roads. The buildings, houses, barns, etc. were close to the hillsides with the road in front and then the farmland on the other side. This area, of course was a valley and very picturesque.

The scenes along the coast were lovely when one saw it from the roadway. We had wonderful sea-food meals. In Penobscot Bay we visited with many shopkeepers. There were antique shops; one after another, another, and another. One shopkeeper said, "These antique shops are closer than the two ends of a cow standing length-wise." We went through a Granite museum in Montpelier, Vermont and at Bar Harbor walked the paths of the park and enjoyed the scenic Atlantic Ocean.

We traveled across Lake Champlain by ferry. We had to wait some time to be boarded, and it was lunch time, so we tail-gated. We had crackers and sardines for lunch. It was a nice crossing and one could view the shoreline with homes and recreational areas.

Gas prices on this trip were about $0.60, and Motels ranged from $15.00 to $21.00.

Upon returning home we heard that Prince dog had slipped his collar shortly after we left. My dad went to feed him and found him by our backdoor. Guarding his domain! He didn't come to the food dish so Dad thought he'd take him by the neck and put his collar on. Prince thought

differently and bit Dad. I think Ellen Dufort took Dad to the doctors' office. He was bit in the hand; several stitches were needed. It looked terrible! It healed well! Prince was still loose when Dad came home from the doctors. He called Tom Bliss to do away with Prince, just so that no one else would be a victim. One just could not take a chance.

1975 MUSKALLONGE LAKE - LAKE SUPERIOR= We traveled with our Shasta to the State Park. Jo Baughan also traveled with a fold-down trailer. She had a flat tire on the trailer. It seems we were near Rogers Dam and it was repaired there. It also was the day after Jimmy Hoffa, a big union boss, had come up missing. We went through a road block check on US-131 that morning. We're sure it was regarding his disappearance July 30, 1975.

We set up camp and went to Lake Superior; it was the warmest I think Superior ever gets. We all enjoyed our wade or swim there. We had good camp fires, eats, etc. The next day Superior was as cold as usual. Roy Baughan and Maureen came up after work, on Saturday. The guys went fishing but none got much to talk about. Only the one Rollin got, a three inch Northern Pike, we have pictures to prove it! We had a fun time!

1976 THE JUNKYARD= Kay Farrell invited us to join them for a long week-end at the junk yard in Lake City. They had a motor home we could stay in. Mark and Maureen came up on Mark's motorcycle.

We have happy memories of this time. We ate in the small house and had a picnic type supper one night. The large bowls of potato salad, and other food was devoured.

This is where Heidi first drove a car. Lisa, Linda's sister, was an 'experienced' driver. She could 'rip' around the many parked junk cars and junk piles. This in addition to it not even being a two track, but an open, over grown field with humps, bumps, and bushes to run over. Such excitement! I rode a trip around, 'twas thrilling as one could hardly believe. Yes, I screamed with excitement!

We went to Lake Missaukee to swim one afternoon. Pat and Kay took us all out for dinner. I think at that meal I had the best bread pudding I've ever had.

1977 KENTUCKY= Barb, Heidi, and I went to Kentucky to visit Shirley. We visited the Shaker Village in Pleasant Hill, Kentucky. An interesting historical part of the past! We had a nice meal on their grounds. The dining area had a beautiful dual spiral staircase in it. We also ate at a Kentucky Fried Chicken place; it was Colonel Sander's first establishment.

KENTUCKY= Sometime! Nate, Barb, Heidi and I visited Shirley again. This time I have memories of having dinner at Pruetts. Mr. Pruett and Nathan had been in the army together in Burma. They had a large home, similar to a plantation home, but in the village of Mt. Sterling, Kentucky. All the rooms were furnished with beautiful antique furniture. Many tables had "Claw" feet, and many pieces were massive.

Carriage ride through Shaker land

1978 Probably-DECATER, ALABAMA= Rollin's mom was on a tour with the Egypt Valley Grange people and had slipped and fallen in the bathtub of the motel. She had fractured some ribs. Gladys, who also had fractured ribs, Rollin, and I went there to be with her. We drove all night. We did some inquiries at the motel and then went right to the hospital. The tour had to continue, so she was more than happy to see us, a strange city, a hospital, and not up to par in one's health. She had to stay in the hospital one more day. We drove around the city some, and ate at the airport restaurant. The food was great, but what I remember most, was how the waiter held the pitcher so far from the glasses as he poured water but never missed the glass. We made the reservations for Gladys and Mom to fly home during this time too. Another thing, the first burrito I ate was on this trip. Rollin and I enjoyed a more leisurely drive home and enjoyed some of the less traveled roads.

   1978 CALIFORNIA= We went to Fresno, California with Barb and Nate for a military reunion. We went via route I-70, I think. We saw Mono Lake in the Nevada Sierras, cacti in bloom, (such vivid colors) and on into Yosemite National Park. The area of Yosemite was spectacular.

   Nate's 888$^{th}$ Ordinance of the Army held its Reunion at the Fresno Travelodge. We stayed with the group attending the reunion, attended the banquet and enjoyed seeing the buddies visit, as well as we visiting too. The 888$^{th}$ were stationed in Fresno in the early days of WWII. They had previously been at Fort Custer, Michigan. The heavy maintenance unit also was based at Camp Beale, near Marysville, California. The unit shipped out aboard the (old) S.S. Mariposa on September 9, 1943. They arrived in Bombay, India October 12, 1943. They went to Ledo, India to work on the "Ledo Road" which was to link India to China. At the end of the war the unit was based at Shingbwiyang, Burma at the 105 Point on the road.

   In the days following reunion we met people Barb and Nate had known in the years they lived and worked in Fresno. These people were Cy and Blanche Manoogean and Lee Cates. We stayed with Lee, Barb and Nate with Blanche. Lee took us shopping. Blanche took us to a processing plant of apricots, figs, nectarines, oh, were they tree ripened sweet!

After saying farewell to these kind folks, we went north toward Washington. At Paradise, California we stayed at Carl Balsam's brother's home. (Carl was Nate's brother-in law). Art Balsam showed us some gold nuggets he'd panned some years before. Gosh, one of them was quite large. He had them all in a safe!

We motel-ed it on this trip and used the camp stove and coolers for meals. We had a lot of nice picnic areas to eat at (sometimes I wish I could remember the specifics). One lunch I remember how much we enjoyed the 'Polish Roses' that Marti had sent with us to eat. Barb says it was the first time she'd had them.

We went north to I-84 and drove along the Columbia River. The Gorge was beautiful and the waterfalls too. There was quite a bit of construction being done there and a pilot car led us through the same.

I think we probably crossed the Columbia River at Tri-City area. We went on up through the wheat country of Washington to Aunt Erna's in Coeur d'Alene, Idaho. We drove around the area of Beauty Lake and Beauty Bay. We ate at a restaurant, up several floors, overlooking Beauty Bay. We went on home via U.S. 2. We broke into the Minneapolis area and it was thick fog! A very enjoyable trip.

Prices for this trip were: groceries, ice, park fees $95.95. Gas total $244.69. (Gas prices per gallon $0.629 to $0.739) Motels, 11 nights, $268.00, (per night $15.00 to $27.00... we also spent five nights with friends. These figures were our one-half share of costs. Miles traveled 5,474.

1979 UPPER PENINSULA= We went to the Soo Locks and around Michigan with Betty, Brut, and Heidi in August. We especially enjoyed going through the locks on an excursion boat. Heidi watched the various freighters and kept a log of their names. She enjoyed doing that as much as the going through the locks with the rising of the water. Memories, memories!

MANY VARIOUS YEARS= We went several years to Traverse City and stayed with Gladys and Carroll. It was always relaxing and beautiful. Since they have their home there, it is neat to look out their living room window and view the East Bay, with sometimes a swan or two going by. We have gone to Dick and Darlene Tuttle's "hide-a-way." They have worked hard to build this; it's a nice home for their retreats.

1980 CANADA= We went to Canada a couple of years for artificial sweetener with cyclamates (cyclamates had been banned in U. S. of A.). This liquid sweetener I'd used for years in some baking, and all of my canning and freezing. I missed it. It left no after taste and the canned fruits were as if canned with sugar.

This trip, in late spring, we went by truck and drove all night. Heidi and Anita Lovell slept in the back of the pickup on air mattresses. We remember the beauty of the day-break. The horizon becoming light and the fog in the air, with the silhouettes of trees; it truly was a picture of nature's beauty! We went to Niagara Falls. We ate in the 'Needle' restaurant and viewed the falls from above. We were in the stationary part; not the revolving one. We took the 'Maid of the Mist' boat trip, under the falls. It was the first time Rollin and I had taken it; very nice; fun! We got a lot of mist from the falls on us. Yes, we went to gift shops, stayed overnight in a nice motel, and we did remember to get the sweetener.

1980 CEDAR POINT, SANDUSKY, OHIO= It was probably during the week that we went to this amusement park. (Betty, Brut, Rollin, and I).

We got there about supper time. We reserved our motel room and went out for supper. I remember each of us ordering a different entree. Brut had boiled dinner. It was a huge portion and we all commented many times, "How good it was, and so seldom on a menu."

The night's rest was great, never, never have we had such comfortable beds.

The next day was fun filled, the rides were thrilling. Rollin and I went on the best roller coaster they had at the time 'The Gemini,' and I guess, over the first big drop, I couldn't get my breath for what seemed like minutes, I couldn't even scream! We bought big dill pickles on a stick from a vendor and then sat and enjoyed them to the last seed and brine drip. It tasted *soooooo good*! At night we ate at a restaurant overlooking a marina. Oh, the water I consumed, was it eleven glasses? We went to The Blue Hole the next day. This was a big hole (similar to a spring), which one could look into the depths of clear blue water. Betty could remember her dad taking her to this when she was a little girl. I'm sure it too has more tourism now than back when she was a child.

1980 INDIANA-KENTUCKY= Barb, Nate, Rollin and I went to Purdue University to say "Hi" to Carmen. Albert was writing a paper, so we didn't see him.

We enjoyed going through Parke County, Indiana to see the covered bridges still in use and some not. The roads were gravel and some blacktop. The fields of corn were planted right up to the road. This was different than locally and quite pretty. If at a four corners all was corn; then one 'inched' out at a stop sign to gain visibility.

We took many local back roads on into Kentucky to see Shirley. One noon we ate at a little restaurant that had a pasta variety platter, what a portion, what a fill!

  We stopped at an area that had a natural arch bridge with foot-paths that we walked. This area was also known for botanical reasons. It had many trees and plant life growing there which did not grow everywhere but in some places, thus to a botanist it was a treasure of knowledge for research. This was within the Daniel Boone National Forest.

Shirley took us to the well known horse farms, or she would guide us to them. We saw some of the famous horses as Seattle Slew, Secretariat, and others. I took a picture of Seattle Slew and only got his rear! Calumet Farms and Walmac were a couple of farms I remember visiting.

1980 OZARKS - OCTOBER 5-12= This trip came  as a big surprise! The Egypt Valley Grangers had a tour planned and needed more passengers to fill the bus. We were asked to go with them. It was October and I took off work for this trip. The Grangers who I remember were Ken and Shirley Anderson (who invited us), Fanny Thomet, Jean Robideaux, Esther Hazlet, Dale & Gladys Shade, John and Marge Potter, the Kellys, Neal, Florence and Nellie Vandepeerle, Roger and Evelyn Crampton Jansma, Maude Fase, and Mona Rooker.

The bus driver was Randy and tour guide was Paula from Jar-Mar tours. They kept us in line and *hopping* all the time.

Highlights were many on this tour. We visited the Arkansas State Capitol building. In St. Louis, Missouri, the view from "The Arch" was great; the paintings within the old courthouse, the theatre-dinner show on the riverboat are all nice memories. We went to Eureka Springs (The Switzerland of America), in Arkansas. The statue, "Christ of the Ozarks" atop Magnetic Mountain, was an eye catcher for miles. It is seven stories tall. Here we attended the "Great Passion Play," in a 4,100 seat amphitheater. What a great production, live horses, sheep, doves, racing chariots through the streets, and great actors and actresses. This town has been noted for its health spas since the 1800's. In the older part of the town the streets are very narrow. Streets were built on the side hills and a home may have its front on one street and the rear on another.

Branson, Missouri (not nearly as full of tourism in 1980 as now in 1994) is known for the great toe-tapping show of the "Bald Knobbers Jamboree." Another great (outdoor) production is the play of Zane Gray's book, "Shepherd of the Hills." During an intermission people from the audience were asked to come join in the Square Dancing. Ken, Shirley, Rollin, and I did this. It was fun! In the afternoon we rode a wagon about the farm which pointed out where some moonshiner's stills had been in the time of prohibition. We went to Silver Dollar City too, which is in the area.

On the way home we visited Grant's farm near St. Louis, where The Anheuser Busch Clydesdale horses are bred and raised.

This indeed was a fun filled trip. We enjoyed the people and played Uno at night in the hotel room with friends. The food was good in the restaurants too.

1980 or 1981 ILLINOIS= Aunt Irene Dieckman and Clara Behrens were here from Illinois for mother's birthday. That year Heidi and I, with Sharon and Amy Ysseldyke, took them back to their homes. We four then went on to Great America in Gurnee, Illinois. We have memories of trying to find a motel, of Amy commenting,

"There's one!" (Its sign outside advertised evening entertainment- topless dancers). Needless to say, we didn't stay there. We also have memories of the fun we had in the one we stayed at. We did have an enjoyable, fun day at the amusement park the next day.

1981 ALASKA= It was Thanksgiving Day in 1980 at Imogene's that Barb commented that Nate had said to her, "Guess I'll never get to do something I've always wanted to do."

She asked him, "What's that?"

His reply, "To drive the Alaskan/Canada Highway."

She answered, "Guess we'd better do it before you can't see or I can't walk!"

Barb then said, "Anyone want to join us?" I knew Rollin didn't have enough vacation time so didn't make any positive comment.

Rollin and I discussed the fact that we'd love to go. (SO WHAT'S NEW?) We decided that we'd write to the Grand Rapids office of the Kent County Road Commission explaining he'd have three weeks due him in July 1981 and asked if his 1982 vacation could be advanced at this time (August fifth being his anniversary date). The reply came back, yes!

We now made plans for Alaska. Heidi would go with us; she was thirteen and one half years old. She asked for money for her birthday and Christmas gifts. She saved her baby sitting money. We'd said she'd be responsible for one third of the state room cost on the boat.

We took our Ford truck with a cap on. Rollin fixed a cot to fit across the front of the back (Heidi's quarters). He made a stone guard for the grille. Nate and he put on a second gas tank. Barb and Nate borrowed Bud Wilkinson's camper. (Our sleeping quarters). We had CB radios for communication. Barb's handle was Dancing Digits; mine was Gum-Drop and Heidi's was Crawling Cutie, due to her crawling through the slider window of truck. Heidi brought twenty seven books (in a milk crate) to read. I think she read them all!

We left on Wednesday, June 24th; it was very, very windy for about two hours.

The day's travel was nice, drove 567 miles and stayed at Albert Lea, Minnesota. They'd had hail and 90 mph wind the night before!

JUNE 25th... We went through lovely farms of corn, bean fields, and grazing land. We stopped in Mitchell, South Dakota to see the "Corn Palace." We saw many antelope. We saw Mt. Rushmore and stayed in Custer State Park, South Dakota.

JUNE 26... We saw mountain goats, buffalo and some deer. The snow covered Big Horn Mountains were beautiful. A mountain thunder storm, we watched form, but we didn't get any rain. We stayed in Bozeman Pass, Montana at night. The view was a panoramic view and we were above the highway and railroad; fun to watch.

JUNE 27... The sun was shining and the scenery beautiful; farmlands in the valleys were irrigated. Followed varied terrain and then beautiful mountains for many miles into Idaho. Stayed with Aunt Erna at Coeur d' Alene, Idaho.

JUNE 28... Went through wheat lands, sage brush, range, more farming, mountains, and then a valley of fruit west of Yakima, Washington. We camped by the Tieton River on U.S. 12 (Smoqualmie); cooked out, had camp fire and s'mores. The river rapids rushing by, gave the evening's music; quiet and peaceful for sleep. One tree right at our camp site was fifteen feet in circumference. Forests have many this size and so straight. Today we also gathered some ash from the Mount St. Helens eruption a year ago.

JUNE 29... It was sunny on US-12. We're traveling through White Pass viewing Mt. Rainier with the sun on it, evergreens sporting their new growth; palisades of rock wall 428' deep; what varied beauty! Saw a deer swimming across Rimrock Lake. Nearer Mt. Rainier we stopped at Box Canyon of the Cowlitz Glacier, a 180' stone wall to the gorge below. We took a fifteen minute walk there. We stopped at the visitor center at Paradise where we saw slides presented by a lady ranger from Michigan. We saw the top of Mt. Rainier without clouds and with floaters passing over it, just beautiful! Oh, there was so much beauty in this area including wild flowers in full bloom. Timber throughout was enormous, they were framing the roadway with an arch, so tall and straight. Stayed at Alder Lake, very quiet; no electricity or water.

JUNE 30... The morning had low hanging clouds over the lower mountains. Then the scenes resembled Michigan on, Washington 7, with little farms near Tacoma.

We arrived at the dock about 11:00 A.M. in Seattle. We walked the waterfront. Here, Heidi was happy to be between Mom and Dad, due to the skid-row type characters. We went in some shops. Met many people awaiting the car ferry, which we would take for the next part of the trip. The cost of our passage was: state room for three, $108.00; passage for three, $414.00; passage for the vehicle $440.00. Supper was on the boat; really enjoying this trip.

JULY 1... Out on boat, Matanuska. There were 532 people aboard. Halved a breakfast with Rollin. We met many interesting and friendly people from all over. The solarium was wall to wall sleeping bags and tents, and even a couple of tents right out on that deck. Saw some whales and bald eagles. Heidi played cards with a young lady and cribbage with Uncle Nate. The day was dreary but nice.

JULY 2... At about 5:15 A.M. the boat was rocking; we were going through the Dixon Straits. Rainy most of the day. Ported at Ketchikan, Wrangell and Petersburg. The towns are nestled into the hillsides and the ocean side buildings were built up on stilts for tide. Saw eagles flying around. Scenery is pretty, enjoy, enjoy!

JULY 3... On the Matanuska, we visited, and viewed. The Ranger showed pictures in the observation lounge, about eagles, history and The Wrangell Narrows. We docked at Sitka. Heidi and I left the boat and walked around on a road to a beach where the people were digging for clams. We dug too and got a half of pail. It was nice talking to the residents. Saw a beautiful rainbow. Mendenhall Glacier at Juneau impressed me; it is twelve miles long and one and one half miles wide. It looked like a running river. It was light until about midnight.

JULY 4... Up and 'attem' with the call of the steward at the door. It's 2:30 A.M., in one hour we'll port at Haines. It was dark as we drove into Haines. We parked and slept awhile. On our days drive we saw snow capped mountains. These were of the St. Elias Range. Lake Kathleen and Lake Kluane both were such blue lakes; the latter was thirty five miles long. We drove about 380 miles, most of the road was gravel, it was muddy only about thirty miles. We were lucky, because we pulled off near a creek and here were drivers carrying water, in used coffee cans, and washing off their headlights. They'd come from the opposite direction, and had had rain. We went through the Yukon Territory; we saw a bear. Stayed overnight inside Alaska about twenty five miles at Dead Man's Lake.

JULY 5... Rainy! Drove to Tok. Called a Rose Woods; she directed us to Slim and Buz Afton's; we also stopped at Scobys. We drove Highway 2 to North Pole, it was decorated for Christmas. We did our laundry at the North Pole, and also stayed overnight. The temperature is about 58°.

JULY 6... Rainy, and then sunny. We drove up to Fairbanks on Highway 3, and visited the museum there. We bought groceries. We traveled the George Park Highway to Mt. McKinley Provincial Park. The roads were dirt, gravel and rutty. We shopped at a trading post, it had many handmade crafts. The heater was on about forty five minutes at night in the camper. This night, we had a shampoo line over a log at the camp site.

JULY 7... Up early to catch a tour bus at 6:40 A.M. (school bus). We saw a cow moose with twin calves, Dall Sheep on high ridges, and three bear. The caribou were great; they pranced and danced playing games. Scenery was 'deep and wide'; the wild flowers growing in the rocks on the hillsides were pretty. At higher elevations it rained and snowed, windy and foggy. Mt. McKinley was not visible at all, nor was the mountain range (which on a clearer day is said to be most beautiful). The road was bumpy, rutty and full of chuck-holes. The driver did not give us much information. The tour was 170 miles round trip.

JULY 8... Clouds hung over the mountains and rain made it less picturesque. We set up camp in Anchorage. Called Mae Ingersol Quinn and Max Fonger, also phoned Wilhelm and Pat Schossal (they had owned property on Indian Lakes Road in Algoma Township when I was treasurer, and this is how we made the contact). We went to visit them. Then they guided us up to Flat Top Mountain to have a view of the city's lights at night. Magnificent!! The road to this mountain was stony, rutty and steep with hairpin turns.

JULY 9... The five of us, in our truck, drove to Portage Lake. Nice weather. Drove the Seward Highway along Turnagain Arm; the tide was out and so the mudflat was extensive. We viewed many Glaciers. At Portage Lake a huge mass of ice had broken loose from a glacier and it was so blue. It was here that we bought the Viking Bear that we still enjoy. We stopped on our return, to Anchorage, at the Alyeska Ski Lodge. We shopped and I had my first giant, delicious cinnamon roll with butter here. We also shopped at a candle factory, bought candles made of seal oil. Further on we saw the results of the 1964 earthquake, abandoned homes, half covered with silt. Then, closer to Anchorage, we again saw Turnagain Arm; the tide was in, so all the mud flat was covered. We visited Mae Ingersol Quinn and family in the evening.

JULY 10... Shopped in the morning in Anchorage. I bought a birch basket at the native shops in the hospital area, I bought nothing at the shops downtown. The apartments and buildings use many hanging baskets with colorful flowers.

Then we traveled the Glen Highway through the Matanuska Valley's farmlands. The gardens proved what we had known; they raise things *big* in this area. At Palmer we visited a museum of transportation on the Alaskan State Fair Grounds. We visited a Russian Orthodox Church and an Indian burial ground next to it. The day's drive was pretty; mountains, canyons, and the Matanuska glacier. We camped at Little Nelchina camp ground. This was a very pretty setting.

JULY 11... Drove the Glen Highway to Richardson Highway, and then we went to Valdez. We drove along the

Alaskan pipeline, some of it was above ground, and some was buried. There were many waterfalls. The two larger ones were Bridal Veil and Horse Tail. There were many glaciers too. The Worthington Glacier was the largest and we could drive right up to it. We saw helicopters dropping supplies to workmen on high tension lines. We also saw an abandoned hand drilled tunnel. It's quite a contrast to the road construction area where blasting now goes through the rock, it was interesting to see this as we drove through it. From the observation lookout at Valdez, we viewed the oil port city across the bay. The Alaskan Poppies (orange, gold, red, pink, and variations of them) were in bloom and the masses of Fireweed were so pretty dancing in the wind.

JULY 12... We drove along the towering peaks of the snow-clad Wrangell Mountains. We were surrounded by the mountains, lakes, rivers and forests. We saw moose and mountain goats. Again in Tok, we saw Buz and Slim Afton. The bunk house, they were building, really come along well in the course of the week. This time Ray and Mable Scoby were home. We bought a miniature dog sled from Ray. He had quite a woodworking shop. They had painted green stones instead of lawn. At night we were in the Yukon Territory again and camped at Lake Creek Camp Ground. Upon entering camp, we were asked if we were tenting. They asked because there had been trouble with the bear. We set up camp and a bear trap was right next to our site. Two rangers were in charge; with a dog. During the night the dog barked and Heidi was to her cap's window and said the rangers were out at once with their guns.

JULY 13... We were on the Alaskan Highway again, going home; they had watered it and graded it with an Adams grader. The St. Elias Range and Kluane Lake we viewed again; the lake was like a mirror and reflected, so beautifully, the mountains, trees, etc.

On to the city of Whitehorse, Yukon Territory, got camp site, went shopping, had money exchanged at the bank (a 19.85 increase); this called for a night out. We ate at the lovely Prospectors restaurant.

JULY 14... We visited the MacBride Museum; it featured all aspects of the Yukon history. We read of the history of the S.S. Klondike, a stern wheeler used for cargo and passengers from Whitehorse (460 miles) to Dawson City. Interesting facts were revealed. There was quite a bit of road construction the first part of the day's drive. We forgot to get ice when we got groceries. We stopped at several little stores but none sold ice. Then before we got to the camp ground, where we stayed we saw a sign *ice*. It was a little home-made sign. The guys wanted to fish some and when they were gone, I said to Barb, "I saw a sign *ice* back a ways. I'm going to go see where it is." Well, it was backing much further than I thought. Over ten miles back I spotted the sign. I meandered down the little road, down a winding hill and finally got to it. They had ice in their freezer. It was in one half gallon milk cartons. It sold for $5.00 a half gallon carton, I got two. We camped at Big Creek Camp Ground about 30 miles west of Watson Lake. The guys didn't catch anything.

JULY 15... We took the Cassiar Highway at the Junction, some gravel and some black-top roads. We drove into the town of Cassiar. It had asbestos mine and a huge sludge pile. Employees all lived in the town; houses were all alike, and many mobile homes.

The day's drive had many scenic lakes, large and small; they were aqua and deep blue, some serving as mirrors. We traveled very dusty roads today. Signs read "use headlights, dust area." We camped by another river. The guys got a 14" Rainbow Trout, we ate it. Camped at Todagin Creek on the Cassiar in British Columbia.

JULY 16... Every type of road today, the Alpine Meadows were colorful. Visited the Indian villages of

Kitwancool and Kitwanga. They had authentic totem poles; among them the famous Mountain Eagle or Thunderbird pole. Homes were dilapidated.

At Kitwanga we left the Cassiar Highway; it was an adventurous road with very few services. A road to remember. The bridges were one way, with plank flooring, and side rails. They were too narrow for a mobile home (trailer) to go through. We watched a mobile home raised high enough to go over one of these bridges. The men would jack the trailer up and put planks under it, until it was high enough to proceed over the bridge; when over, they had to remove the planks and let the trailer down. On Yellowhead Highway 16, at the Buckley River we saw native Indians use long spears to gaff salmon in the turbulent rapids of Moricetown Falls and Canyon. Interesting! Camped at Smithers.

JULY 17... Traveled on good roads with similar views. At Burns Lake we washed the trucks. From here on a lot of farms, there were all types of hay bales. Many acres being cleared. Stayed at Prince George.

JULY 18... In places many forests being cut for timber. Stopped at a couple of creeks, fellows fished, we refreshed! Mt. Robson, 12,972 feet, the highest point in the Canadian Rockies it stood out majestically for miles.

Stayed at Jasper, a tourist town nestled within the mountains. The Rocky Mountains here have gray tops and are very jagged. Trains are traveling all the time; watched seven during the evening with one hundred cars or more on each, also one passenger train.

JULY 19... Took a tram up Whistler Mountain, 7,432 feet. Quite a sight. Saw the tree line due to elevation as we went up.

Again the scenery through Jasper Park, etc. was lovely. I enjoyed very much the Athabasca Falls which cut through a tiny gorge of rock and formed **'pot'** circle type cuts where the whirlpools cut steadily for eons of years.

The Columbia Icefield was massive. The Icefield Parkway must be among one of the loveliest scenic roads. A view from (a turn-out) Sunwapta was something. The tiny dots below, were cars on the highway, it showed just how great the mountains are, how majestically huge, and reminded me of God's masterpiece of creation and of the song, "How Great Thou Art." Thanks to God too, for health, eyes and the opportunity to view this part of His great creation. Camped at Rampart Creek in Banff National Park.

JULY 20... Sunny, cool. Saw many lakes of aqua blue and several glaciers. On to Lake Louise, many tourists; the gardens of flowers were pretty. We walked through the Chateau with the lovely shops, etc. We drove further on Highway 93 and into Kootenay Provincial Park. Camped. In the evening we took a ride to see the wild animals, all close to the road, in total we saw two black bear, a mule deer, seven mountain goats and a deer, all with the naked eye. This Park, as were the others, was beauty, beauty, beauty! Many evenings we popped corn. Yummy, a climax to a great day.

JULY 21... Drove into Banff, a town with mountains surrounding it. The hotel there was neat with its lovely shops. The floral gardens surrounding the hotel were gorgeous. Then the lake with its magnificent color will never be forgotten. Drove to Calgary, and soon after, the mountains were part of the past and we were passing farms ranches, fields of grain, many cattle, irrigated crops and fields' summer fallow.

We were just ahead of a thunderstorm most of the day. Clouds were interesting to watch. After we set up camp for the night, winds blew strongly and it poured cloud bursts, soon the sun was shining.

JULY 22... Sunny, drove through grain country. Then in the flat land where it was cross-patch effective planting. Wheat fields were lush green. Farms closer together, wind breaks around them. Camped east of Portage La Prairie, Manitoba

JULY 23..Driving through Canada; prairie country, ranges, wheat fields, then rocks, lakes and rivers and more pines, just very nice. Camped about 80 miles west of Thunder Bay, Inwood Provincial Park. Walked around the lake. Yummy, chicken livers for supper.

JULY 24... Drove on, stopped at the Niagara Falls of the North, the drop of 128,' not too much water in the river though. Saw a huge bull moose grazing right by the roadside, but cameras were not available for quick accessibility. At and after Nipagon, fog really socked in.

JULY 25-26-27... We continued east in Canada. Then we did leave Barb and Nate in the Upper Peninsula and they went and visited some friends on the St. Mary's River.

Miles traveled this trip 8,487 in addition to the inside passage miles on the boat. Gas prices were $1.349 to $1.699. We averaged 17 miles per gallon.

1981 –FLORIDA= In August, about two weeks after we returned from Alaska, Betty Mieras, Heidi, and I left for Florida. We were taking Baughan's freezer (full) to their home.

We drove straight through. Betty and I still laugh at the silly things we said and sang about to keep awake! In the mountains (early morning) a sight I enjoyed was the valley completely enveloped in fog. It looked like a flat white floor with greenery on each side.

It was nice seeing the kids again. We swam in their pool. Mark took us to Disney World. We visited Tom, Vera Mae, and Toni Dunagan. Tom was Mark's supervisor at Lear-Seigler in Grand Rapids, Michigan, and was instrumental in Mark getting work at Martin-Marietta in Orlando...

Maureen and Travis came back to Michigan with us for a week or two. We had a break under a big tree at a rest stop, 'twas nice! We spent a night in a motel. Mark drove up, for the closing on the house mortgage, and took them back.

It was such fun surprising Rollin, as Travis walked into the bedroom to wake him that morning. Travis fell down the steps almost immediately and how I praised God he wasn't hurt.

Gas prices $1.219 to $1.309 on the above trip.

1981 CANADA- ALGOMA RAILWAY= On a Thursday in October we were driving on old US-31 through the north counties of the Lower Peninsula. What beauty in all the leaves of fall.

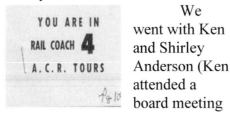

We went with Ken and Shirley Anderson (Ken attended a board meeting of the Michigan Township Association) and after that we went into Canada to experience the Algoma Railroad ride. This railroad traveled from Sault Ste. Marie, Canada, to Hawks Junction. A total of 165 miles (it went beyond Hawks Junction but we rode only to Hawks Junction). The railway meandered through the Agawa Canyon. We couldn't get tickets for that day; we got there too late. We purchased them for the next day.

The day on our hands proved fun and interesting. We traveled the local rural roads around Sault Ste. Marie, Canada, some roads we made turnarounds on.

The rail ride was beautiful. The lakes, sky, and Mountain Ash trees (with their huge clusters of large red berries), gave us much to look at. The fall colors were at their peak, so the trees showed off their leaves in hues of gold, orange, red and the evergreens peeked through for the added touch.

We drove home after the tour so we arrived home late, Monday morning came early for all, as we were all still employed.

1982 -FLORIDA - SPRING BREAK= April 2-10 Connie, Lee, and Nate Poulin with Timo, an exchange student from Finland came over with their fifth wheel (Timo was attending Fruitport School, living with Kelvin and Ruth Deters). Heidi, Rollin, and I loaded our luggage in and off we went to Florida. Mike Hart and John Maison saw us off.

We left wearing sweat shirts. Soon we traveled through a heavy rain storm, and wind. Lee was a good driver. We drove straight through. The Baughan's were awaiting us. Had a nice time; we slept in their home. Poulins and Timo in the trailer.

On the Saturday evening that we arrived, April 3rd, we called Michigan and they were having a blizzard. Anne Norton was married at Peace Lutheran in Sparta and the guests went home, rather than to the reception. Later, when home, the bus drivers told of the bad visibility and blizzard that I had missed.

Kids went to Disney World and to Rosie O'Grady's. We all went out to eat (Barb and Nate came up too) at a Japanese restaurant that prepared food in front of us. Very entertaining. One thing not planned was when the chef was salting one of the orders, the salt shaker's cover came off and all the salt fell out. He had to start the order over. Heidi's biggest memory here was she saw a cockroach!

I remember reading to Nate the story "Peter Pan" over and over again up in the fifth wheel. Coming home an incident I recall, was going through Atlanta, Georgia and not taking the by-pass as it was late at night. Well guess what? Tail lights, stop lights, red, red, red; the Atlanta Braves were just through playing their ball game. We didn't have any trouble though, Lee just stayed in the far lane, and we looked big!

  1982 – FLORIDA= It was in August; Heidi, Betty, Brut, Rollin, and I left to go to Maureen's in the blue and white Ford truck. We had two lawn lounge chairs along with luggage in the back cap. Two of us sat, or lied down or whatever on the lawn chairs. I believe with a sleeping bag on them; it proved satisfactory and even rather comfy. We drove straight through with the adults changing positions and driving.

  Brut, Rollin, Mark, and Heidi went crab dipping yet that night.

  We slept in twin beds, Betty and Brut slept on cushions in the (quite unused) living room.

  We swam in the pool. Visited the Dunagans, as well as they at Baughans. Betty, Heidi, and I went to Sea World. One day we ate breakfast early, then Betty, Brut, Rollin, and I went to Disney World. As we left the trolley from the parking area, Rollin was in a cold sweat; an insulin reaction so soon after breakfast? Yes, because after eating a hamburg and drinking some juice all was well. We did have a fun time there, we older kids!

  We went to Busch Gardens. I remember the cat (Lynx) on the tree branch sleeping within the building area as we proceeded up to the elevated monorail. The monorail was to view wildlife of the world; in an expanded area. Then remember the chutes ride, that left Brut especially wet. They bought a souvenir *dry* towel after the ride.

  That evening we'd planned to meet Mark and Maureen and Travis at Branch-Ranch Restaurant for our evening meal. We did so well; we both exited at the same time from the opposite directions onto the road to the restaurant, following one another! The meal here was served family style. The vegetables were served in 8x8 aluminum baking pans. Food was abundant and tasty.

There always seemed to be a cloud burst at sometime during the day or evening hours. This time it was in the evening driving back to Baughans.

Returning to Michigan we stopped at Shirley and Glen Sampson's apartment in Lexington, Kentucky. We visited the Kentucky Horse Park and also some of the well known horse farms Calumet, Walmac and Claiborne were some. One stable was very new. The most noticeable thing about the stable was the amount of oak that was used. The trim, doors, stalls, mangers, etc. were all oak with a gleaming finish. It was just beautiful and sparkling clean. It was the Gainesway Farms.

We played cards at night with Glen.

1982 – CHRISTMAS= Baughan's came to Michigan in November for an early Christmas. I remember making snow-people with Travis in the front yard. There was a lot of cold weather but not a lot of snow the rest of the winter. The "people" stood a long time before melting.

We must have had a nice Christmas, don't we always?

1983 – FEBRUARY= I came home from the afternoon bus runs on February 18th, and on the table was a note 'baby boy-Brent Daniel'. It took me a second to realize it was Mark and Maureen's!

Then I asked, "Is all O.K.?"

Rollin came out of the hallway with tears, "No, baby is not doing well." It was sad. Mark called Barb and Nathan (wintering in Ruskin, Florida) to ask them to come and stay with Travis. Mark had just told them that things weren't going well. As they hurried to Orlando, Barb wondered who was not doing well, Maureen or baby. Later Nathan commented many times that it was the only time that Barb had ever told him, "Drive faster, drive faster!" Otherwise she was always telling him to, "Slow down!"

We called Mark and Maureen many times at the hospital and they also called us. Mark and Maureen had the feeling many times that I shouldn't come because the hospital personnel were trying such'n'such. Then at 3:00 A.M. the 22nd they called; I should come. I'd done all the calling regarding air schedules, cost, etc. the afternoon before (thanks to Marti's insistence). In preparedness, I also called Betty Mieras to see if she had any cash I could borrow. She did not, but said she knew her Uncle Bill always had cash on hand. She called him and borrowed two hundred dollars from him for me. I felt better having some cash with me. I just have to insert here what my mom said to me when Maureen was going to move to Florida. She said that it probably would take no longer for me to get to Florida flying, than it had taken her mother to get from the Alpine Station (now 7 Mile Road and Vinton Avenue area) with the horse and buggy to their home at 9852 Pine Island Drive. Alpine Station was a railroad stop, and from Chicago her mother had come by train.

  I was Township Treasurer then, and had to distribute taxes to schools and government units, from the tax collections. I had already written the checks for the units and schools. Martha Henning was the township clerk, and bless her; she just said, "No problem, send Rollin over with your records, etc. and you go!" I did.

  Mark and Maureen met me at the airport (I'd had trouble with my left leg for a few weeks--but all went well). We picked up Travis (from where I don't recall), went to their home and then to the hospital. Mark and Maureen both held Brent, while Travis and I admired such a little baby (normal size; new born) with all the monitors attached. We returned home and had only been there a short time when the call came that Brent was failing. The kids went back. He only lived the days February, 18-22, 1983. He had Sturge-Webber Syndrome with Hemangioma.

  Funeral arrangements were made. I stayed with Travis. I was with the kids at the funeral home visitation and at the home as friends called there. The extended family, who wintered in Florida, Aunt Barb, Uncle Nate, Aunt Helen, and Uncle Scott, attended the funeral.

1983 FLORIDA= Spring break March 30-April 9; back to Florida for a visit. I remember Maureen and I went shopping. We bought two dresses for Grandma Rosell and she wore the gray and pink one so much. She even commented, "Malcolm often said I looked good in pink!"

The guys went shrimp dipping.

We had Travis' birthday party and sun bathed and swam in the pool.

Baughans came to Michigan June 30 and into July.

1984 EVENTS= Maureen and Travis had come back to Michigan with Mark's folks on March twelfth. While they were home we had an extended family hay ride on March twenty-fourth at Dufort's farm. Then at spring break, they rode back with the three of us. Loren Marsman and Mike Hart also drove down this spring break. We had CB radios and did a lot of yakking to them and to others.

The kids went to Disney World and we all went out to eat. Can't really tell a lot of specifics as these trips all seem to run together.

1984 FLORIDA= In July we left again for Florida! We were expecting a new grandchild. We arrived there and waited.

We enjoyed the pool, visits, and the highlight was learning to play Hand and Foot; Mark just knew we'd enjoy it. We did!

Derick Lee was born July 29th. We were all thrilled. It was nice to be there and enjoy the little one. (Baughans were home for Christmas in 1984) The highlight of the Christmas visit is the hayride for the extended family, with Santa visiting at our home; it's somewhere else in this volume!!!!! Probably with some Christmas memory.

1985 FLORIDA= In January, Mike Hart went to Florida and stayed with Mark and Maureen until May.

March 28-April 7, spring break, the three of us again went to Florida. Always enjoyed a visit to or from the Dunigans, and now again Travis' birthday. Both the Holmes' and Wilkinsons' came to the party, when they wintered in Florida. We enjoyed the little guys and played with them outdoors and in. As stated before these Florida trips just run right into each other!

   1985 TENNESEE= Barb, Nate, and we went to Nashville. We stayed at Shirley and Glen's house a night; and mowed the lawn (they were selling it, as they are now in Michigan). We then drove to Carol and Virgil Cauthen's (Dolly Krueger-daughter of a friend of my mom's). We stayed with them. We attended Grand Ole Opera, and toured the park. Actually, we enjoyed the entertainment at the park as much as the Grand Ole Opera. Carol took us on a nice tour of Nashville pointing out stars homes, etc. and telling that some of their children went to school with her children. They were both gracious hosts and we enjoyed our stay.

   1985 PARKE COUNTY, INDIANA= Three or four days in July, Betty, Brut, Rollin, and I went in our pickup (with cap) to Parke County to view the covered bridges. We again had lawn loungers in the back. We traded positions.

   We stopped at a Memorial Park on the way down to eat. Where?

   We heard the insects like Cicadas singing in volume the one evening as we roamed on the rural gravel roads. It was actually something I'd never heard in our area.

   We all enjoyed the bridges as Rollin and I had a few years before. We had one lunch at a little town or a four way cross roads, it was delightful to visit with the area people. They mentioned that in fall, when the colors of the trees peak, the little roads are bumper to bumper with traffic. They have four tour routes marked in colors green, black, red, etc. We stayed in a motel two nights.

1985 FLORIDA= a g a i n! Christmas. We drove through the night, it was cold and clear. It was a fun Christmas. This was the first year Baughans were in their new house. Travis got the big machine for Christmas (green with big handle bars). Derick got a trike (Henry Bloom died while we were visiting here). This was the year that Connie and Nate Poulin were with us a few days at Maureen's. Nate and Travis played outdoors somewhere and came home **black**. Connie and Nate rode back to Michigan with us.

Myself, Rollin, Travis, and Derick

1986 APRIL= Heidi and Mike's wedding. The Baughans were up for it.

1986 or 1987 LOUSIANA= Not sure which year! It was kind of a quickie trip decision! Connie (Wilkinson Poulin) was going to pick up a Bass Boat for a friend. She asked if I'd like to go. Why not? Nate, Ethan Deters, she, and I went down for it.

We stayed in motels two nights. I know one had a pool and we spent the evening in it, just having a good time. The boys did some book reading. We bought several pounds of fresh shrimp in the area on our way home.

It was a fun trip with no problems. We went through many areas I'd never been in before. I saw rice being grown; some of the fields were flooded.

1986 CHRISTMAS= Baughans flew-up for Christmas.

1987 FLORIDA= Mike and Heidi took our car with a trailer and the jet skis to Florida. They came back with Maureen and boys in Baughan's van.

Maureen and the boys were here for Grandma Rosell's birthday party. Then July 21, we went back to Florida with Maureen and the boys in the van.

While in Florida, July 24 and following we all went to the Keys in the van. We stayed on Island Islamorada at the Holiday Isle Motel and drove on day trips from there. It was a delight to view the waters from the height of the van. We visited parks, saw mango trees in swamps, etc. We went on a tour in the glass bottom boat out to a Coral Reef. The Reef was something to behold and the fish were breathtakingly beautiful. On Key West we enjoyed shopping and took the picture of us and a sign stating how far it is to Cuba.

Rollin, myself, Travis, and Mark holding Derick

Myself and Rollin

While in Florida, Bruce called to tell of their new daughter, Brenna Rae.

As we were ready to leave Maureen's, we found our CB had been stolen the night before. We awaited officers for the report. After that was given, we took off.

We filled the gas tank in mid afternoon, and then drove in heat and a thunderstorm. At a point the car faltered, spit and sputtered; we pulled off and Rollin put in some dry gas stuff and again topped the tank. We continued about 28 more miles and again the same. Macon, Georgia was the place. We pulled off again and an older gas station attendant called a wrecker from a station back a few miles.

It was about 4:30 P.M. and Rollin needed to eat, as his blood sugar was lowering. We ate from the cooler. The wrecker came and at their station two fellows declared we'd have to wait until Monday for the Chrysler dealership to open. I assured Rollin we had money for a motel in a suitcase.

Then a man from near the counter came over and asked Rollin if he could take the car for a ride. We rode with him; he drove, accelerated hard and the car did well. He said that though, the car doesn't 'vapor-lock' it acted the same. This was due to overfilling the gas tank, and the gas expanding. He said he felt we could continue home (we always drove straight through to and from Orlando) because it was evening and the temperatures would go down. We did, and with no trouble we were in Grand Rapids Sunday A.M.; eating at the 68th Street, McDonalds.

We went right to Kentwood to see Brenna Rae. I said to Linda, "I'm a terrific (terrible) grandmother; I can't even take a picture of baby; I left my camera in Florida."

She replied, "That's not all you left; Maureen called and your suitcases are in the loft!" Honestly! The confusion of the officers checking the car, probably hurrying, due to starting later, put us in a forgetful mood!

Brenna was a sweetie. Babies are such precious beings!

We knew we were to care for Christanna on Monday, and that also was a bit of a concern as we sat in Macon. She had asthma and Marti tried not to have a babysitter have the extra responsibility of decisions, should Christanna have an attack.

Bruce had installed central air in our house while we were gone. A treat for this lady who seemed, far too often, to be wet with perspiration. As I say, "I don't perspire, I sweat!"

1988 OHIO= Trips once or twice per year to Florida have come to a halt. The Baughans moved to Burton, Ohio.

We went there in July and celebrated Derick's birthday; we had bar-b-que pork and beef ribs dinner in a grove of trees north of the house.

We went to a town festival. We toured an Amish Cheese factory and went to a pioneer village. We had fun at the kid's home catching fire flies and picking blueberries.

In October, Rollin and I went there while Maureen and Mark went to Washington State because Mark had a job interview. We were there about three or four days.

Then in November we were there for Thanksgiving. So were Mike and Heidi. We had a sweet potato soufflé, so delicious. A highlight of this time was going out, picking out, and cutting down the Christmas tree, for Pre-Christmas! (It was a Charlie Brown type of tree.) Why, because this family was moving to Washington State. They will be in Michigan for Christmas. We took all of Maureen's frozen food home to our freezers when we left.

1989-WASHINGTON - June 20-July 19= Rollin and I drove our 1983 Dodge pickup to Goldendale, Washington. It was packed, loaded! We drove to Des Moines and rested in the cab from, 2:30-6:00 A.M. Then we rang the bell at Lorraine Dufort Dahl's home. We had a delicious breakfast and spent a couple of hours of visiting. We left there about 11:00 and continued driving while the temperature of the day increased. We stopped at a rest area in mid-afternoon thinking we'd rest a bit more and not be in the heat for awhile. Well, it cooled off fast and we only rested a few minutes and were on the road again. (It was June 21st, the longest day of the year, then add the hours gained when crossing the time zones; we had daylight a long time!) In the higher elevation, we drove about a half hour with snow coming down.

One thing I remember was getting into Laramie, Wyoming and putting in 30.6 gallons of gas into a 30 gallon tank. Yes, we were wondering if we'd make it to a gas station! I'd say, as others have, we came in on **fumes**!

We rested in Laramie from 3:00-6:00 A.M. on a side street; our noses were cold upon awakening! We ate breakfast in a 'neighborhood' restaurant and all the patrons were commenting on how cold it was; 34°. We agreed!

We stayed the next night in Pendelton, Oregon. It was nice to shower and rest well. The next day we were off to Maureen's. We had no problem with her directions to their home. We arrived to a locked house and no one home. We thought it would be neat to back the truck into the garage so it'd be out of sight and a surprise. Oh, we were about 1/3 into the garage and in drove Maureen and the

boys. Maureen and they had been at a restaurant for lunch. They'd just ordered and Maureen looked out the window and was almost sure it was our truck (blue and white with cap and a back door) that went by. She wanted to mention it to the boys, but thought best not to, just in case it wasn't us. She could hardly get through lunch fast enough.

We were impressed by Mt. Adam's snow capped peak as we drove from Goldendale to their home. While there, we found ourselves gazing out to the south the first thing each morning to see if Mt. Hood was visible.

We burned a large pile of debris, limbs, etc. Rollin and I watched the fire and raked into it, into the wee hours of the morning. We heard the coyotes; really neat. We heard them several times.

We had an enjoyable time. We took in many scenic areas for our first time. The various falls, the Columbia River Gorge, Mt. Hood, part way to Mt. St. Helens, Mt. Adams, Glenwood area; all very pretty. We met some of their friends and neighbors.

I had a bad sinus infection for four days; just lay and slept. I went to the doctor for medicine; it was during the July 4th holiday.

The boys had chickens. Chores of feeding, gathering eggs, etc. brought back memories!

We came home via Yellowstone National Park and saw the results of the 1988 forest fires. We drove through the Big Horn Mountains; oh, the wildlife we saw. The beautiful scene, "When the Moon Comes over the Mountain," was really awesome. There was a long area of severe thunder storms from eastern South Dakota and down through Iowa (I-29). The lightening was all around us, all four directions; all types, snake, heat, etc. Spectacular!

THE CRASH OF FLIGHT 232
After an engine exploded at 37,000 ft., Haynes guided the crippled DC-10 for 45 minutes, until seconds shy of touchdown, the plane tilted and crashed, erupting into a huge fireball.

Haynes meets the press a week after the crash with wife Darlene and Laurie.

The day after we got home there was a jet crash at Sioux City, Iowa, an area we'd gone through 12-15 hours before. We commented, should it have been then, certainly lightening could have been a cause, but as it was, it was not. The flight number was 232.

1990 WASHINGTON -July 9, Barb, Nate, Rollin, and I left for Washington. We had a good trip out. Nate drove their new car. It was hot outdoors, 100° plus. 'Twas comfortable in the air conditioned car.

Derick in Mark's lap, myself, Rollin, Travis, Barb and Nate Wilkinson

We went on some day trips about the area. On one such trip, driving on the Old Dalles Mountain Road, I spotted the loveliest wild black berries near the road. Nate turned around and we picked eight quarts among the four of us. We put them in the metal cookie tins we had in the trunk and also in the cooler. Nate, Rollin, and I went there again a couple of days later. Maureen went to rent a sander for use on the deck in The Dalles, and she dropped us off and we picked. The berries were nice but some were over ripe.

Nate and Rollin sanded the deck and sprayed it with Thompson's wood preserver. Barb made several pies which we enjoyed and she gave some to the neighbors too.

One night we left before sun down, with Jeff and Debbie Teal's Dodge flat bed truck, to view the sunset. The hay bales made it a hay-ride. We traveled a two track after leaving a county road, up to Gray Back Butte, a fire lookout was there. The view was lovely as were the mountains and sunset.

Judy came from Idaho to visit. She stayed in a motel in Goldendale. We had a nice afternoon and evening.

This stay proved uncomfortable one day for Nate. He felt so poorly that he didn't care to eat lunch. He lopped around on the davenport with pain. Maureen and Barb took him to the hospital; he apparently passed a kidney stone though not while it was monitored. He came home late the next afternoon.

We came home via Washington-14, US-12 and then I-90, and US-59. We stopped about an hour and a half at a lady's home near Pringler, Iowa. Barb and Nate had met her on their trip to Europe. Then I-94, I-80, etc. home.

Gas prices $1.079 to $1.179; motels $25.00 to $40.50

1991= Just to note, Baughans came to Michigan; for our 40th Anniversary.

1992 WASHINGTON - April- We flew into Portland, Oregon and Judy Dieckman Waughtal met us. She'd moved to Long Beach Peninsula, Washington (from Idaho) in the summer of 1991.

We stayed with Judy until Sunday. The kids came Friday night about ten o'clock. While we were together, we enjoyed the ocean, the beach, seeing the towns, and eating seafood.

Judy's home is nice and she seems very happy and content with its purchase.

Oh, it was beautiful! Spring was a few weeks early. The wild flowers were beautiful on the hillsides, the landscaped flowers and shrubs were breathtaking too.

The kids had a varied (to say the least) job list for us to do, if we cared to. We did some of them, very much at our pace. We both read several books. As usual too, I had cracked hickory nuts and packed them, so I picked two quarts plus of nut meats. (Will mention here that I had hickory nuts with to pick in both 1989 and 1990; as well as most of the trips to Florida, oh, then sometimes I had socks to darn!)

Hilside covered with spring flowers

The third of April we picked up Aaron at the Portland airport and came back to Goldendale via the scenic route US-30. He enjoyed that.

We met Mark and Maureen at the local park and went to a restaurant to eat. We attended the play, Sound of Music, put on by the community. I enjoyed watching it and it was a relaxing evening. It was put on in what was the old school and reminded me of our old gym stage (my old high school on Alma, now torn down). The props had to be simple, due to space, but they were sufficient and effective for the play.

Mark took Monday off and the boys and he left early to ski at Mt. Hood.

Mt. Hood ski area

There had been a ten inch snowfall in that area. Maureen, Rollin, and I went later arriving there about eleven or eleven thirty. Before the area of the Timber Line Lodge (built in the 1930's by the WPA), Maureen put the vehicle in four-wheel drive rather than have Dad put chains on, as the sign had requested.

The little boys were on the small learners' hill with an instructor. Aaron was on the Mountain. I think he enjoyed it. He said he went 'puff' down to his waist in one snow drift.

Rollin and Mark left about 2:30. The boys, Maureen, and I left later. The slopes were closed due to heavy snow squalls at about 3:30. We shopped awhile in the shop, after the boys got their gear returned. Then traveled back home.

We took Aaron on local roads; went to a couple of natural arches and to some small ice-caves. The boys had fun snow-balling, hiking,

Aaron, Travis, and Derick

Rollin, Aaron, myself, Travis, and Derick

and just making fun. One P.M. we went shopping in The Dalles. Aaron got some Columbian brand T-shirts. Mark gave him a tour through the plant.

Baughans were getting ready to fit the yard for re-seeding. Mark and Dad tilled the hard soil, this brought up countless stones. We 'stoned' the yard. Aaron's comment, "These sure are lighter than what I've picked up in Michigan." How true, these were lava rocks. Aaron had earned much of his air fare stoning a field and putting them into our ditch area for landscaping. He drove our little tractor then.

Rollin did some sawing for the deck rail. I did some weed spraying. The kids were finishing the upstairs bedroom; off the loft. They have really remodeled and made the home more sunny and pleasant. The entry room which they added (with a basement) surely has given them more storage space. The house has no basement.

We took a weekend and went to Leavenworth, Washington. The town is likened to a Bavarian Village with many shops. We stayed at Wenatchee on Friday night. Rollin and I visited Kay VanderJagt Turner and her husband Mike. Oh, they have a beautiful home and view. We truly enjoyed the visit. We then went on to our destination. We shopped and enjoyed Saturday. We stopped at Cashmere, Washington and toured the Aplet Cotlet factory on our way back to Wenatchee.

Maureen, Mark, and Travis went to visit some friends. Derick, Rollin, and I had pizza sent into the motel. Derick had an upset tummy so it was good he hadn't gone with his family.

One day Rollin and I took Mark to work. We were off then to Gordon Colby's at Otis, Oregon. We stopped first to see relatives of Janet Hammerlind Vanderhyde. They were Ben and Genevieve King, a delightful couple who lived in a home overlooking a valley and the mountains behind. We stayed with Gordon. He took us around a Forest Reserve, shopping and out to see an elk herd. We had a great time visiting too. The ocean was too rough or we would have taken a boat out to see the whales, in migration.

Returning to Goldendale we stopped at McMinville to the Lavender Tea Room, owned by a Keith and Trese Blanding (these people are the children of a lady who sent me a copy of the article from The Grand Rapids Press regarding my retirement; she lives over on Fuller Avenue a couple of blocks west of VanHorns). The home was a restored old home; the decor was lovely.
    Trese herself waited on us. A menu was brought out with a fresh flower blossom on it. The bill also had a fresh flower with it, but of a different species. The home itself was painted soft lavender and the vestibule had a huge bouquet of lavender lilacs in it. The other rooms had beautiful bouquets of fresh flowers too.
    1992- WISCONSIN= In June we took a long weekend trip with Betty Mieras doing the chauffeuring. We left about 4:30 P.M. and stopped for supper in Holland. It was a very good meal, but we did chuckle and remarked, "Good thing we're not in a hurry or on a schedule." Service was kind of slow!

    We stayed in Michigan City. Then the next day we went to House on the Rock in Spring Green, Wisconsin. It was something else; so vast an exhibit one could hardly comprehend. To think that it was one man's collection almost 'blows' one's mind. Exhibits included: replicas of the Tower of London's Crown Jewels, the world's largest carousel (it took two and one-half years to complete, it is 35 feet tall and 80 feet in diameter, weighs

35 tons, has over 20,000 individual lights on it, instead of horses it has 269 carousel creatures both real and mythological); tiffany lamps, furnished dolls houses, paper weights, pipe organs and oodles and oodles more. Very, very enjoyable. The exhibits were nicely arranged.

We visited the Cave of the Mound, and walked the guided tour. As said before, caves fascinate me and I enjoyed this one too.

That evening we were just driving about the country roads and chanced to come upon a very nice restaurant. The food was delicious and we got there just at the right time, especially without reservations.

The country side of Wisconsin with its rolling hills was beautiful. The dairy farms with the three or four Harvester Silos were a sight to see. I really enjoyed the rural-ness of it all.

On the way home we stopped in Waterloo, Wisconsin to visit with Jim and Elaine Springer. They weren't home so we found where Elaine's mom, Ruth Berner lived. Betty was kind to let us 'look them up'. We visited about one and one-half hours with Ruth. She showed us pictures of her children-grandchildren. She also phoned her sister-in-law Lillian Schnoor and let me visit with her (Ruth's husband Arthur and Lillian were my mom's first cousins).

Betty had been to Oshkosh, Wisconsin to the International Air Show and she knew we'd enjoy the Air Museum there. She drove right to it and we toured it. It really has so much history and wonderful displays within.

We continued to enjoy the scenery.

We stopped at Albert and Carmen (Klein) Bugaj's for supper and the night. It was nice to see their home and visit. It was fun to watch and enjoy Lydia as she played and climbed 'her tree'.

We had breakfast there and then traveled on home, a very enjoyable trip! (We have a video of House on the Rock.)

1992 - WASHINGTON-October -We chose to go Amtrak to Wishram, Washington. The trip was nice and we met and visited with many people. We were a little disappointed that we went through Glacier National Park at night. Food was excellent.

Mark met us early at Wishram, and took us to their home; davenport was out, ready for us to snuggle in for a 'nap-back,' which we did.

We were there when Mark, Travis, and friends went

elk hunting. It was a great year, they brought back three (various sizes). The adults, eight including us, readied it for the freezer. We started about 9:30 A.M. and finished about 4:00 P.M. The meat was cut, ground, weighed, and

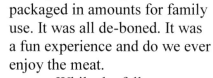

packaged in amounts for family use. It was all de-boned. It was a fun experience and do we ever enjoy the meat.

While the fellows were elk hunting, Rollin, Derick, Maureen, and I again went to Leavenworth. Scene was different, than in April, all flower boxes were in bloom and less snow in the area of the mountains.

We stayed in a motel there, shopped the P.M. when we arrived. The following A.M. we went out and found an art and craft show in the park. We spent much time there enjoying the talents of many people.

A few miles after we left Leavenworth there was a pickup truck in a turn-off area. I said, "I think he had

Golden Delicious apples on that truck." Maureen whipped a turn-around and we ended up buying two bushel and being given one-half bushel of sort outs. These are sold in boxes, not baskets. Rollin and Maureen had to re-pack the jeep to get them all in. Rollin and I canned several quarts of applesauce but we all ate many out of hand. They were so flavorsome!

We attended some soccer games of the kids, also Grandparents day, and visited all of Travis' classes. One of his teachers, Mrs. Pond, really impressed me. (She said she had been to a seminar in Portland recently and one session

dealt with the Holocaust. The speaker had said that this was such an inhumane thing that it surely did not happen. The students in her class had studied it, and she had a bulletin board of pictures of it on display. She remarked that the technology of photography at that time was not so sensitive and could not have portrayed the faces of the people so frightened and horrified or haggard or with such malnutrition. It did occur... but if we don't continue to teach it as such; there will be a time that those who survived it will not be living to vouch that it happened. How true!) We also attended the harvest day party on Halloween with Derick. Mrs. Lovelace was his teacher; one who really challenged each student.

Gordon Colby came up for a visit. He stayed in the kid's fifth wheel. We had a relaxing time while he was there.

We flew home on Halloween. I wore a sweat shirt that Marlynn Dufort Barkow made me; it had Boo-Boo on it with a Halloween scene. There were many compliments offered about it. The flight was very clear and beautiful.

1993 FLORIDA= March and April we spent six weeks in Florida. (It was here that I began writing this VOLUME of memories!) We flew into Tampa. We headquartered at Barb and Nate's.

We spent three nights and four days at Avis and Bob's in St. Petersburg. Gladys and Carroll were there too. They took us all around to places of scenic beauty and interest. We had a nice time. We really enjoyed some clam chowder soup at a restaurant one noon.

We also spent a day with Bill and Linda Bronkema in Bradenton. They took us to LuAnn and Tim's home and also to Wayne and Sharyl's. Little Nathan, son of Wayne, was a cutie. Leona was our young princess all day! When Rollin walked into their home, here is Leona waving her index finger at him (When they lived next door to us on Fonger Road this started, when she was in the kitchen and Rollin in the T.V. room). They took us around to the areas that Bill does lawn care and places of interest in Bradenton. We saw the driveway to the J & J Park where my mom and dad enjoyed several winters.

At Barb's we relaxed a lot, ate out on Wednesday nights also after church on Sunday. We really enjoyed playing cards with them as well as their friends. We went shopping and I bought some clothes for Rollin and me.

Rollin 'puttzeed' along with Nate as he repaired things for people in the park. They went grocery shopping and to a flea market for fresh produce. Those fresh, ripe tomatoes, strawberries, and other veggies, were *Oh, so good!*

We had a delicious meal at Harry and Vivian's, friends of Barb and Nate, that had lived in the park but now live elsewhere.

We left for home on a Sunday, staying at a motel for the night. Monday after eating our evening meal we felt we'd go on to our home and Barb and Nate could stay and leave Tuesday for their home.

Upon arriving home, our answering machine had a message from a lady wondering if we were interested in selling the little gray house. Then in about forty- five minutes she called again. Things were rolling, almost too fast!

1994 -WASHINGTON –April= We flew again to Portland, Oregon. Judy Dieckman Waughtal and son John met us. They had a rental car; her car was in need of repair so it was in an Astoria, Oregon garage.

We meandered down scenic Highway 4 in Washington, to use up some time in order to pick up the car at 4:30-5:00 P.M. We had not seen this area of Washington.

The next day we gabbed and rested. Then Friday, we went to Cannon Beach on the coast in Oregon. We shopped some and had lunch while there.

In the evening, the Baughans, Vern, Sue and Ben Sartain came to visit us. The young folks had a motel down the beach a way (Travis had chicken pox at this time).

Saturday morning about ten of us went to the beach to dig for Razor Clams. It was a fun experience, got 67 clams among us. It was quite a sight to watch the beach fill up with all the vehicles and people to clam. We'd walk out as the tide was out. The little bubble coming out of the sand indicated a clam below! This prompted one to dig or tube for it. We used PVC plastic tubes to pull up core samples of sand that hopefully would contain a clam. When the waves would approach all would take off for the drier beach. I couldn't walk fast so I got quite wet with a few of the more forceful waves (still babying the hip recovery). It was a laughable sight! Razor clamming is allowed only a few days a year and only when shellfish population and the tides are right. There had not been a clam season for a year or two in this area.

We had what's become our annual Fresh Seafood Dinner at Judy's. (Cioppino!) So delish!

Sunday P.M. we left for Baughans. Our month with them went quickly. Highlights were a weekend camping at Crow's Butte, viewing two of Travis' track meets, and a lunch at the school's cafeteria with Derick. In the great tournament of Hand and Foot; I'm sure the guys were ahead. We had a nice motel room in Portland, Sunday May first then, off for home on May second.

1994 YELLOWSTONE NATL PARK- AVERY. IDAHO-WASHINGTON- June 22nd, Wednesday= Janelle and Christanna VanHorn, Rollin and I flew to Portland Oregon. We picked up the car rental and drove to Baughans. Oh, what fun not having a shift lever on the steering column. Each time I'd forget about that, the windshield washers would come on! (This is a memory for the VanHorn girls, because it happened so often and it was so laughable!) Thursday we ate, gabbed, and packed Baughan's truck and the fifth wheel. Friday, Maureen, Travis, Derick, Janelle, Christa, Rollin, and I left for Yellowstone National Park (Mark could not go; he needed to be at the plant for negotiations).

We drove all day Thursday and well into the night. Then on Friday we arrived in Yellowstone and got our camp site. We set up camp and then went about the park some.

All day Saturday we toured the interesting, beautiful acres of Yellowstone. I think one of the prettiest areas is the Grand Canyon of Yellowstone. The waterfalls, hot springs, etc. are all so fascinating and awesome that one cannot tell of the greatness of any or all.

The kids got along well together and helped with the various chores of camp. In the vehicle we never had a cross word, though two always had to buckle up together. Nor were there any arguments about who was going to sit by whom. It was great!

Maureen had the menu well under control.

We went to Jackson Hole, Wyoming and going there viewed the beautiful, majestic Teton Mountains. We shopped there, and took pictures of the arches of elk racks on the four corners of the village park. Upon returning to Yellowstone we only waited for about ten minutes to view Old Faithful *spout off*. Such a sight! We covered the park almost completely and enjoyed every minute of it. The wildlife we saw were elk, bison, bear, coyote, moose, antelope and maybe more. The three days were full but very rewarding.

We then went to Avery, Idaho where we set up camp at Turner Flats Camp Ground (men's elk camp) on the St. Joe River. Oh, how the kids played in the river, went fishing, made s'mores, whittled on sticks and all in all just were kids camping. Fun, fun, fun!

These four grandkids had a fun time, but I think what Rollin and I marveled about the most was how well they got along. There was never a complaint about two persons in one seat belt or who was sitting by the window, etc. You understand the four of them sat in the back seat the whole trip while on the road!

Back to Maureen's on Thursday afternoon. Friday some went and picked fifty-five pounds of big Black Bing Sweet Cherries. They canned some and we ate, ate, ate.

The kids and I made Hobo stoves out of large coffee cans with an air vent cut out at the bottom. We also made Hobo burners by cutting corrugated cardboard the height of a tuna can and circled it round and

Baughan boys and VanHorn girls

round to fill the tuna can. We melted paraffin and poured it into the tuna can. The VanHorn girls and the Baughan boys cooked hamburgers on them for our supper. I think that the kids have that experience as a good memory.

Community days were to be in Goldendale, and the kid's snowmobile club was having a float in the parade. All four kids worked on it with the adults, one or two times. The parade was on Saturday and the kids all got to ride in the parade. Nice time, the float received First Place.

On Sunday we took the day and went to Mount St. Helens' area (the mountain erupted May 18, 1980). What devastation! Two hundred thirty square miles of timber lost in literally seconds... trees 15 miles distant were scorched to death by temperatures of more than 550°! The column of ash braided its way 16 miles up into the sky; day turned to night and the ash fell like snow over parts of Washington and Oregon. This havoc killed 57 people and caused $3 billion worth of damage. One cannot imagine the true destruction and the force of this eruption. The Visitor Centers are most interesting and I'm sure they make it more real for those of us who can only use our imaginations. Our rented car had a flat tire when we returned to the parking lot. Rollin and Mark had it fixed in no time.

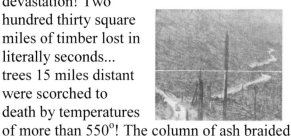

The four Michiganders left Maureen's. We went to Judy's for an afternoon, night and most of next day. The girls fully enjoyed her dog Ky, walking the beach; and talking to John. We had a nice visit again.

1994 NEW JERSEY= Mary Colby Larson had asked some time ago if there was a tour through the Lowell Seniors if we would like to know about it. I'd said yes. She let us know of one going to Wildwood, New Jersey with Atlantic City on the itinerary. Sounded good.

We left at 5:00 A.M., September 25, for the bus at Lowell. There was a nice group of twenty one from the Lowell Seniors, and then we picked up five more in Dearborn and four in Perrysburg, Ohio. We stayed the first night in Straussburg, Pennsylvania. The next A.M. we took the Straussburg Railway on a tour through the Amish farms. We shopped and enjoyed.

On the road again we went to Wildwood. The itinerary there was full. The highlights being a trip to the quaint old village of Cape May. We took a trolley ride through the older section of homes, and a boat out to the waters of the ocean. On the boat I had the new experience of feeding the Sea Gulls; crackers from my mouth! They just swooped down and whipped it from my teeth's grip.

We went to two Casinos, The Resorts and The Trump Castle, in Atlantic City. We played the nickels and quarters to the extent we planned and used up the amount that jingled down now and then. We called it an experience.

We visited the Liberty Bell, Independence Hall, Congress Hall, and the Betsy Ross House in Philadelphia, Pennsylvania.

We went to Longwood Gardens (I wouldn't mind going there each month from April through October). That evening we had dinner at Renaults Winery, and received some recipes for dressing, etc. We had some good wine served there in tasting time. We enjoyed two evenings of entertainment. The one night we left the show and our sides ached from laugher.

On the route home we visited Valley Forge National Park. We saw the reconstructed cabins that were like those Washington's men used the winter at Valley Forge and other points of historical interest. We stopped a brief time at the Hershey Grounds and gift shops in Hershey,

Pennsylvania. There is so much to see there too. The whole area of this trip we had never seen before!

As we traveled on the bus; we were not to use the word 'bus,' when we did we paid a dime into the kitty. Can you imagine there was twenty-four dollars in it the last day? It was used as bingo prizes the last afternoon. It was split and two games were played. Rollin won one. It surely put fun into the trip at intervals when things were quieter.

1994 WASHINGTON= We arrived home from the east on the first of October. We unpacked, laundered, and packed. We left for Goldendale, Washington at 4:30 P.M. on the third. How's that for go, go, go!

The 1995 Dodge truck's arrival (it arrived September 23rd) was the determining factor of going or not going to Washington. The kids did not know we were coming! The Michigan kids kept track of us though.

We drove a night, day, and a night and parked in Baughan's yard at four o'clock in the morning. Mark came out and saw a truck…wondered "who and what?!" He went back in and got Maureen. They came closer to the truck and he said, "Maureen, it's your folks!" We really surprised them. Fun!

Mark and Travis went elk hunting in Avery, Idaho with the friends. No luck though. We did, however, hit a deer on the way home from a soccer practice, yes, with the new truck!

We relaxed, took in football and soccer games, and helped two mornings in the classroom where Maureen works, shopped, and enjoyed every minute of it. The boys are fun to be with. The weather was nice out there (as it was in Michigan too).

Average gas price on this trip to Mark and Maureen's was $1.23 per gallon. It was 2190 miles to their home—the new truck got 15.9 mpg.

1995 WASHINGTON= March 28-April 18. Must have enjoyed things in general. Maybe sprayed weed killer in the yard areas etc. Went to activities of the kids etc.

1995 UPPER PENINSULA= (also 1994, 1993, and 1992) Drove up in the car, and spent a couple of nights with Bob and Gwen in their 5th wheel, at Grand Marais. The beauty of the area is always a delight to view. We went out and dug some wild leeks, cleaned them and enjoyed some even after we came home.

1996- We bought a 5th wheel in late winter, and in May went camping at Grand Marais, and again in fall to Thompson Creek. Both of these times we were with Bob and Gwen and in the spring Marv and Lois Colby also were there so... we all enjoyed our stay. Barb, Nate, Rollin and I also went to Buckley with it.

1996 WASHINGTON= June 13-28th. We enjoyed the usual, but the extras were going to the track meets at Cheney, Washington and the area of Lewiston, Idaho. We went in Baughans 5th wheel for both weekends. It was fun to watch the boys compete and to meet some of the group that participate and those who support them.

1996 NOVA SCOTIA= Barbara and Nathan had been invited to the Wambacks 50th Wedding Anniversary party. They asked us if we would like to go along. We did! It was a beautiful trip and 'twas nice to see the eastern coast again. It amazed me how many tons of wild blue berries they have in both Maine and Nova Scotia, cars were along the roadside and people were back into areas picking them.

We toured Halifax and I was so impressed about the explosion of about 1919 (I think). Two boats exploded in the harbor. Hazel's parents were young, her father worked for the railroad and was in a rail car at the time and was thrown from side to side. The railroad yards were miles from the harbor. The surviving people went home to find their homes destroyed and their loved ones killed and dismembered. If I'm not mistaken her grandparents were killed as was an uncle or two. They told that a cold winter storm followed. The city of Halifax was helped a great deal by the people of Massachusetts. They sent workers, lumber, medical supplies and personnel, and other numerous things. These supplies came by the water/boat. To this day the Halifax city sends the city of Boston (I think) a large Christmas tree for decorating in gratitude for their help in the disaster. There is a lovely park of many acres made in the area where the survivors were housed (in tents) during the rebuilding. We also went to a fort and saw the cannons shot, and to the harbor area where lovely memorials have been erected for all those who have perished at sea.

An interesting place we visited was Peggy's Cove, a tourist attraction. It truly was a place that rocks were interesting and very, very, very huge. The lighthouse on the point was beautiful (years later Swissair Flight #111 crashed into the sea at this point). When the TV News announced this, it brought the scene into perspective... I'd been there.

The Wambacks were very hospitable people. In the past they had their home as a bed and breakfast. Rollin and I had an upstairs room and private bath, and Barb and Nate were on the ground floor.

The party was held at the Wamback's daughter and son-in-laws home. Their grandson whom I had met in 1993 (in Florida) has of course changed... grown!

I composed a poem, and left in our room before we left. It said in part "The party... we crashed."

Rollin did have a couple of insulin reactions coming home. During one I remember being in the back seat and thinking, "I wonder where the last blue hospital sign was, and how soon before we see another." God was good; he again made all things well!

## ANNIVERSARIES

1976 - 25TH ANNIVERSARY= The children had sent out invitations to all the wedding party, family, and to our close friends. Ours never got to us but was returned to Marti, after the event. Marti and Ron had made place cards. Ron had painted violets and she wrote the names. They added beauty to the tables. The centerpiece was pretty and the room was set up nicely. They had a nice table of memories, also a time for verbal tributes and memories. A bountiful buffet satisfied our appetites. This festivity was held at the Clubhouse of White Creek Estates, on White Creek Avenue, Cedar Springs, Michigan. The VanHorns had a mobile home there.

Connie Poulin, Judy (Dieckman) Waughtal, Nellie Lamphear (Rolin's Mom), myself, and Rollin

Judy Dieckman Waughtal, maid of honor from Idaho; Mary Couturier Colby (Gordy), bridesmaid from Utah; Evelyn Straus Williams (Wayne), bridesmaid from Cedar Springs, Michigan and Connie Wilkinson Poulin (Lee), flower girl from Nunica were there. Bob VanAtta (Avis), groomsman/usher from Kentwood; Donald Tuttle (Sue), ring bearer from Rockford, and Harry and Ellen Dufort, master and mistress of ceremonies from Sparta also attended. Dick Holmes, groomsman/usher from Maryland had had surgery and could not attend; and Ed Mueller, best man from Lowell was not there.

Others there were Mom Lamphear, Dad and Mom Rosell, Aunt Helen and Uncle Scott, Gladys and Carroll, Barb and Nate, Imogene and Maynard, Betty and Brut, Gwen and Bob, Ken and Shirley, and our own kids, Marti, Ron, Bruce, Linda, Maureen (Mark, friend, was signing up for school, made it much later) and Heidi. There was much visiting for an hour or two and it was a lovely party!

40TH ANNIVERSARY= The anniversary open house was held early (July 7, 1991) due to the Baughans being here from Washington. It was held at Bella Vista Church on Belding Road, Rockford.

The kids worked hard to get the area all ready after Sunday church services (as I recall, Loren Marsman helped right along with our kids). It looked so nice. The tables

were decorated with colored table cloths, white streamers and bows, with mirrors and balloons as center pieces.

The lunch was catered by Ginger Manson and gals. Tasty! The cake depicting our forty years was made by Rose Frey; Marti's neighbor across the street.

How things changed in the fifteen years since our twenty-fifth. Evelyn Williams and Mary Colby had both died of cancer, Harry Dufort had died and Ellen due to failing health could not make it; Judy Waughtal had just moved to Washington from Idaho and didn't come, Connie Poulin was on a trip, and again Ed Mueller was not there. Bob Van Atta and Don Tuttle were there, also Dick Holmes from Maryland.

There were two TV's showing our old movies, on video tapes. My wedding dress, wedding album and other wedding memorabilia were set up on a table for all to view. There were writing tablets on the tables so people to jot

Back: Ron VanHorn, Aaron VanHorn, Heidi (Lamphear) Hart, Mike Hart, Bruce Lamphear, Linda (Farell) Lamphear, Mark Baughan, Travis Baughan
Front: Marti (Lamphear) VanHorn, Janelle VanHorn, Christa VanHorn, Rollin, myself, Brenna Lamphear, Corissa Lamphear, Maureen (Lamphear) Baughan, Derick Baughan

down a memory. Memories had been asked for and many came in before the occasion.

A book of remembrances was made up, with pictures copied to compliment some of the experiences. I'm sure the kids were up late finishing it and I can only imagine Marti was up the latest!

The presentation that Marti gave was nice. The statement I liked best was, "I remember when Mom was expecting my youngest sibling. It seemed she was coping just a bit differently than my great excitement expressed. Well, now I'm at the age she was and I must admit I understand." (Up-stretched hands!) "Lord, please, don't send me a precious bundle now!" "Heidi we all love you, it wouldn't be the same without you!"

There were about 130 people who made this day so memorable. Thanks again kids, for your love and the work you put into it.

I've read the memory book over many times. I added some written items to the area of the Fortieth Anniversary Book and also some cards we received. Nice!

The party was over, and the clean up was too. Our family all met at Marti and Ron's. We'd opened up our gifts. The weather changed, dark clouds and winds came and I was told to go to the basement with the grandchildren. Lights went out. It was not a tornado. The winds though, were so strong that many, many trees and lines came down.

Marti and Ron were without electricity for four or five days. They used Mike's and our generator to help keep things somewhat normal.

45TH ANNIVERSARY-1996= The Baughan's came home over spring break and we decided to celebrate our anniversary early. We thought it would be nice to take the immediate families out for dinner. We went to Mountain Jack's in Grand Rapids. The meal was delicious and served well.

Linda had a neat cake decorated, with our wedding picture framed with frosting, for the dessert, quite unique! We were given the largest white flowering azalea plant I've ever seen from the VanHorns'. It adorned our dinette for months. Heidi had received estimates for lawn service (cutting grass) from lawn care businesses. She presented us with a certificate for lawn care from all of them. There was a meaningful poem on it. It referred with humor to my 1995 lawn mower accident. They also felt Rollin should not be mowing due to the dust, etc. with his susceptibility to pneumonia. It truly was a gift appreciated. The business was J & L Lawn Service, and they were great to work with.

## MY PARENTS' WEDDING ANNIVERSARIES
## SEPTEMBER 24, 1919

Their 25$^{th}$ was observed with an open house at 9852 Pine Island Drive. Many relatives, friends and neighbors attended. I was 14 at the time and thought that this was quite a milestone.

Their 50$^{th}$ was celebrated with an open house at Mamrelund Lutheran Church. Their family had grown to encompass all their grandchildren.

For their 55$^{th}$ they took

their family to a dinner at a restaurant on West Leonard Street in Grand Rapids. All children, grandchildren, and their spouses, who could attend enjoyed an evening of celebration.

They did celebrate their 58$^{th}$ Anniversary at the then popular Sveden House Cafeteria on Plainfield Avenue. All close loved ones were there expressing their congratulations of such a milestone. A very special little one was in attendance. Their first great-grandchild had been born just a month before: Aaron James VanHorn.

Barbara, Carrie, Malcolm, Imogene and Irene (The Rosell Family)

## RETIREMENT PARTIES

Rollin retired after 27 years with Kent County Roads and Parks Commission.

He retired December 3l, 1990. In February 1991 a retirement party was held for him. It was at the Cedar Springs VFW Hall. There were about 95-105 there, including our local kids.

There was a buffet dinner with a decorated cake for dessert. The cake was decorated with various tools on it.

The program was humorous and serious. The plaque, picture of Rollin and his county pickup, and a poem read by Paul Rea were very nice tributes.

There was humor with the presentation of the gag stuff. The push broom, complete with the coffee cup, rear view mirror, etc. The apron with all the items to help me about the house was hilarious. As always, Russ Merlington did a great job as Master of Ceremonies.

Other items given to Rollin were a gift certificate to Meijer Thrifty Acres, a 'Retiree' license plate for the car or truck, and the afore mentioned toy green pickup complete with equipment number and county road and park logo on the door; really neat!

Irene: My bus driving terminated, before Christmas vacation, in 1991. A Grand Rapids Press interviewer and photographer (called by some parents of the Kindergarten. run) rode with me on my morning elementary route.

The last day driving, I received various gifts and mementoes from the students.

Ridgeview Elementary and Central Elementary had banners, booklets and cards made by students or classes, to give me. My eyes were *teary!*

The kids at Englishville Alternative High School had a big card signed by all, and gave me an Englishville High School logo T-shirt.

That night was the bus drivers' Christmas party. Upon arriving home from it; I came into the kitchen and there was a computer banner with "CONGRATULATIONS, ON YOUR RETIREMENT" hanging on the bulkhead. Baughans had sent it to Heidi for her and Dad to put up. A nice surprise!

My retirement party was held in February 1992, at Maxwell's Restaurant, north of M-37 and M-46 junction. The buffet dinner was great. They had pickled herring and what was left over the owner gave me to take home!

A neat 'bus' cake was made by Ginger Manson, Carol Lamper and Jan Houghtaling. They gave me a money tree (skillfully leafed by Carol Whipple), the amount really surprised me. I also received some mugs for retirement and friendship.

I had worked several weeks before, to draft a last

will and testament (type of entertainment) bequeathing items to those who would still be driving the buses etc. Rollin handed me the items as I read a verse for each driver, assistant and mechanic. I heard afterward that it was enjoyed!

I received many, many cards and have included them in my scrapbooks which span my twenty-seven and one-half years of driving bus for the Sparta Area Schools, Sparta, Michigan.

## ALGOMA SUNSHINE CIRCLE

This is a group of local ladies that meet once a month. It was organized in 1923 (probably). Ellen Dufort mentioned that when Bob Dufort was born in January 1924, he was the first to receive a gift from the Sunshine Circle. My mom, Carrie Rosell, Ellen Dufort, and Lottie Fonger were some of the charter members. The group made quilts from the time it began to give to families who were the victims of house fires. We received one from them after our house fire in 1977.

I never joined the group until after retiring from bus driving in 1991. The group meets at member's homes for a potluck dinner (lunchtime) once a month. The hostess usually furnishes the main meat dish and the beverages.

They have silent auctions twice a year, a birthday penny box and dues which is used for contributions to charitable groups. I always felt/feel that it is a very friendly local of ladies.

## KENT COUNTY ROADS AND PARKS RETIREES

I think in 1989 the Kent County Roads and Parks organized a Retirees Group. During the first years I could not attend many of their gatherings, I was still driving bus.

In 1992 however, Rollin and I began attending regularly. The meetings have been varied, and interesting. Many of the activities Rollin and I would never had done alone. This group of people is very friendly and caring. In 1994 and 1995 I was an elected trustee, and then in 1996 and 1997 I was elected treasurer. I found the board great to work with. We have become much more acquainted, and consider them all friends.

## ALGOMA TOWNSHIP HISTORICAL SOCIETY

The Historical Society of Algoma Township was organized in (I think) 1988. I was asked to be a part of it; others were Lambert (Carl) Friske, Eloise Covey, Lyle and Doris Squires, Bob and Lela Peck, Bill and Agnes Brown. Many others through the years were/are active in gathering information and artifacts. Eloise and I did a great share of the categorizing of items and making out inventory cards. Linda Friske VanderJagt set up the categories. She did a great job.
 At a later date display cabinets were made for the hallways of Algoma Township Offices (currently located in the old Algoma Central School-Algoma Avenue and 13 Mile Rd.). The items displayed represent logging, farming, homemaking, schools, churches, wars, roads and other aspects of life in my community of yesteryear.

## POSTSCRIPT
## NATURAL GAS LINES

Just as a matter of record, due to not knowing where to insert it... Natural gas lines were extended into our area, and on Pine Island Drive, in late 1993. We had a gas furnace and hot water heater installed in the house at 9400 Pine Island Drive, January 25, 1994.

## THESE ARE MY MEMORIES THROUGH DECEMBER, OF 1996!

Memories, by year, from 1997 – 2010

### 1997

This year surely was varied and held new experiences for myself.

January 27$^{th}$ Rollin and I enjoyed having Betty Mieras and her sister Luella Dean for scalloped oyster casserole. It's a way Rollin can have oysters without using milk (RENAL diet...milk only at breakfast).

March 20-April 7$^{th}$ we were in Washington State. This time we visited the John Day Fossil beds...so interesting. It's one of the largest fossil beds. We also went to Baker City, Oregon to the Oregon Trail Interpretive Center; a great display... what a lot of history, hardship, and determination.

Back: Brenna, Janelle, Aaron, Corissa
Front: Christa, Emily, Bethany

The year in general was enjoyable because of attending some swim meets, (Northview High School) Janelle and Christa were in these. One was against Spring Lake and cousins Annie and Cara Wilkinson were opponents. Recitals, had Corissa and Brenna participating with piano and then to the concerts of choir and chorus at the Grandville High School. Both girls were also in plays that we attended, and Brenna was in track also. Special persons day were always a great way to see the accomplishments of the students in the classes.etc. We attended the Kent County

Road and Parks retires gatherings and I attended local Sunshine Circle ladies whenever I could. Bethany and Emily were beams of sunshine when we'd be with them. I have fond memories of imaginary tea parties with teddy bears and dolls. The neatest memory is an imaginary camping trip. We were in our living room. We packed the truck and trailer (the davenport) then read the map and arrived at the check-in building. The manager (grandpa) was questioned regarding hiking trails, the creek, and the sites for parking. We set up camp. The girls chattered and felt they were doing the "real" thing. About three months after Rollin died the girls and I again went camping at the same camp with the same format...the girls remembered the details well...grandpa was again the camp manager and questions were asked him.

Meijer Gardens had the "Butterflies" display and it is so beautiful, interesting and educational. We took Bethany to view them.

Bethany and Emily at Halloween

The "ZOOMIE" or golf cart, Rollin & I purchase in April of 1997. We used it primarily to go from our house to the Hart's across the field from SW corner of the 40 acres to the NE corner. We passed the pond and sometimes we saw a turtle peek his head above the water, or a couple of ducks taking off as we approached. There was one "patch" of water lilies, which would blossom in the summer. Rollin only had use of it from April through September. He did enjoy having Bethany and Emily ride with him. I must mention that Heidi, Bethany and Emily came to visit us using the "Zoomie"...zooming across the fields! It was refreshing as the wind blew through their hair.

OUR AREA especially experienced a most rare weather storm. October 27, 1997 night dropped 9" of heavy, wet snow. As I heard cracking outside during the night, I looked out and flakes were coming down. These flakes were not flakes but "GLOBS." I must say it was definitely a sight to behold!

The trees had not dropped their leaves and the branches hung down to the ground. These were all the various trees...oaks, maples, locust, evergreens etc. It was quite the news and topic of conversations throughout our area. The branches bent way down with the leaves touching the ground; this reminded me of HULA SKIRTS. We had no electricity for 69 ½ hours. Mike kept the generators going for the freezer and refrigerator (theirs, mine and his parents).

In October, we had the sad news that Charlene Mieras Taylor has breast Cancer. Her $1^{st}$ chemo treatment was Nov. $10^{th}$ I'm so sorry. Later I heard Debbie Benson Dines' hubby Ray has pancreatic cancer. He had surgery the $26^{th}$; not all the tumors could be removed, chemo/radiation is next.

Barb and Nate went to Florida; Imo and Maynard were on vacation to Hawaii, at the time of Rollin's birthday. Aunt Helen asked me to Freedom Village for evening dinner. It was especially nice to be with family on the date of 12/12 and even more so because Dick and Mary came from Washington D.C. area for the week-end. It was so nice to see them.

Christmas Eve was at my house. It was heartwarming. The Christmas gift to our kids from Rollin and I was given, along with a poem I'd written to explain it.

Rollin would have been so happy. Christmas Day I was with Heidi, Mike and the girls. In the afternoon we went to the Van Andel Museum in Grand Rapids.

We spent a couple of fun/work days up at 'the lot' with Bob and Gwen. We tried to clean up the lot so (hoping to put it up for sale. We took hamburg and fixings with us for lunch and had an open fire burning all the day.

Every Wednesday evening Barb, Nate, and we alternated going to each other's home. We had our pot-luck meal and then usually played cards. When Imogene and Maynard could they joined us too. Others we were with quite often were Bob and Gwen Dufort and Betty Mieras.

We've really appreciated the black top drive way and had it re-sealed. It's so black!

Rollin fell in a rut of the front yard on May $19^{th}$ he broke his leg. We went to ER at 4:00 P.M. had it set and back home. I didn't make it to my $50^{th}$ high school reunion on May $30^{th}$ due to this.

Grandson Travis traveled to Europe with International Track and Field group and participated in track (hurdles and relays) events others. The highlight was eating with, (sat next to) the Olympic Hurdler. The visit was so great, Travis said.

The Retirees, in June went to Ludington's Lands Inn Motel, and traveled on to Manitowac, Wisconsin on the boat Badger. We entered into some of the activities of the ferry and also went out on the deck to enjoy the water and weather…a fun time.

The highlight of our year I think was Aunt Helen and Uncle Scott (Holmes) $65^{th}$ Wedding Anniversary. It was August $23^{rd}$, 1997 and was held at a Holland Motel. They looked SOO young for observing this anniversary. There were "old friends" from the Muskegon area, and "new" friends from Freedom Village, relatives as Karen & Bill Fisher, we "Rosell" girls and our spouses and then their immediate families. It was so festive! There were

Maynard Klein, Rollin, myself, Imogene Klein, and Helen Holmes

eight to ten seated at each round table. One of the grandchildren hosted each table..........Shawn and Reed with Lacy and Murphy were ours.

Uncle Scott's tribute to Aunt Helen was very endearing. He told of their simple wedding with only the best man and maid of honor and of the trip back to Ann Arbor with a wedding present tied to the back fender of the car (a pause, followed by) a bushel of potatoes. We three sisters looked at each other and grinned...they were from our parents, Malcolm & Carrie. Their children and grandchildren's presentations varied; but each told of a loving bond and of close family ties and remembrances...

The dinner was delicious and the evening a delight (it was Rollin's last extended family party).

My second hip was ready to be replaced, so on July first it was done. Dr. Thomas Malvitz was the surgeon. Oh, how great to have no pain in the groin; it had been excruciating! I had asked in Rollin could stay in my room during my hospital stay. They'd had a cot put in the room for him. He did have a couple LOW sugars in the early A.M. Juice to the rescue! I stayed an extra day (until the $5^{th}$) due to no natural B/Ms before. Bruce stayed with us the

5th and 6th---babied us....made the meals and served us, just like D-O-W-N-T-O-W-N. The 7th and 8th day some of the VanHorns did the same. From the 9th day we had a lady from Kelly Home Services stay with us from 10:00 p.m.to 7:00a.m. She was a black lady and a real jewel! We decided "this route" because if Rollin needed to go to ER I was not mobile enough to handle the calls etc. There was a documentary made at Bronson Hospital some years ago about KNEE and HIP surgeries. I viewed it on August 18 and it was very informative, and most interesting.

Dates to remember in 1997: Sept. 1st, went to a Tractor Pull with Bruce and Linda and family (Linda's dad, Pat) was one in the PULLS. Sept: 6th, Anita Lovell's wedding—very pretty and a nice reception. Sept. 7th Kaleigh Dufort's 3rd birthday party. These were dates of "lasts" before Rollin passed away.

Rollin's health throughout 1997 required many, many doctors' appointments and lab tests. One of the expensive medications was PROCRIT, taken by injection; the amount determined by the lab tests. I was happy he could administer it so well. He surely was great for obeying both the diabetic diet and the taking of the insulin shots for 34 ½ years, and the RENAL diet for 20 months. I took Rollin to ER 13 times from January 1, 1997 to the last time September 10, 1997.

September 10th was a Wed. night and we'd been to Barb/Nate's for our weekly meal and card games and came home. Phone rang it was Gwen regarding our lot sale. We went over to chat about it. I did mention to Gwen that Rollin had a cough. We left for ER at 1:30 a.m. --- diagnosed as pneumonia with the comment he'd be on intravenous, antibiotics and would be home in a couple of days.

He had a bad day Thursday; had a heart attack, and then Friday was quite good. He told me Friday night "as much as I hate to leave you and the family, I just can't battle the four things (diabetes, heart, pneumonia, and kidney failure." Then he also said, "I want you to call Maureen and see if she can come. I don't want to wait until the doctors ask that the family be called in and then have her over 'the Dakotas' when I pass." The next statement he made was: "I don't want to leave my family, but GOD KNOWS BEST!" "I do hope I'll live long enough to talk to Dr. Oren Mason." Dr. Mason was not on call that weekend. Rollin did have an "in room" dialysis for 3 hours on Friday, it released most or the TOXINS they hoped it would; thus hoping to insure his life until Maureen got there.

Heidi called Maureen and she called to say the best she could do was fly into Grand Rapids at about 10:00 Saturday night. Bruce picked her up at the airport and brought her to the hospital.

All the kids were there all or most of the time. On Sunday the 14th, I kidded Rollin that he wasn't taking me out for our 46th wedding anniversary...adding, "I guess you are though 'cuz' I'm eating your supper."

On Sunday P.M., after the family met with the medical personnel, we decided to stop all medications and no life support ...except for Rollin's comfort. I was so happy that just before our meeting; both of Rollin's sisters (Gladys & Avis) came to visit him and I asked them to join us at the meeting. Monday was a beautiful day. All visitors were given a KISS as Rollin lifted the OXYGEN mask to do so. Visiting were: our kids were so caring and loving during Rollin's hospital stay and all times thereafter, his sisters and mine, Deb Benson Dines, Betty Mieras and Gwen Dufort. Tuesday was quiet with more pain relievers given---at 5:50 pm Dr. Oren Mason said his goodbye to Rollin; then he told me he'd not see him in the morning. Rollin passed away peacefully at 6:14 PM. Many prayers were answered and we had our 46th wedding anniversary on Sunday, September 14th 1997.

Family, friends and neighbors were all SO supportive and loving. The day of the funeral was very threatening. Tornado alerts were sounded, rain, thunder etc. In spite of it many were to the service—some did write and say they'd not come at the last minute due to the weather. The service was comforting. Marti gave a beautiful—"5 senses" tribute to her daddy, the other children's input was included in it too (Christa wrote a beautiful tribute, see below). The ladies of Bella Vista Church served a nice "finger-food" type luncheon. Many dishes of food were brought to the house for the family. Memorial contributions were heartwarming; the amount of monies sent to American Diabetes Assoc. in Rollin's memory totaled over $1300.00, the church received $400.00 and there were many lovely floral tributes. I must mention here that several weeks later, Maureen and her Washington friends were talking and the subject of paying an amount for flowers came up. Maureen asked what she owed and they said it was for her father. She called me and asked if I remembered getting an arrangement…I said "no." The florist in Goldendale called Ostmans in Sparta to check into it….it was discovered the order had been stapled to the back of a filled order. Ostmans called me and apologized to me. They would be sending me an arrangement in the future. It coincidentally was a Christmas centerpiece and it arrived on Rollin's birthday December $12^{th}$. I have enjoyed it and still have it (2010).

## A TRIBUTE TO FROM GRANDDAUGHTER TO ROLLIN AFTER HIS DEATH

"Grandma- this poem is just some good and bad memories I hope that it will bring joy and not pain."

### REMEMBERING HIM

Remember his smile
And his glasses all bright and shiny
Remember the way his hair was combed
And the smell that filled the air after he shaved
Remember his prickly kisses from when he didn't shave
The hats he always wore
Remember the major farmers' tan that he always had
The games he played to make any child happy
Remember the finger "wiggle" that always meant "Hello"
And the weeds we picked that we used to tickle his nose
Remember the way he shuffled his cards.
The ring he always wore
Remember the insulin bottle clicking on his rings rolling in his hands
The way he felt proud around all of his loved ones
Remember him teaching me how to drive his tractor
The ache that I got in my stomach whenever he got sick
Remember him for the things he did for me
The ache that was all in me when he got really sick
Remember walking in to the hospital
The room and all the machines beeping and buzzing
Remember the last prickly kiss
He was here just 5 months ago

This poem is dedicated to my grandpa; the best there ever was in the world!

With all my love, grandpa- Christanna B. Van Horn

The KCR&P Retirees group had a trip to Branson, Mo. planned for Sept. 29-Oct $2^{nd}$. Rollin and I had cancelled our reservations due to his health. Now, after his passing they called me to see if I'd enjoy going with them. Dar and Lorraine Nellist were unable to go due to illness. I called my family to ask them what they thought, and they said I should go. Then I called various friends and it was Eloise Covey who could go with me. The trip was nice. The Veterans Tours surely had reservation for great shows, and eating places. The KCR&P group is always loving, caring, and compassionate. I'm happy Eloise could go; she is a lovely person.

I had a family work crew working on October $3^{rd}$ and $4^{th}$. The boys and granddaughters shingled the roof. It was a long, busy day for all of them. THANKS to all.

1998

The family took me out for my birthday the evening of January 2. Most of the VanHorns were skiing but Marti was there, as were all the others (not Mike as he was working). The $3^{rd}$ I helped Northview swim team gather Christmas trees for recycling.

A season of my life continues. The truck that Rollin ordered and then we enjoyed so much was the vehicle I'd keep. I had sold the car a few months before. Then maybe I should sell it and buy a MINI VAN. I did enjoy the height of the truck and the way it drove. I did put it out by the road to sell...many lookers, no takers!!!

It was kind of funny, a call came to me asking if the $5^{th}$ wheel was for sale; yes, but I had not advertised it yet. The caller was George Layman who had bought the Ford truck a few years ago, who stated he thought if the truck was for sale maybe the $5^{th}$ wheel was too. He bought it, as well as some other accessory items.

The truck didn't sell. Winnie Knight, Betty Mieras and I took a ride up to Bert and Henry Sprik's at Barryton, Michigan. We jabbered about how we did enjoy the truck, why, we could even take a trip with it! Oddly and for no particular reason, the next morning I went to the Chrysler dealers in Grand Rapids and I traded it in for a Plymouth Voyager Van. The van gave me about 11 1/2 years of use, 120,000 miles.

As in the months past the church areas of people, friends, family, retirees, etc. were there and enjoyed various activities. Bethany and Emily (with their mom) always were there for me; living so close they did many things for me as well as gave conversations and PRETENDS.

During the early months of the year I bought a gas range & a microwave oven. The boys installed. I also replace the kitchen window—an OMNI.

Dear friend Gwen had been ill at various times; she went to ER with diarrhea and cramps. Bob too, was under the weather. Pneumonia and after that his physical disclosed colon cancer. I was glad they had the syrup season behind them. There wasn't much I could help them with so I tried to keep the cookie jar supplied and visit them often, though sometimes only a few minutes.

Emily Hart had tonsil/adenoids out on May 22; Bethany and I played at my house.

In late May, I went to Mark and Maureen's. Very soon we went to Travis' State Track and Field Meet. He took 1$^{st}$ in the hurdles so is WASHINGTON STATE HURDLE CHAMPION. It was so great to attend that event! June 5$^{th}$ Travis graduated from High School. There was an open house and I met a couple of new neighbors of theirs. Roy and Jo Baughan, Steve, Loretta and children and Judy and John Waughtal all were there too. It was nice.

June 19$^{th}$ Mark, Maureen and I left with their 5$^{th}$ wheel to meet Bruce, Linda and family, they also brought Janelle and Christa VanHorn at Estes Park, Colorado.

Mike, Heidi and girls flew in and rented a car and motel there. We had a most enjoyable time. Upon arrival Mark asked Bruce how far he'd driven; Bruce said 1100 miles, Mark chuckled and said we drove 1110 miles. We celebrated birthdays (even Bethany's); went to peak of a mountain on Trail Ridge Drive and went out looking for wild life. Mark's brother Steve and family were at the same camp ground so they ate a couple of times with us. I rode home from Rocky Mountain Park with the Lamphears in their motor home. A memory for all of us was made! I was home on June 26$^{th}$.

I was of course in Washington when, on May 31$^{st}$ thunder storms, accompanied with 130 MPH straight line winds razed havoc in the Sparta area about 5:00 a.m. (this encompassed a large area both in length and breadth). In areas, many to most of the trees were felled and yet less than ½ mile there may be none down. These were oaks, maples, evergreens and locust; it was reported that a 100 year old tree was broken in Rockford; about 11 old barns were destroyed in the area. Electric was off 6 ½ days; total of 10 days to restore it to the total area. Again the sounds of generators and chain saws were heard everywhere. Mike kept my freezer and refrigerator going.

My 1$^{st}$ year exam on the left hip was very satisfactory. Praise God.

During July the Grand Rapids Symphony had their concerts on Friday nights at Cannonsburg Ski Area. The first time Betty Mieras got information but she couldn't go so Winnie Knight and I went. The next time Betty, Heidi, the girls and I went Char and John Taylor joined us. It was fun to watch Bethany and Emily dance and keep time with the marvelous music. The evening was GREAT the climax was fireworks right at dusk. The crowds there were enormous. People sat on the slopes, on the level ground or in lawn chairs. There was food available to buy or one could bring their own. It's like "grand central station;" it was amusing to see all the various foods people brought for their party as well as all the differences in the people themselves. We'd get there early; the groups kept coming and the total at some of these concerts top 4,000 in to the 5,000. The third concert attendees included Betty, her sister Luella Dean, Dorothy Ringelberg, Winnie and I. Each concert has a special artist or group. One concert evening it was a BANJO player...I thought of Uncle Bob VanAtta all evening.

I attended the 50$^{th}$ wedding anniversaries of Ken and Shirley Anderson; Betty and Art Teesdale in August the wedding of Wendy Bascom and Chad Kik. Mike's Grandma Edna Durham died August 10$^{th}$ and Luella Dean on August 31$^{st}$. At church we served 3 funeral luncheons in two weeks: Amy Wiggins in October and Bill Teesdale in November.

I busied myself with some freezing and canning. I picked some nice raspberries at Joel Lunger's. It was a hot summer. Other activities: Avis and I spent a couple of days with Gladys and Carroll in Traverse City. We visited, ate and played Hand and Foot (cards); I gathered leaves with Corissa and identified them; went to a couple of swim meets at Northview High; attended a Civil War reenactment program at the Kent City Historical meeting; also an Alpine Twp. Historical programs on OLD BARNS; a visited a 100 year old rake factory in Freeport with the retirees; I helped a day at Pine Ridge Camp baking, another day fall clean-up, while there I noted many black Walnuts under several trees, so I picked up 3 grocery bags of them, I drove over them with the tractor tires to get shucks off, then cracked them when ready and they were filled with great meats! I'll go there any year to get more; Sept. 28$^{th}$ -Oct. 3$^{rd}$ with retirees went to Branson, Betty was my roommate; the organ concert at Meijer theater of VanAndel Museum was beautiful, Gwen Dufort, Kay Meek, Gert Beckett and I went. We also attended an Andy Williams show at

VanAndel Arena; 3 bus drivers retired and I attended their party; they were: Ginger Manson, Joyce Winkler, and Maxine Reister (I gave them a goodie bag); The Wallinettes, Gladys and Carroll's church group went to the Festival of Lights in Battle Creek, a very festive ride and viewing of Christmas!

Ron and Marti's 25$^{th}$ Anniversary we had at my home with the immediate family dinner. I made custard for homemade ice cream. Bruce and others churned it to a YUMMY treat.

Heidi had some of the Holmes cousins on Friday after Thanksgiving for lunch. It was such a fun time. Becky was there, as was Beth and Carlos, also their parents Randy and Kay and Dick and Mary. What an afternoon of visiting and reminiscing. Bethany and Emily were such nice little hostesses. Imogene came to visit too, that made it even nicer.

Myself seated behind Scott Holmes, Bethany Hart, Helen Holmes, and Emily Hart

Christmas Eve at my home had the kids gathered. Kids did the work. I was fighting a bad cold/cough/sinus since November 19$^{th}$. Horrid! Each family asked/told me to be with them on Christmas day but I just wanted to cough, blow and sleep in my own home!

## 1999

January came in with a "WHIRL," blizzard on the 2$^{nd}$ and 3$^{rd}$; there were no churches that held services on the

3rd and on the 4th most schools and some businesses closed. I did leave Wednesday the 6th for Washington. Snow was coming down, the very damp kind, as Betty Mieras took me to the airport. It was very slow traveling on the on the East Beltline, (45 minutes to go 4 miles. Upon entering the terminal ,the "loud speaker" said "anyone going on N.W Airlines to Minn./St. Paul come immediately to the front of the line"—I was one—I made it!! Then in Minneapolis the departure gate radioed that I was on my way—being driven in an electric cart. Travis was still home on Christmas break and it was nice to see him and the rest. Derick and I played some games and he was a GREAT help as Maureen, he and myself made 70 dozen cream wafer cookies. I took many dozen cookies home packed with care (in boxes) in my one suitcase.

As last year, I was busy every other Tuesday caring for children at MOPS (Mothers of Pre-Schoolers), at church I worked in Nursery like I have for years! The kids are so cute and different. Also, of course, there were monthly meetings of Algoma Twp. Historical Society and the inventory to record. KCRP retirees birthday, get well and anniversary cards I send out at proper times. Retirees went to a play at Turkeyville, had a Valentine lunch/ party, & potlucks also went to a White Caps base ball game; I still take many (more elderly) neighbors and church people to Drs., Labs ,etc.; I never tire of being to the grandchildren's sports, concerts and plays.

There were showers, weddings, anniversaries and graduations, and of course funerals. Charles Courtade died Feb. 23rd Jack London died April 1st, Mike Farrell passed April 16th in a motorcycle accident, Frances Vanderhyde, Shirley Anderson, our dear Charlene Mieras Taylor, and Ray Dines.

March 2nd I flew into Sarasota, Florida, I stayed with Barb and Nate and helped them drive home. While there I enjoyed being with friends of theirs who I'd met in 1993.

The Baughans came in on Saturday April 3rd. Maureen went with me (and surprised the extended family) to Gladys and Carroll Tuttle's 60th wedding anniversary on April 8th. It was prime rib sit down dinner at Wallin Congregational Church in Grand Rapid. It was nice.

Janelle VanHorn graduated from high school May 27th. Those years F-L-Y by! Aaron graduated from Davenport University on June 8th. It was so impressive to have his mom present him with his diploma.

In June we rented a motor home and Mike, Heidi, Bethany, Janelle, Christa and I set out to meet the clan at West Yellowstone. For one meal we had Hobo pizza and s'mores over a fire pit on the way out. Thirteen of the family were together and camped in Bozeman, MT., West Yellowstone, and Jackson Hole, WY. We visited Rocky Mountain Museum and toured the campus of Montana State University (Travis is a student here, but he was in Alaska working a summer job, in the fisheries I think). Camping, playing and visiting were highlights of our time together. YELLOWSTONE NATIONAL PARK: God's created beauty (contained in one large area), can one describe it…I truly do not think so! This natural beauty was being enjoyed day after day, and it was fun to see wildlife roaming in their natural habitat. THE GRAND TETONS: Glorious, snowy, jagged peaks, the youngest mountain range in the United States. JACKSON HOLE: A beautiful village nestled in the mountains, where one can "Shop 'til One Drops." Emily celebrated her 4th birthday 6/18. I went back to the R.V. before the others. The seven grandchildren played games or rode hot-wheels and had volleyball games versus their parents. Nine days together---memories!

I went with Gwen and Marlana to Milwaukee, Wisconsin to the "restored" Circus Wagon Parade. The horses that pulled these beautiful wagons of a former era were something to see in and of themselves. Many hours were spent restoring these wagons, and it was interesting to hear where some of them had been found and the condition they were in!!! Jeff and Robin Dufort's horse club sponsored it.

November $16^{th}$ I was off to Hawaii, to Rich and Dena Ingersol Clements with Betty Mieras. The flight across the water from Los Angeles to Honolulu was a gorgeous picture all the way. They met us and we stayed in a hotel the first night. We stayed in the Clements home the rest of the time (though they were getting ready to move so we did stay a night or two at friend's home. What can I say but BEAUTY, BEAUTY, BEAUTY: THE WATERFALLS, THE MOUNTAINS, THE RIVERS, THE SPECTACULAR FLOWERS, THE GREENRY, PLUS THE WEATHER, made these two weeks a great experience. Dena and Rich showed me every beauty spot on their island of Kauai and also the historical areas Honolulu.

I was in Hawaii when Imogene and Maynard had their $50^{th}$ Anniversary celebration. Our Lamphear family gave them "A Bulb Garden" each month, Heidi wrote, designed a cute card to be enclosed with their card.

## 2000

The usual –over all-: concerts, sports, birthdays, MOPS, meals for church shut-ins, open houses, wedding, showers, visiting sick and shut-ins, Retirees (parties and regular monthly meetings . Jean Soderstrom and I went out to lunch, as did Betty Mieras and I; I enjoyed the Barber Shop Quartet Concert…what harmony! I enjoyed when I could care for Emily; off the bus or whatever. The family had the Annual clean up day at my home on Mother's Day, I also joined Linda Traxler and Carole Whipple (after their bus runs) for breakfast, oh, yes, then the Historical meetings and programs.

Trips for this year follow: Betty and I went on a Mississippi River Cruise. We toured Dubuque, Iowa, stayed the night in a hotel and the following morning boarded the paddlewheel boat for a day long cruise, back on land we visited the Amana Colonies in eastern Iowa (Nat'l Historic Landmark of German settlers, seeking religious freedom in America). The food and area are similar to many of the Amish areas. I really enjoyed JOHN DEERE Pavilion Museum and the talk on its history as farm machinery leaders.

FRANKENMUTH day with Gladys's church group, fun!!!

Mark and Maureen were here about a week in July; all the family was together at my home on July $30^{th}$.

In July, at my home, we had a Camp Fire Girls reunion. Carl Jean VandenBrock Hattan was here from Louisiana. Others attending were Carol Bristol King, June Bristol Cole, Arlene Tewsley McIntyre, Sue Ringelberg Schmidt, Evelyn Darling Ring, Bonnie Dayton Simmons and regrets sent by Mary Babylon. Also joining us was Dorothy Ringelberg. I served a tasty lunch and we had a fun afternoon "gabbing."

SEPTEMBER Betty and I flew to Portland, Oregon. We rented a car. We went to Eleanor's (Dena Ingersol Clement's) friend. We stayed in her home at night. The following day we all spent the day touring the country side. I was amazed when I saw a row (about 15- 18) of combines ready for the harvest! Next we went down the coast to Gordon and Avis Colby's. They told us we may enjoy visiting the newly opened OREGON's aquarium and sea life' so we went and truly enjoyed it. We'd rented a motel and then went to Colby's to visit. Gordie came out to the car and asked for our luggage to carry into the house. We said it was at the motel; he then stated we should go back, cancel our stay there, as we were staying at their home; this we immediately did. The view from their home was of the Pacific Ocean. Conversation flowed for several hours, rest was refreshing, breakfast tasty and then we were on our way to my cousin Judy's for the night and then view Mt. Saint Helens (the volcano). The view down the mountain side was too much for Betty so we turned around and went through Steven's pass, then to Leavenworth. We shopped the shops and travelled on to Cashmere where they make APLETS AND CAPLETS, we purchased some, yummy! We did then, tour Mt. Hood and went down the Klickitat Grade, Trout Lake, Glenwood etc. as we stayed at Mark and Maureen's.

## 2001

In general, 2001 and 2000 were very similar.

Trips were Fort Atkinson, Wisconsin to a play, but I can't remember the name of it!

In September, Retirees again went to Branson, Missouri. Bob and Pat Anderson of VETERANS tours make every moment pleasant. An unexpected surprise, at our first rest area break was Bob tipping his coffee cup and down the full length of his pant leg it d-r-i-b-b-l-e-d. He received much good natured teasing about this and drew much attention.

Games played are fun. The horse race meets with noise and cheers as "their" horse moves on. Norm Ostrom was on the "winning horse" team both going and coming home! When bingo is being played all anticipate the calling of their third card. Bob and Pat "go all out" to have us enjoy the trip; and they do no less with the gifts they give as prizes.

We had a "sing-a-long" using the KCR&Ps song books (which Heidi helped me put together). Here too one could feel the "one-ness" of all aboard, especially when all the patriotic songs were chosen rapidly, to be the next request. Those songs rung out with the spirit of sympathy, praise and thankfulness as U.S.A. continues to REMEMBER SEPTEMBER 11$^{TH}$, 2001 (This was the date of the terrorist attack in New York City, and The Pentagon building, Washington, D.C. In the future it is referred to 9-11-01).

A standing statement (or joke) is: "What? Is it time to eat again?" One can't imagine the food that is put before us...unless you've been on a VETERANs TOUR. What is also amazing is that all; yes, ALL the meals are included in the tour's price. Bob suggests to us to leave a voluntary tip at a few of the places, otherwise even that is included!

The SHOWS, (as Bob conveys before arriving at Branson) are all good, it's just that some are better than others." All the main shows were great! Then there were breakfast or dinner shows that were great too. One show was a dance troupe from Ireland (an added surprise). They made us sit in awe with their fast, faster, and fastest movements and precision. What dedication, what talent!!!After this beautiful, awesome, fast moving show; comments were heard such as, "Wow, I'm almost weary from just watching them!" Could it be we are all SENIOR CITIZENS? The shows that had banjos and fiddles were, OHHHHHH what talent... "Orange Blossom Express" was played to the fullest two, three or four times. Enjoyed? Ahhhh huh! The Presley family with their own Cecil and Herkimer (comedians) had tears of laughter flowing down our checks or our sides were hurting. Then in the grand finale, to see them as their true person...what a switch!

I must not forget our YOUNG bus driver, Steve. He had a most beautiful voice and at the end of the first sing-a-long we asked him to sing a solo. He sang "America" and "America the Beautiful." At that time, there were requests for the next time ...one being "Amazing Grace."

At the Edward Allen dinner show, Edward was on stage near the table that our bus driver was seated. Edwards hear him singing and motioned him to come up and join him on stage. They then led all in the restaurant in singing "Amazing Grace." Needless to mention, it excited us.

<u>JUST FOR REPETITION NOT TO BECOME TOO BORING I STATE THIS: FROM YEAR 2002-2009</u>

These years (as even some previously) have so much repetition that I'm using these GENERAL PARAGRAPHS for the following: I drove many people to doctor appointments, lab tests, nursing homes to visit friends, picked up some to attend their church services etc. Many of those that I transported had passed away by 2009.

Areas of church: nursery on Sundays ($2^{nd}$ service), MOPS care of children every other Tuesday, funeral luncheons and meals to sick or shut-ins.

People I've tried to visit regularly: Marian Schuur, Gert Sprik, Sven & Dorothy Nelson, Winnie Knight, Dorothy Ringelberg, Reva Huey, Donna from BVC and now and then a few others.

I enjoyed many various musical and instrumental concerts at Bethany & Emily's schools as well as some others: the organ concerts in Grand Rapids and the Nazarene Church's Christmas and Easter dramas and music concert. Track meets at Grandville High and plays at Sparta.

Most years in August I've picked blueberries at "Marvin's" on Stebbins Street north of Sparta.

I have been very happy to be available to put Bethany or Emily on or get from the bus during Elementary and Jr. High years.

In the years 1999 to 2003 I went to several activities with Ginger Manson and the group from Fulton Manor

Home. Ginger drove the bus for them and also worked in activities area some.

Many of these years in June I picked strawberries at Dan & Patti Wilkinson's…free for the picking. I also picked "fall raspberries" at Joel Lunger's on 13 Mile Rd. I called them "Golden Nuggets": sooooo yummy in frozen jam and just to eat after defrosting them.

## 2002

The year off to a great start; Betty Mieras treated me to the wonderful talented show of "Champions on Ice." It was her gift to me for my birthday. I've always marveled and been intrigued with ice skating. The costuming of the performers is so beautiful, and flow with the movements of their acts.

During the first months of the year, Jean Hansen Seelman worked with me on arranging the 55$^{th}$ class reunion. It was held at the Swan Inn on Alpine Ave. A nice dinner was served and the group of classmates and the spouses enjoyed it. They also spent hours after visiting and catching up.

In the month of May, Marti had Aunt Helen and Uncle Scott to a presentation at Davenport University. It went well and I'm sure the Holmes enjoyed it. We then had lunch at the cafeteria.

Again to Alaska, this time a cruise with Evelyn Ring as my roommate - August 1$^{st}$-14$^{th}$.

I was home in time to help celebrate Barb and Nathan Wilkinson's 60$^{th}$ wedding anniversary at Dan and Patti's. Very nice! Guests always enjoy seeing one another. Time passes quickly, since in our busy world of today we do not visit in one another's homes.

The retirees went to Fort Atkinson, Wisconsin in October to the dinner theatre. We viewed on stage "A

Fireside Christmas" and "The All Night Strut." As always, it was a pleasant trip with great people.

2003

January 9, 2003 my dear sister Barbara passed away at Hackley Hospital in Muskegon. Imogene, Maynard and I had visited her on the 7$^{th}$. Her memorial was 1-13-03 at Spring Lake Presbyterian Church. I truly miss her. We couples did a lot of things together including many trips. I went to visit Nathan frequently, every week or two. Our conversations many times were about our trips and other times together. MEMORIES, MEMORIES!

## MY TRIBUTE TO MY SISTER BARBARA AT THE TIME OF HER MEMORIAL

Barbara Wilkinson, (a person of Swedish and German decent), but she was known by other names. She was known as wife for over 60 years, daughter for 70 years (until her mom died in 1990's sister for 78 years and grandma for 24 years, and also as neighbor and friend.

She was born October 8, 1920 in Algoma Township, Kent County, Michigan, in the house her parents, (Malcolm and Caroline Rosell) bought in 1919. She was a World War II war bride, marrying Nathan Arlo Wilkinson on August 21, 1942. (She herself hand wrote the invitations).

She and Nathan lived in Fresno, California while Nate was stationed there. She worked for Civil Service detailing U.S. troops' transfers and deployments. When Nathan served his country in India (Ledo Road area) she returned to Michigan. After viewing home with her parents and upon the advice of Nathan's parent (Nervi and Dell), she exercised her power of attorney and purchased a house (much smaller than now) at 14901 Boom Road. She and

Nathan moved into this home when he returned to the states (as of 2010 this house had be demolished by new owners).

Into this home came cries of babies, of laughter, and of activities of one son and three daughters growing up. Home it was; with baked goods every week, garden produce and lovely flowers. In 2001-2002, others picked the flowers and brought them in.

With the children in school she became a secretary at Jeffers School (a rural 2 room school where her children attended at the time), and later at Holmes School in Spring Lake, Michigan.

Most of you knew her as:
- An optimistic, upbeat person
- A member of the church choir for years
- A Michigan Extension Service member
- A lover of her flower gardens
- A harvester/freezer and canner of their own garden bounty
- A canner/freezer of other fruit and produce not raised by them on Boom Road
- A gracious hostess and entertainer of family and friends
- A traveler who enjoyed the beauty of God's creation
- A friend who'd bring or send baked goods or a casserole to others at times of sickness of death
- A Great-Auntie who sent cards weekly to a great niece recovering from surgery
- A person who loved life

With Barb, you, as a relative or friend, have worked, traveled, visited, rejoiced and celebrated various occasions, their $60^{th}$ Wedding Anniversary possibly being one of the most recent. You have loved her, appreciated her, cared for her, gone the second mile with and for her---you have been a dear loved one.

One can envision Barb, at this time, in the house of many mansions-greeting family and loved ones who have gone before.

May we all feel the sweetness of memories of Barb and may they soothe the emptiness we may feel from her passing. Let us remember the testimony of her faith and peace with God as her powerful, enduring witness to us of our certain home, which she is now experiencing.

I pray God's blessing upon all of you. I thank you for visiting the family today. Thank you for when/where you touched Barb's life or she touched yours.

A tribute to my beloved sister, with love, Irene

In May, I went to Washington. Maureen had a PASTA EAT for the Sr. High Track Team. There were 16-18 kids there. It is always nice to put faces to names one's heard. I had fun just listening to them, also watching them. I went to both District and State Track meets. Travis and a friend attended the State meet and left from Cheney to be at the University of Missouri by or before June $6^{th}$, 2003

Mark has really been enjoying teaching $7^{th}$ grade history.

Aaron has bought a house and is settled into it. Janelle is in college at Grand Valley and is working too. Christanna graduated in June from Northview High School and is working for Spectrum Health. Corissa is in her $2^{nd}$ year at Hope College; Brenna is a Jr. in high school at Grandville. Bethany is in $5^{th}$ grade at Sparta Middle School and Emily is in $3^{rd}$ at Sparta Elementary. Bethany is doing minutes to hours of her physical therapy daily at home.

Derick graduated from High School, he was valedictorian and his speech was great and of course Grandma was proud and happy. My only first cousin on my mom's side, Judy Dieckmann Waughtal who lives on Long Beach Peninsula in Washington State, (sees the Pacific from her home) was to his graduation. It was at the time the recessional began that I was going to stand up and I had excruciating pain go down my leg. I was fearful that it could have been my left hip (replaced 10 years ago) "giving out." After several weeks at home I finally had an appointment with the hip surgeon and learned that it wasn't my hip. Then in August I went to a pain/spinal doctor. It was a herniated disc causing a sciatic nerve problem. This Doctor Randal Palmitier gave me one shot of cortisone in the spine and it was at least 90% better. It was uncomfortable yet some days/months later for 5 to 15 minutes a day; this continued even into December. This sciatic nerve pain slowed my summer down a lot. A half hour was enough outdoor work and I'd need to come in and rest (SLEPT!)

On November 15th, an extended cousin from Wisconsin and I met in Lansing. Elaine Berner Springer Baumann and I had a great visit. I'm thrilled she thought of meeting there. She was there for two of her grandson's wrestling competition.

## 2004

Scott Holmes playing his violin

Sadness covered our extended family in the first third of the year. Our Aunt Helen (Rosell) Holmes passed away on March 25, 2004. Her families from various states were to the funeral. Uncle Scott did well and I understand he gave a violin concert for HIS family that evening.

Then it seems his health faltered and went

downhill. I did go visit him each of his last five days. He passed away April 5, 2004 just 10 days after Aunt Helen.

The morning of the $5^{th}$, Mary Holmes called and said Clark would be flying into Grand Rapids and renting a car to drive to Holland (Freedom Village) to be with his Grandpa, so I didn't need to if there were other things for me to do. I was on my way out the door when she called, so I did go.

Upon my arrival at the nurses' station I asked how Uncle Scott was; I was asked my relationship…then the Hospice Nurse told me, "It will not be long." I went into his room and asked him a few questions. He did answer a couple with a squeeze of my hand---then passed.

A gentleman friend of Uncle Scott came by and I told him…It was about lunch time and he suggested we go have lunch and visit. I'd told him Clark would be there in early afternoon. Clark arrived and we visited a little. We then removed Uncle Scott's belongings that were in the nursing unit back to their apartment.

Both Aunt Helen and Uncle Scott's Memorial services were at Freedom Village's Chapel. I remember Douglas and Pat Klein gave them a lovely tribute. Bethany Hart also gave one (I think at Uncle Scott's). One thing she mentioned was that when she and Emily visited them with her mom or grandma; we always had lunch at the small cafeteria. Uncle Scott would joke with us and ask, "Is it going to be a grilled cheese sandwich and a shake?" The answer was YES please! I also gave a tribute at one or the other service.

In July and August I had cataracts removed by Dr. Scott Weber at Grand Rapids Ophthalmology, East Beltline, Grand Rapids. What a great improvement in sight!!

On July $30^{th}$ 2004, a beloved and respected doctor of our area passed away, Dr. Thomas Fochtman. Dr. Fochtman was very well respected by Grand Rapids area specialists. His wife Cecile said that he ate and slept his practice. His daughter Sandra remembered him as soft-spoken, but you always knew when he was angry. "When dad called you a jackrabbit, you were in big trouble. He never used foul language," said Sandra. He and his associate, Dr. E. Eary were my family's physicians. They were the doctors who came into association with Dr. Bull. Their office was called to deliver each of my four babies.

A SHORT TRIP= My sister Barb had lived in Fresno, California when Nate was stationed there. She was very close to a friend named Lee Cates. Lee was going to be in Minneapolis for some gathering and had hoped she could come to Michigan to visit Nathan (it couldn't be done). When I heard this I talked with Connie and we decided we'd go to Minneapolis and visit her there. That we did! It was a nice visit and a great time of reminiscing. I'm so happy we did it. We also stopped for a little visit with Ruth Berner and her daughter Elaine.

Gwen Dufort and I went to Branson, Missouri with the retirees in November. As always, the shows were great. We did view the last performance of the Lawrence Welk show at Branson.

All of the grandkids are progressing in the areas of their lives…Oldest one in the field of employment—Next ones in college or post grad or high school and "my little girls" are already in $6^{th}$ and $4^{th}$ grades at Sparta.

2005

The plays I attended were: Brenna's "Annie Get Your Gun" and "Alice in Wonderland." Plays involving local talent are always impressive and enjoyable to me.

Tuesday, March 8, 2005 there were whiteout conditions on U.S. 131. 84 cars in a pileup with one dead and thirty-three injured. The southbound lanes had 47 cars and the northbound lanes had 37. A press reporter was in the crash and wrote a first-person article on it. Also, in the car that hit the reporter was a Rockford Ambulance paramedic. Rockford school buses retrieved uninjured stranded motorists. In the 1.5 mile long crash scene, 22 ambulances and more than 60 law enforcement officers responded. This was just south of the 10 Mile Rd. overpass.

Stanley Turowski and wife Bessie bought the acreage adjoining the south/rear property line of our acres. Bessie was a Kotchka and that acreage was known as the Kotchka farm on Grange about 1/3 of a mile South of Fonger Rd. Stanley had been forced to join the Russian army in Poland when he was just 16 years old. He lost almost all contact with his family. He was with the Russian army in Argentina when two cousins in Michigan helped him reach the US. With the help of Sue Blackall and Katie Lezman, members of his church, he was able to contact a grandnephew in his hometown. Katie had been a Polish exchange student and her mother, still living in Poland, assisted by calling the hometown to find someone with the last name Turowski. This grandnephew had wanted to contact Stanley, but didn't have the address. The two Turowski family members plan to keep in touch.

I attended high school with a girl named Joann Lamoreaux and she had three brothers in service WW II. In their home's front window was a flag with 3 stars on it. This indicated that there were persons from the home in service of any branch. During the war if a serviceman was killed the stars were replaced with a gold star. As surprising as it may be, all 3 stars were replaced by gold.

Memorial Day 2005, at the little Lamoreaux Park, west of State Street in Sparta, the service was dedicated to them. Three busts of these heroes were unveiled for the first time. The attendance of Sparta and the surrounding area made a large crowd.

Washington State: August ll-25$^{th}$. Derick and Jordan's wedding was the 20$^{th}$. Mark and Maureen had the rehearsal dinner in their yard under a large canopy. Bruce, Linda, their girls and Matt were there. They'd driven out in their motor home and were camped at a campground on the Columbia River. I stayed at a motel in Goldendale for two nights before the wedding. Brenna stayed with me. It was so nice to have her help the morning of the wedding...and just to be together. Six of Mark's Michigan family also attended the activities.

Heidi, Bethany, Emily and I toured the "Russell Home" on Boltwood, just south of the Veterans Home on Monroe Ave., Grand Rapids (it was the Comstock Home prior. Mrs. Russell maiden name was Comstock). The home had been sold after the Russells' were older or had passed. The new owners had not made it into apartments as most of the larger old homes have been. These gracious owners, Tom and Melanie Smith, took us throughout the 3-storied home. This is the same one mentioned before as Ruth, Marti, and I toured it on the egg route with Mrs. Russell. Since this one I have taken a group of neighbors and friends to tour it too. One of them, Dorothy Houvingh, mentioned that her mother had danced in the ballroom as a young lady. This statement gave Melanie a thrill, to have Dorothy relate what her mom had told her as they passed by the beautiful mansion.

At this point I don't know about 2006!
HEY! I found some notes for 2006....WOW!!!

From December $22^{nd}$ 2005 to February 7, 2006 we had above normal temperatures...forty eight days; Feb. 2, 06 it was 41 degrees. 53% of days since December $1^{st}$, 2005 with no sunshine –to February 2, 2006.

Gas prices: Jan. - Feb. - March varied from $2.16 to $2.49

On January $27^{th}$, 2006 Western Union Telegram service ended. Western Union was founded in 1851; built its first transcontinental telegraph line in 1861. It was as incredible and as astonishing as the computer when it first came out. It was for more than 150 years flowing with messages or joy, sorrow, and success came in signature yellow envelopes hand delivered by a courier. Telegrams reached their peak in 1920s and 30s.

In January, Heidi and I went to Antique Road Show's appraisals at Comstock Park High School. I took the child's SLEIGH from Aunt Jennie Hackinson; it appraised for $1,000 to $1,500.; keep that in mind my children!!!!!!

Dear friend Wayne Williams passed away February $1^{st}$. He was married to my dear friend from $3^{rd}$ grade on EVELYN STRAUS. Ken Anderson passed on Feb. $5^{th}$; Marian Schuur (sister Barb's dear friend) passed on Feb. $19^{th}$, and Jim Emery on March $25^{th}$. This shows the age era I'm in. Heh?????

Betty Mieras and I started volunteering at Alpha Family Center in Cedar Springs on Monday afternoons. This is a center for un-wed gals; it gives encouragement to not abort their little ones, and various other help as food, diapers clothes and lots of advice.

April 17, 2006 Nathan Wilkinson died. His memorial was the $21^{st}$. Randy Holmes came to it. O n Sat. the $22^{nd}$ Randy and I traveled all around the Muskegon, and Big Star Lake area. It brought back many memories for both of us but especially Randy.

In May, I went with the Rockford Seniors on a day trip to the Music House Museum, Williamston Dinner Theatre and Old Mission Penn. etc. Eloise Covey went too.

June found Evelyn Ring and me traveling to niece Lydia's High School Open House in Peshtigo, Wisconsin. The gathering was very nice. While in Peshtigo, we went to the Peshtigo Fire Museum and on the way up there we stopped to see Roger Cole in the U.P. As we came home we stopped at Trout Lake and toured the old, old hotel on the grounds.

July 15th the Historical Society sponsored a Hymn for the Township churches. It was well attended and some of the churches had special music for us to enjoy.

August 5th was the beautiful wedding of Corissa and Matthew Gilmer. It was held at Holy Cross Lutheran Church in Grandville and the reception was at Noto's delicious food and great evening. I gave them a picture of a wedding that Corissa drew when she was camping with Bruce, Rollin, I that I had had framed. The ladies had long, flowing dresses and looked elegant.

Then came the trip to Washington; Sept. 28th-Oct 12th. This was the first flight that I've taken there when the sky was free of clouds and so very clear. I saw the farmlands and the valleys and mountains in a different perspective. Marti picked me up carrying a winter jacket and scarf to keep me warm. Michigan is the state that has changeable and unforeseen weather……..

Bethany Hart (age 14) went deer hunting for the first time (with her dad Michael). Within an hour she had shot a 3 point buck with one shot! I don't know who was the most pleased, she or her dad---or even Gram. Mike shot his deer six days later. He shot from a blind that Ron made out of brush from Van Horn's yard. That hunting blind went up in smoke in the winter, since it was actually part of my brush–burning pile.

December 14th I went to the Fire Academy Graduation of Christa at Dart Auditorium. Now she's a fireman and EMT.

2007

There was no snow until the third week of January. Then winter was bad in February. Also, April 11th, we had five inches of snow.

Janelle asked me if I would talk to one of her classes regarding my hip replacement surgery and the therapy /recovery. This I did. I emphasized the need to be faithful to the exercises given us to do and also to continue them the full term. I stated that I was extremely satisfied with the results of both of my replacements! I mentioned also that I had not been able to cross my legs for years and I still only cross them at the ankles. I still use a small/flat pillow between my knees when sleeping on my side! QUALILTY OF LIFE...SUCH A DIFFERENCE no pain in Groin (hips didn't have any). I can now walk, do gardening and even walk stairs as an adult (1 foot only per step).

The play that Bethany acted in this year was "Hurricane Smith and the Garden of the Golden Monkey." Again, a play enjoyed by the audience.

My first trip to WASHINGTON D.C. = Betty Mieras and I were taken to G.R. Airport by Marti on April 26th; she "wheeled" the two of us to the departure gate. We boarded the flight for Cleveland and were on the runway when the pilot announced that we would be going back to the terminal. This was due to a thunderstorm in Cleveland and we would be unable to land there. We left the plane and waited for quite a while to be cleared to go to Cleveland.

In Cleveland, we had to wait for a flight to Washington D.C. We had a fellow and a gal push out wheelchairs to the GATE. They were such nice people I'm sure we'll not forget them. Eric (Lynn Piell's husband) met us at the airport and drove me to meet Dick Holmes at a predetermined place. Therefore now we were both with our loved ones.

It was so nice to spend time with Dick and Mary. We had a lot of time just to visit and catch up on our families. I visited with them at both Clark and Jean Anne's homes. The grandchildren were all sweet and active. Of course, the various tours they gave me of D.C. were nice; Dick knew where all the one –way streets were and of course all the historical and interesting monuments etc. The War Monument s were so heart-warming and made one so aware of the lives that were lost for our freedom….that far too often we take for granted. I am thrilled to have been there, and I do regret that Rollin and I didn't go there.

Open Houses: Charlie and Maggie Browns $60^{th}$…about June 3 or 4 and Bob and Sharon Yssseldykes in September.

$60^{th}$ High School class reunion was July 13, 14, 15. This was at the time of Sparta's Town and Country Days. Jean Hansen, Seelman, Soderstrom and I were the committee. Friday night those that wished to could go to the bar-b-que at Baleyeat Field and visit with classmates. Saturday at lunch time we went to the Garden Patch and each ordered from the menu. The number attending was very good, and we had the full dining area to ourselves. Then…some went to view the T&C parade and others went to the American Legion Room (north room of the Civic Center). After the parade more joined others at the ALR, and we visited for a couple of hours. Sunday morning those who desired went to Perkins on Alpine for breakfast together.

On a sad note we had 4 classmates pass away since March $1^{st}$: Sero Lutkes, Barbara Bull, Martha Lee Nason (and right now I can't remember the $4^{th}$… the total I don't recall now either).

In August, I rode with Bruce, Linda, Brenna, Matt & Corissa to Missouri to attend Travis Baughan and Keli Payne's wedding. We camped next to the Baughans. I attended the rehearsal dinner l it was tasty and I enjoyed visiting with Mark and Maureen.

The wedding was beautiful and the reception was held at the same location so there were no travel needs. I kiddingly mention that I don't know if I were as excided over the wedding as I was the fact that my W-H-O-L-E family was there. Kyle, Christa's boyfriend took a few great pictures of the whole family...nice!

WEATHER NOTE= October-warm; October 6$^{th}$ 85 degrees in the daytime hours and 71 degrees at night. On the 7$^{th}$ it was 83 degrees and we'd had no killing frost. December 1$^{st}$ was Anna Wilkinson's wedding in Spring Lake. It was horrible weather, driving home it rained, snowed and worse yet it was sleeting and the windshield was full of ice. Under those conditions the miles always seem to be twice as many.

## 2008

The year in general, again like many of the previous years. I volunteered at Alpha Family Center in Cedar Springs, attended plays locally, went to volleyball games when I could, worked in nursery for MOPS, attended some travelogues, and went to seminars on Long Term Care also one on Alzheimer's, then took people to doctors and labs and nursing homes.

The village of Sparta had the Vietnam War Memorial on display August 21, 22, and 23. I went to see it at Balyeat Field. The viewing of it was very heart wrenching and yet warming. One cannot even begin to comprehend the numbers of soldiers killed in our many, many wars. I was grateful to see this tribute.

Many family members went to Walker Arena in Muskegon to enjoy a program by Cathy Buckley's program. She is a hearing impaired comedian. It was a very pleasant evening...sponsored by Michigan Disabilities connection, where Marti's is employed.

Aaron Van Horn and Rachel Newland were married on October 25$^{th}$. It was a lovely day for the wedding and a lovely wedding. Mark and Maureen came for it. Bruce picked them up at the airport late Friday night. They came home with me after the reception, we gabbed awhile and then went to bed; up early to get to the airport on Sunday morning….so it was truly a f-l-y-i-n-g trip for them!

2009

Again the year in general was the same as previous years.
A dear neighbor-friend passed away, Winnie Knight, in June.
I was in Washington October 15-26$^{th}$, worked leisurely in the Iris Garden and read a book or two.

**Maynard and Imogene Klein**
Sixty years as husband and wife were observed Nov. 25 by Maynard and Imogene (Rosell) Klein of Casnovia. A family dinner was held in honor of the occasion. Children of the couple are Doug and Pat Klein and Carmen and Albert Bugaj. They have four grandchildren and three great-grandchildren.

Imogene and Maynard observed their 60$^{th}$ wedding anniversary (what a great milestone!) The children, grandchildren, and great-grandchildren with Ida McDougal and me enjoyed a tasty meal at Sayfees on November 28$^{th}$ in honor of it. The evening was filled with conversation and laughter. The little ones were so well behaved their parents could/should have been proud.

On a sad note; Jordan wanted a divorce from Derick---proceeded---finalized in April '09.

The Algoma Township Historical Society dedicated the VETERANS Memorial Park on Grange Ave. just south of the Algoma Cemetery. The monument also gives honor to the Algoma Baptist Church and has the bell of the old church incorporated into it. The service for this was very touching and heartwarming. The crowd of people in attendance was estimated to be 225 to 275.

## 2010

No "earth shattering" activities!!
The usual of: (a) church activities.
(b) Out to breakfast or lunch with friends or groups, (one was a fall breakfast with the former Kent County Road and Parks retires. It was enjoyable and nice to see everyone that was there.
(c) Mystery Trips and to plays at Turkeyville (Horizon Club IBWM Bank and Sparta Community Education.
(d) Sunshine Circle.
(e) Travel/transporting to Doctors-Labs etc. with others.
(f) Historical society of Algoma and a couple of gatherings with Tyrone, (Kleins).

Mark and Maureen Baughan were to China with an Education Group in March. They truly enjoyed it!

Matt Gilmer had work duties for some weeks in Africa. Corissa traveled there to spend some time for them to enjoy, as vacation.

In June my niece, Connie Wilkinson Poulin, took a group of friends to tour the Hackley and Hume homes in Muskegon. She is a tour guide there and it was her day off so was allowed to do this. We met and ate at the Institute of Culinary Arts restaurant, very near the historic homes. We all enjoyed both.

The evening of August 7$^{th}$ I heard sirens travel north on Pine Island, but they did not go far. I then took the car to see where they may have stopped. I sometimes, now think of Frank and Reva Huey due to their health. However Fonger was completely blocked by cars and people and there was fire further to the east. I went home and then went through the fields and parked there. There were fire trucks in front of 1288 and smoke and flames coming from the house. Fire trucks from Alpine Twp. and Sparta Village assisted Algoma Twp. Fire Department. They fought it well. (Yes it brought back many memories...Rollin and I had built it in 1951-2 and had lived there until 1956 when we traded homes with my folks. Yes it also brought back memories of the fire we had in 1977 at 1274 Fonger when Maureen jumped through the front window.

Bethany was at home and went to watch the fire. She wrote an article about it for the newspaper she was interning at, The Rockford Squire. The article follows:

The home I've always known as the "little gray house" at 1288 Fonger St. caught fire at around 8 P.M. on August 7, while the Pelton family was at Berlin Raceway. The Pelton family has lived in the house for three years. But, in the past, the little gray house was owned by three generations of my family. My grandparents built the 24x28 foot house in 1951 and 1952, and later, after the house was no longer owned by anyone in my family, an addition was added. My great-grandparents also lived in the house for a long time after switching homes with my grandparents. My parents lived there before I was born as well, so the home has special significance to my family.

Fortunately, the only occupant at the time of the fire was a black cat, which ran out the door as soon as firefighters opened it. The two dogs in the backyard and the cat were unharmed. Firefighters saved two boxes of baseball cards and many of the pictures off the walls. David and Debbie Pelton live in the home with two of their three sons, Mark, Jake, and Josh. Thankfully, no one had decided to stay home while the rest of the family went to the races.

"We lost a few wedding pictures, but most importantly no one was hurt," said. "This is the first time we've been through this, and right now we're sort of numb."

Jake and Josh Pelton both graduated from Rockford High School before the family moved to Fonger Street.

Currently, there is no idea of the cause of the blaze and the Peltons are waiting for insurance to determine if the house is a total loss. The part of the house that was built by my grandparents suffered less damage than the addition, but there is still smoke and water damage to contend with throughout the house, along with broken glass and vent holes in the roof.

Saturday night, as I watched the house burn with my mom and grandma, I wondered how they must be feeling as the place where so many of their memories were made was so unexpectedly ablaze. I cannot imagine their loss, just as I cannot imagine the Pelton family's loss.

Bethany Hart

WEDDING= Kyle and Christa's wedding, October 2, 2010. A very pretty wedding—smiles were abundant.

At the reception people who lost their lives in military service with Kyle while he served years in Iraq and/or Afghanistan. A fellow firefighter who was killed while serving on ambulance crew with Christa was also honored.

Christa and Kyle each made up a plate of food as a tribute, one for military personnel and one for paramedics who had died in the line of duty. These plates were taken to a special table, and they got to "eat" first.

One day in late fall, Betty Mieras and I went to Mecosta area and visited Floyd Hardiman and wife. He is the grandson of LUKE BANNISTER the black hired hand that my dad had in the late 1920s and early 1930s. It was a pleasant few hours.

Christmas Eve was great; only missing were Janelle (and Tom); she had to work. Everyone was happy…we began at 5:00 P.M. so that Kyle and Christa could be back to work duty on time. The wrapped "on the floor" gifts for my granddaughters went fine. These were Christmas décor items that I felt I no longer would use.

Christmas café and program at Sparta Nazarene Church I enjoyed very much!

Christmas luncheon at Linda Stotz (Betty Mieras's niece) was delicious, time spent visiting was enjoyable and the home's decoration was pleasant to the eyes.

CHRISTMAS= "The Bloom family party." It was nice to see the extended cousins as always great food and yes, they still have the impromptu children /adult program!!!!!

This article reminded my why these efforts are worthwhile:

And, to think, that I began my story in 1993! I'm hoping to give my descendents my writings on Mother's Day of 2011.

## Mom's life story is gift that keeps on giving

**Dear Abby:** I have a suggestion for people who are stuck for gift ideas. Several years ago, I asked my mom for a very special Christmas gift. I asked her to write down her life story — things she had done as a child, the experience of hitchhiking from New Mexico to Tennessee during the Great Depression, and all the other experiences of her life. She did, and I printed it for her. That year she gave each child, grandchild and great-grandchild a copy. It was the best Christmas present ever and one that's still cherished by us all.

Both my parents are gone now,

but we have Mom's wonderful stories to remember. Without her book, those memories would be lost forever. I encourage everyone to record their family history and memories for your loved ones to read. You'll never regret it, and it will be enjoyed for generations to come.

— **Andrew in Johnson City, Tenn.**

**Dear Andrew:** That's a terrific suggestion. And if the parent or grandparent isn't comfortable with writing, the same goal can be accomplished by setting up a video camera and interviewing the family member by asking questions about his or her youth.

JEANNE PHILLIPS
DEAR ABBY

THE GRAND RAPIDS PRESS    TUESDAY, NOVEMBER 16, 2010

## TRAGEDIES IN THE NEIGHBORHOOD ~ GRIEVING FAMILIES
## I DO NOT REMEMBER THE DATES AND MANY OF THE DETAILS OF THESE...

I was probably in my early teens when the neighborhood was shocked and joined together to seek and to find, a missing man, presumed to have commit suicide. Hank Montgomery lived on the west side of Pine Island Drive; the North West corner of Rector and Pine Island. Mother went up and stayed with Wilma (Ted) his wife as many men searched the field and woods. He was found with a dynamite stick blown up in his back pocket. I have been told that after Pearl Harbor, he and another neighbor man had gone to help clean up the mess at Pearl Harbor...this would give the fact of my age being more like 14-15 years old.

    Burt Hetland, son on Arnold and Grace, who lived in the "STONE HOUSE" on Pine Island south of Rector committed suicide in the upstairs bedroom via gun shot. He was depressed because an older neighbor young man (whom he admired) had been killed in a motorcycle accident. After the fact his mom made the comment to me, "If Burt knew the grief he has caused our family; he never would have done this." One can't imagine the grief a family and close friends go through. Burt was in his mid-to late teens, a junior or senior in High School.

    Orley McMillan, North East corner of Pine Island and Rector killed his family (I don't recall how many children there were). A young son Orley lay on the floor and played dead, thus he survived. My Marti thinks she was in the $2^{nd}$ grade and one of the girls was in her grade. My, oh, my, how sad!!

    Laura Jo Sutcliff lived west on Rector Road from the corner of Pine Island and Rector was kidnapped from her home during a summer. She may have been abducted in '64 or '65. She was not heard of for many years, then…..the man did it again (I believe in Allegan County), authorities found a receipt near a scene of an investigation. He was apprehended. He did lead them into Newaygo County and to where he'd buried Laura Jo.

Art Woltanski lived on 11 Mile Road just west of Pine Island. I was told he was drunk and on the "toilet" when their house totally burned down. He remained on the toilet and burned to death.

The Fishers lived on Algoma Avenue just north of 13 Mile Road. The twins, Donald and Diane were on Betty's bus route. On the p.m. run she had let them alight at their home this particular day. Later that evening she learned that Donald had killed Diane, a gun shot hit. All of these sad experiences in our basically quiet and peaceful neighborhood make us think!!!

Oh my, there is yet another one. Nancy Kinney, wife of Rick and mother of Jeanne and Ginger, suicidal death from carbon monoxide found in the garage on Grange, the old Bloom/Dufort farm.

## POST SCRIPT
## THE JOB I FORGOT TO MENTION

I did sell wedding invitations and accessories for many years, to both relatives and former bus riders. It began when brochures came with greeting card orders that Marti and Bruce sold to others. I think my first order was for Connie Wilkinson and Lee Poulin. Some humorous memories: one bride and grooms' names for napkins were "Dick and Jane" (names used in very early reading books of $1^{st}$ Grade); another was when I mentioned to a couple that in the invitation one used both first and middle names. The fellow then said that he only wanted his first name used. I then questioned: "Is that because when you were younger you were always called 'Glen Allen' when you were in trouble?" He answered yes.

## MOTHER'S "BUTS"

Mother came from Oak Park, Illinois, a suburb or Chicago in 1919 when she and dad married. They lived with Aunt Jennie Hackinson for several months. They purchased 35 acres of sandy land in Algoma Twp. Mom had left the amenities of electricity, running water, and flush toilets. Quite a change to kerosene lamps to light at sun down, pump water for use in the house—(at first had to be carried into the house from an outside pump), and of course the use of the "OUT HOUSE" or the potty in the winter. Yet when she went out of doors at night she used the "BUT" I've never seen the "milky way" in such beauty!!

During the last 1 1/2 years of her life, her eyesight became very poor and she commented, "I wish my vision was better so that I could read my devotionals, write letters and cards and watch a few T.V. programs ("Wheel of Fortune, and Jeopardy") then her "BUT" think of how many years they have worked for me!!! (She was probably 92 year to 92 ½ years when she made the statement.)

## THOUGHTS OF MY DAD

I remember with loving feelings that he would come in from the field at noon; he'd often give my mom a pat or her shoulder or buttocks and give her "smooch" on her neck. He was a loving hubby and dad!

Another remembrance was he would instruct Imogene and me about various farm chores and then praise us if jobs were done well.

# BITS OF ADVICE TO LIVE BY

From Betty Mieras. She gave me a "line" to remember too; "If you do a deed, or make a comment in love, caring or with compassion and the recipient misinterprets it; then it isn't your fault, but THEIRS!!!

From Aunt Helen: I was mentioning that the barn at 1288 Fonger had been used as a building for practice fire fighting for the Algoma Twp. Fire Department (the new owner had given the permission to do so). I commented that it made me feel somewhat "blue" as I could remember as a youngster when it was built. She then stated, "But Irene, it has/had served its purpose!"

## SAYINGS AND SUCH TO PONDER

### Cancer

Cancer is so limited...
It cannot cripple LOVE
It cannot shatter HOPE
It cannot corrode FAITH
It cannot kill FRIENDSHIP
It cannot suppress MEMORIES
It cannot silence COURAGE
It cannot evade the SOUL
It cannot steal ETERNAL LIFE
It cannot conquer the SPIRIT
Author Unknown

## THE MOST

| | |
|---|---|
| The most destructive habit | Worry |
| The greatest joy | Giving |
| The greatest loss | Loss of self-respect |
| The most satisfying work | Helping others |
| The ugliest personality trait | Selfishness |
| The most endangered species | Dedicated leaders |
| Our greatest natural resource | Our youth |
| The greatest "shot in the arm" | Encouragement |
| The greatest problem to overcome | Fear |
| The most effective sleeping pill | Peace of mind |
| The most crippling failure disease | Excuses |
| The most powerful force in life | Love |
| The most dangerous pariah | A gossiper |
| The world's most incredible computer | The brain |
| The worst thing to be without | Hope |
| The deadliest weapon | The tongue |
| The two most power-filled words | "I Can" |
| The greatest asset | Faith |
| The most worthless emotion | Self-pity |
| The most beautiful attire | SMILE! |
| The most prized possession | Integrity |
| The most powerful channel of communication | Prayer |
| The most contagious spirit | Enthusiasm |

Author Unknown

## GALLERY OF PICTURES

These couples have been mentioned, some many times, throughout my written memories. The years within my memory book may have them at various ages in their life. The following pictures I cherish because of my memories of them as couples.

Bob and Meryl (Paulson) Perlstrom

Just for comparison ~ PRICES IN 1930

| | | |
|---|---:|---|
| New House | $ 7,146.00 | |
| Average Income | $ 1,973.00 | Per year |
| New Car | $ 610.00 | |
| Average Rent | $ 15.00 | Per month |
| Tuition to Harvard University | $ 400.00 | Per year |
| Movie Ticket | $ 0.25 | Each |
| Gasoline | $ 0.10 | Per gallon |
| United States Postage Stamp | $ 0.02 | Each |
| Granulated Sugar | $ 0.65 | For 10 lbs. |
| Vitamin D Milk | $ 0.56 | Per gallon |
| Ground Coffee | $ 0.46 | Per pound |
| Bacon | $ 0.25 | Per pound |
| Eggs | $ 0.15 | Per dozen |
| Fresh Ground Hamburger | $ 0.13 | Per pound |
| Fresh Baked Bread | $ 0.09 | Per loaf |

# PRICES OF CARS AND TRUCKS PURCHASED THROUGH THE YEARS OF OUR MARRIAGE AND AFTER ROLLIN'S DEATH

## CARS

1948 Dodge purchased by Imogene and Irene Rosell from Colby Garage, Sparta
  $2,226.66
1952 Dodge Wayfarer purchased 03/09/53 from Mrs. Charles Pocock (6,800 miles)
  $1,700.00
1955 Plymouth purchased 01/14/55 from Speerstra Motors, Lowell
  $2,444.28
1957 Plymouth Savoy purchased 08/06/57 from Highland Plymouth, Grand Rapids
  $2,400.00
1960 Dodge Seneca purchased 03/05/60 from Jackson Motors, Lowell
  $2,371.70
1963 Dodge 330 purchased 07/30/63 from Jackson Motors, Lowell
  $2,394.00
1966 Plymouth Fury II purchased 03/30/66 from McQueen Motors, Lowell
  $2,603.00
1969 Plymouth Fury III purchased 01/09/70 from VanAndel-Flikkema, Grand Rapids
  $2,875.00
1969 Plymouth Satellite purchased from private party
  $ ?
1973 Plymouth Fury purchased from Imperial Motors, Grand Rapids
  $ ?

1977 Plymouth Fury purchased 02/14/78 from VanAndel-Flikkema, Grand Rapids
$4,698.25
1977 Plymouth Volare purchased 05/30/78 from VanAndel-Flikkema, Grand Rapids
$3,644.00
1984 Buick Skylark purchased from private party (William L. Schaap)
$7,800.00
1986 Plymouth Reliant purchased from VanAndel-Flikkema, Grand Rapids
$7,744.08
1991 Dodge Dynasty purchased 12/18/91 from VanAndel-Flikkema, Grand Rapids
$10,600.00
1998 Mini Van (White) purchased from VanAndel-Flikkema, Grand Rapids
$25,284.00
2009 Van (Red) purchased from K&M Northfield Dodge, Grand Rapids
$22,000 before rebates, $18,000 after rebates

TRUCKS AND VANS

1961 Dodge purchased 07/19/65 from McQueen Motors, Lowell
$ 680.00
196? Chevrolet purchased from Clifford Preston on Fruit Ridge
$ ?
1969 Chevrolet 3/4 Ton purchased from VanAndel-Flikkema, GR
$ ?
1979 Ford F-150 purchased 07/26/79 from Vanderhyde Ford, Cedar Springs
$6,193.00

1983 Dodge purchased from private party
  $ ?
1995 Dodge purchased 09/23/94 from K&M Northfield Dodge, Grand Rapids
  $23,000.00

The valuation for the 40 acre property with the white house (1270 Fonger, also known as 1274)
1954      $ 2800.00
1955      $ 3000.00
1960      $ 3500.00 (an acre sold before 1965)
1965      $ 3800.00 (a few more acres sold)
(Dog licenses were $1.50 for a male dog in 1965)
1970      $ 7000.00
1975      $11,000.00
1980      $17,400.00
1985      $38,800.00
1990      $43,100.00


PROPERTY TAXES BEFORE AND AFTER PROPOSAL A-1993/94

9-10-93    $1422.53
12-30-93   $1395.12
9-?-94     $641.13
12-?-94    $666.15